Lying and Truthfulness

In this book, Stewart Clem develops an account of truthfulness that is grounded in the Thomistic virtue of *veracitas*. Unlike most contemporary Christian ethicists, who narrowly focus on the permissibility of lying, he turns to the virtue of truthfulness and illuminates its close relationship to the virtue of justice. This approach generates a more precise taxonomy of speech acts and shows how they are grounded in specific virtues and vices. Clem's study also contributes to the contemporary literature on Aquinas, who is often classified alongside Augustine and Kant as holding a rigorist position on lying. Meticulously researched, this volume clarifies what set Aquinas's view apart in his own day and how it is relevant to our own. Clem demonstrates that Aquinas's account provides a genuine alternative to rigorist and consequentialist approaches. His analysis also reveals the perennial relevance of Aquinas's thought by bringing it to bear on contemporary social and ethical issues.

Stewart Clem is Assistant Professor of Moral Theology at Aquinas Institute of Theology, St. Louis.

ADVANCE PRAISE FOR *LYING AND TRUTHFULNESS*

"In this meticulously researched work, the author presents the case for rehabilitating a Thomistic perspective on lying that counters standard interpretations of Aquinas's position. In recovering these Thomistic insights, Clem makes an important and significant contribution to scholarship, both as a secondary work dedicated to understanding Aquinas more clearly, but also through a novel contribution to moral theology by bringing Thomistic insights into fruitful and creative dialogue with contemporary political and social issues of our time."

Celia Deane-Drummond, University of Oxford; director of the Laudato Si' Research Institute

"This book marks a breakthrough. Pushing past the inadequate alternatives on offer today with respect to the ethics of lying, Stewart Clem grasps the neglected point that Aquinas discusses lying within the context of the virtue of truthfulness. From this perspective, the untapped richness of Aquinas's perspective – which developed markedly over the course of his career and which is quite different from other medieval viewpoints – becomes apparent. Clem provides a profound, balanced Aristotelian and Christian way forward out of the morass of indifference to truth. A tour de force!"

Matthew Levering, Mundelein Seminary; author of *Aquinas's Eschatological Ethics and the Virtue of Temperance*

"With *Lying and Truthfulness*, Clem joins the ranks of scholars such as Williams, Griffiths, and Tollefsen who have penned outstanding recent monographs devoted to moral analysis of lying. Akin to Griffiths's book on Augustine, Clem has written what is now the go-to book on Aquinas on lying and truthfulness. Clem presents Aquinas's thought both in historical context, and as a resource for contemporary issues, well-trodden perennial questions (e.g., the Gestapo dilemma), and more recent topics (e.g., 'bullshit') alike. Clem's innovation is a treatment of lying primarily within the context of the virtue of truthfulness, though he does this with careful attention to action theory, a combination too rare in moral scholarship today."

William C. Mattison III, University of Notre Dame; author of *The Sermon on the Mount and Moral Theology: A Virtue Perspective*

"Honesty and truthfulness have been surprisingly neglected by scholars for many years. In his important book, *Lying and Truthfulness*, Stewart Clem skillfully addresses a number of central issues related to lying, truth, speech, equivocation, and deception. His book should be of great interest to Aquinas scholars as well as contemporary moral philosophers and theologians. Highly recommended!"

Christian B. Miller, Wake Forest University; director of the Honesty Project

"Stewart Clem's *Lying and Truthfulness* is a deeply impressive first book which reflects both a mastery of Aquinas's thought and a command of contemporary literature on the ethics of lying. As Clem shows, Aquinas's analysis of truthfulness and lying was innovative in his own time and is surprisingly relevant to contemporary discussions of the topic. This book breaks new ground in our understanding of Aquinas, and at the same time offers an original contribution to contemporary philosophical and theological ethics. This is an indispensable book for anyone who wants to understand either the history or the potential future of truthfulness as a moral and social ideal."

Jean Porter, University of Notre Dame; author of *Nature as Reason: A Thomistic Theory of the Natural Law*

Lying and Truthfulness

A Thomistic Perspective

STEWART CLEM
Aquinas Institute of Theology, St. Louis

Shaftesbury Road, Cambridge CB2 8EA, United Kingdom

One Liberty Plaza, 20th Floor, New York, NY 10006, USA

477 Williamstown Road, Port Melbourne, VIC 3207, Australia

314–321, 3rd Floor, Plot 3, Splendor Forum, Jasola District Centre, New Delhi – 110025, India

103 Penang Road, #05–06/07, Visioncrest Commercial, Singapore 238467

Cambridge University Press is part of Cambridge University Press & Assessment, a department of the University of Cambridge.

We share the University's mission to contribute to society through the pursuit of education, learning and research at the highest international levels of excellence.

www.cambridge.org
Information on this title: www.cambridge.org/9781009261388

DOI: 10.1017/9781009261418

© Cambridge University Press & Assessment 2023

This publication is in copyright. Subject to statutory exception and to the provisions of relevant collective licensing agreements, no reproduction of any part may take place without the written permission of Cambridge University Press & Assessment.

First published 2023
First paperback edition 2025

A catalogue record for this publication is available from the British Library

Library of Congress Cataloging-in-Publication data
NAMES: Clem, Stewart, author.
TITLE: Lying and truthfulness : a Thomistic perspective / Stewart Clem, Aquinas Institute of Theology, St. Louis.
DESCRIPTION: Cambridge, United Kingdom ; New York, NY, USA : Cambridge University Press, 2023. | Includes bibliographical references and index.
IDENTIFIERS: LCCN 2022027049 | ISBN 9781009261401 (hardback) | ISBN 9781009261418 (ebook)
SUBJECTS: LCSH: Thomas, Aquinas, Saint, 1225?–1274. | Truthfulness and falsehood – Religious aspects – Christianity.
CLASSIFICATION: LCC B765.T54 C539 2023 | DDC 189/.4–dc23/eng/20220824
LC record available at https://lccn.loc.gov/2022027049

ISBN 978-1-009-26140-1 Hardback
ISBN 978-1-009-26138-8 Paperback

Cambridge University Press & Assessment has no responsibility for the persistence or accuracy of URLs for external or third-party internet websites referred to in this publication and does not guarantee that any content on such websites is, or will remain, accurate or appropriate.

Contents

Acknowledgments		page ix
List of Abbreviations and Translations		xiii
	Introduction	1
	The Aims of This Book	3
	The Readership of This Book	5
	The Organization of This Book	7
1	Lying and Contemporary Christian Ethics: A Thomistic Critique	12
	Life in a Fallen World	15
	Speaking the Same Language	21
	A Universal Moral Norm	25
	Disordered Speech	27
	Speaking Trinitarian	32
2	The Ambiguous Legacy of the Eighth Commandment: "You Shall Not Bear False Witness"	36
	Biblical and Patristic Sources	38
	Augustine on Lying and Bearing False Witness	40
	Medieval Interpretations	51
3	Aquinas on the Sins of Speech	60
	The Eighth Commandment and the Prohibition of Lying	61
	The Virtue of Justice and Its Potential Parts	71
	Sins of Speech	77
4	Aquinas on the Virtue of *Veracitas*	91
	The Nature of Truth	91
	The Virtue of Truthfulness	96
	The Nature and Definition of Lying	102
	Lying as a Sin against Truthfulness	105
	Other Vices Opposed to Truthfulness	114

5	Lying, Asserting, and Evading: A Linguistic and Moral Analysis	123
	Equivocation and Lying	124
	Equivocation and Thomistic Moral Theology	133
	The Nazi at the Door	138
	Resolving the Dilemma: Three (Failed) Proposals	143
	Reframing the Dilemma	149
6	A Thomistic Framework for the Ethics of Lying and Truthfulness	154
	Eight Thomistic Theses on Lying	154
	Thomistic Vignettes: Brief Case Studies in Lying	161
7	A Thomistic Theory of Bullshit	170
	Bullshit as a Vice Opposed to Truthfulness	171
	The Structural Sin of Truth Indifference	176
	The Rehabilitation of *Veracitas*	181
	Conclusion	186
	Truthfulness as a Habit	186
	Mortal and Venial Lies	189
	The Thomistic Insight	191

Bibliography   195
Index   209

Acknowledgments

Aristotle once wrote that "those who wish well to their friends for their sake are most truly friends."[1] I have been blessed with many friends who have contributed to this book not only with their well wishes but also by giving their time and sharing their intellectual gifts. The ideas I develop in this volume took shape over the course of several years, and the finished product bears the marks of insights I have gleaned from my interactions with a number of scholars and friends. While they might not agree with everything I have written, their contributions have made this book better, and for that I remain deeply grateful.

This work has benefited from conversations and written comments from more people than I can adequately recall. My interest in the thought of Thomas Aquinas has been cultivated by the mentorship of some of his most astute contemporary readers: Jean Porter, John O'Callaghan, Joseph Wawrykow, Reinhard Hütter, and James Cain. My thoughts on the ethics of lying, truthtelling, and related topics have also been sharpened by conversations with Victor Lee Austin, Susan Blum, Dustin Crummett, Celia Deane-Drummond, Warren von Eschenbach, Kevin Flannery, Agustín Fuentes, Paul Griffiths, Stanley Hauerwas, Russell Hittinger, Tim Ingold, Sean Larsen, Alasdair MacIntyre, Gerald McKenny, Darcia Narvaez, Philip Porter, Matthew Puffer, Miguel Romero, Kevin Scott, Michael Sherwin, David Solomon, and Eleonore Stump. I owe a special thanks to Craig Iffland, who endured my musings and frustrations as I waded through the literature on the topic and, more importantly, helped

---

[1] Aristotle, *Nicomachean Ethics*, trans. W. D. Ross, in *The Complete Works of Aristotle*, ed. Jonathan Barnes (New York, 1991), 1156b26.

me to articulate my ideas when they were mere prototypes of what would eventually appear in this book.

I had many fortunate opportunities to field test the material in this book throughout the writing process. I am especially grateful to Christian Miller and Mark Murphy for the opportunity to share my work at a special "Abstractaganza" session, under the auspices of the annual Theistic Ethics Workshop, and to my fellow participants, Chris Tucker, Joshua Blanchard, Todd DeRose, Anne Jeffrey, and Tom Ward, who challenged me and helped me fine-tune my argument in response to the Nazi-at-the-door dilemma. I would also like to thank Amitava Dutt and Georges Enderle, who organized the interdisciplinary "Lying and Truthfulness" reading group at the University of Notre Dame, and to all the participants who engaged my work with their helpful questions and critical feedback. The "Evolution of Wisdom" colloquium, co-hosted by the Center for Theology, Science, and Human Flourishing at Notre Dame and the Institute of Advanced Study at Durham University, provided a wonderful opportunity for interdisciplinary collaboration, and I learned much from my involvement there. Many thanks also to Keri Day and Christophe Ringer, organizers of the "Ethical Dimensions of Truth and Post-Truth" panel at the 2017 annual meeting of the American Academy of Religion, for inviting me to speak on the contemporary implications of my research. I am grateful to the audience members, as well as those present at the recent annual meetings of the Society of Christian Ethics and the Society for the Study of Christian Ethics, who asked insightful and probing questions that allowed me to refine my arguments and present them more clearly.

This project would have been impossible without the institutional support I received, and I would like to thank, first and foremost, Aquinas Institute of Theology, the Pius XII Memorial Library at Saint Louis University, and the Notre Dame theology department for ensuring that I was never lacking in scholarly resources. I also wish to thank the Center for Theology, Science, and Human Flourishing at Notre Dame for graciously providing resources and office space during a crucial stage of this project. I am grateful to the Vatican Library for access to the manuscripts I consulted while conducting research for Chapter 2 and also to the Rome Global Gateway at Notre Dame for the financial assistance that enabled my travel to the Vatican. I also received financial support from the Delores Zohrab Liebmann Fund and the Episcopal Church Foundation, and it is thanks to their generosity that I have not only been able to develop this project without interruption but also to share my results and interact with numerous scholars across the globe. I am also grateful for the support I received through the Human Distinctiveness Project, co-directed by Celia Deane-Drummond and Agustín Fuentes. This project was funded in part by a grant from the John Templeton Foundation, which initiated multiple collaborative efforts in which I was fortunate to be a participant.

A few portions of this book have appeared in print elsewhere. I am grateful to the *Journal of Religious Ethics* for permission to reuse the material in my essay, "Lying to the Nazi at the Door: A Thomistic Reframing of the Classic Moral Dilemma,"[2] and to the *Journal of the Society of Christian Ethics* for permission to reuse portions of my essay, "Post-Truth and Vices Opposed to Truth."[3]

As this project neared the final stage, Matthew Levering and Bill Mattison read the complete manuscript with close scrutiny and offered insightful suggestions for improving it. The clarity and specificity of their feedback was truly a gift, and I am grateful that such exceptional theologians and readers of Aquinas found it worthwhile to invest in this project. I also want to express my gratitude to Beatrice Rehl and Cambridge University Press for taking on this project and for facilitating such a smooth publication process. I owe many thanks to Evan Bednarz, who edited the entire manuscript in preparation for publication and offered several helpful stylistic suggestions, and to Josh Ostertag, who reviewed the manuscript and made corrections during the copyediting stage.

I began my research for this book when I was a doctoral student in theology at the University of Notre Dame, and I am deeply grateful to my PhD advisor, Jean Porter, whose expert guidance ensured that the project remained coherent and focused. Her sensitivity to Aquinas's historical context, as well as her attentiveness to the complexities of his thought, has inspired my own approach to the Angelic Doctor's writings.

I owe the greatest debt of gratitude to my family. From the beginning, my vocation as a scholar has been grounded in the unwavering support of the Clem and Schulke families, who at every turn have helped me better understand the nature of this vocation. It is cliché to refer to one's written work as a labor of love, but my family has constantly reminded me by their love that this work is worth doing. My

---

[2] Stewart Clem, "Lying to the Nazi at the Door: A Thomistic Reframing of the Classic Moral Dilemma," *Journal of Religious Ethics* 49:1 (2021): 6–32.
[3] Stewart Clem, "Post-Truth and Vices Opposed to Truth," *Journal of the Society of Christian Ethics* 37:2 (2017): 97–116.

parents, Tim and Debbie, inspired my interest in theology and ethics from a young age, by their words and by their actions. My children, Lydia, Sophia, Agatha, and Lucia, and my wife, Molly, are the constant reminders in my life that without love, I am nothing (1 Cor. 13:2). I dedicate this book to them.

Abbreviations and Translations

Unless otherwise stated, translations are my own. Full citations for the following texts can be found in the Bibliography. Further details regarding translations and editions can be found in the footnotes where the relevant texts are cited.

THOMAS AQUINAS

In prec.	*Collationes in decem praeceptis*
DM	*Quaestiones disputate de malo*
DV	*Quaestiones disputate de veritate*
In Cor.	*Super primam epistolam ad Corinthios lectura*
In Eth.	*Sententia libri Ethicorum*
In Gal.	*Super epistolam ad Galatas lectura*
In Iob	*Expositio super Iob ad litteram*
In PH	*Sententia super Peri hermeneias*
In Rom.	*Super epistolam ad Romanos lectura*
In Sent.	*Scriptum super Sententia magistri Petri Lombardi*
SCG	*Summa contra Gentiles*
ST	*Summa theologiae*

ARISTOTLE

NE	*Nicomachean Ethics*
PH	*Peri hermeneias (De interpretatione)*

AUGUSTINE

CM   *Contra mendacium*
DM   *De mendacio*

BONAVENTURE

Collationes   *Collationes de decem praeceptis*
In Sent.   *Commentarius in IV libros Sententiarum*

CICERO

Inv.   *De inventione*

PETER LOMBARD

Sent.   *Sententiarum libri quatuor*

Introduction

Is it ever permissible to tell a lie? What if no one is harmed as a result? What if it is necessary to save someone from danger? What does it mean for a lie to be permissible? Permissible according to whom? Or to what? What exactly is a lie, anyway? Is there such a thing as a "pure" lie – a discrete act, distinct from other kinds of moral action? What does it mean to be truthful? Am I still being truthful if I try to mislead while technically adhering to the truth? How should we interpret the crisis of truthfulness in the twenty-first century?

The present volume offers answers to these and related questions with the help of the medieval scholastic theologian, Thomas Aquinas. Although Aquinas is frequently invoked in scholarly treatises on lying, his views are seldom understood. While a few Thomists have attempted to defend Aquinas's views on lying without modification, their arguments have gained little traction outside of groups who share a commitment to a particular brand of Thomism. Moreover, most of Aquinas's interpreters have assumed that his answer to the question *Is it ever permissible to tell a lie?* is straightforward: *No*. These interpreters, depending on their sympathies, then proceed either to refute or defend (or perhaps dismiss) his position. But rarely does anyone challenge the standard interpretation. This volume offers a challenge to the status quo by proposing a new interpretation and defense of Aquinas's position, one that is focused on the virtue of truthfulness.[1]

---

[1] Thomistic philosophers and theologians have unduly neglected the virtue of truthfulness and its role in Aquinas's thought on lying. This is an unfortunate omission, given its contemporary relevance. Some of the best recent work on the virtues of truthfulness and honesty has been written by moral philosophers who are not writing from an explicitly

To be clear, I do not argue that Aquinas would answer *Yes* to the question of whether it is permissible to tell a lie. While my interpretation goes against the grain of contemporary scholarship, the aim is not merely to be novel. Indeed, one of the key insights of this book is the observation that Aquinas's moral analysis of the lie is not easily translated into the language of contemporary ethical discourse.[2] To ask whether a lie is permissible in certain contexts already assumes a great deal about the nature of morality. In order to discern Aquinas's views on lying, we must first realize that there are other modes of inquiry pertinent to lying – whether and when it is good or bad, right or wrong, lawful or unlawful. In making the effort to understand Aquinas on his own terms, in his medieval theological context, we will be rewarded with many insights that have been lost in contemporary debates on lying.[3]

In short, this book offers a defense of the following view: To be a truthful person – to possess the virtue of truthfulness – is to make assertions about what one believes to be true, or to conceal what one believes to be true, in appropriate ways and at appropriate times. There are many ways to act against this virtue, and the paradigmatic way to act against the virtue of truthfulness is to tell a lie. A lie is told whenever there is a

---

Thomistic perspective. See, for example, Christian B. Miller, *Honesty: The Philosophy and Psychology of a Neglected Virtue* (New York 2021) and Steven L. Porter and Jason Baehr, "Becoming Honest: Why We Lie and What Can Be Done about It," in *Integrity, Honesty, and Truth Seeking*, eds. Christian B. Miller and Ryan West (New York 2020), 182–204.

[2] Philosophers have attempted to translate Aquinas's theological ideas with varying degrees of success. Colleen McCluskey, for example, whose *Thomas Aquinas on Moral Wrongdoing* (New York 2017) provides an excellent analysis of the subject, is perhaps a bit too optimistic when she writes, "Thus, at least some of Aquinas's explicitly theological terms can be accommodated without much strain by nonreligious theories. Aquinas holds an account [of sin] that both theists and nontheists could accept, at least in principle" (9). While I agree with her that some aspects of the mortal–venial distinction can be translated into nontheological discourse, and that these translations may even be illuminating for nontheistic philosophers, I also maintain that some features of Aquinas's thought on sin, moral wrongdoing, and (more specifically) lying are irreducibly theological. See, for example, my analysis of the classic "Lying to the Nazi at the door" dilemma in Chapter 5.

[3] For readers interested in Aquinas in his medieval context, I commend Randall B. Smith, *Aquinas, Bonaventure, and the Scholastic Culture of Medieval Paris* (New York 2021). Also, R. W. Southern's *The Making of the Middle Ages* (New Haven, CT 1953) remains a classic. See also Jean-Pierre Torrell, OP, *Saint Thomas Aquinas, Vol. 1: The Person and His Work*, 3rd ed., trans. Matthew K. Minerd and Robert Royal (Washington, DC 2022) and *Saint Thomas Aquinas, Vol. 2: Spiritual Master*, trans. Robert Royal (Washington, DC 2003). For an illuminating history of practical thought about lying and perjury in the Middle Ages, see Emily Corran, *Lying and Perjury in Medieval Practical Thought: A Study in the History of Casuistry* (New York 2018).

lack of correspondence between *what one believes to be the case* and *that which one intends to assert*. Telling a lie can never be a morally good action, regardless of the action's consequences, because it is incompatible with the virtue of truthfulness. The paradigmatically truthful person will seek to hide the truth when appropriate, but she will never willfully tell a lie. There may be instances in which telling a lie is understandable and forgivable, but this is not the same as calling it a morally good or praiseworthy deed. There are many lies, however, that display attributes in addition to those found in my proposed definition of lying. These lies are not only opposed to the virtue of truthfulness – they are also opposed to the virtues of justice and charity. We often deploy more precise terms to identify these acts: perjury, slander, blasphemy, and so on. These acts are direct violations of justice and are opposed to the will of God. They ought never be done. Within these broad parameters, however, there is still much that needs to be said. For example, we must consider the multifaceted uses of human language and symbolic communication, as well as the fact that we live in a fallen world that often seems to encourage (or even demand) untruthfulness. These considerations will be taken up as the argument of the book unfolds.

THE AIMS OF THIS BOOK

The primary aim of this book is to rehabilitate Aquinas's position on lying and demonstrate its contemporary relevance. Why does his position need rehabilitating? In the first place, Aquinas is often dismissed, alongside Augustine and Kant, as holding a rigorist position that is unfeasible and insensitive to the realities of daily life.[4] I aim to persuade my readers that this is not the case. As a corollary aim, I hope to rescue Aquinas from his own defenders. These defenders include contemporary advocates of Aquinas who uphold a rigorist interpretation of his position, namely, that Aquinas's view is best summed up by the maxim *lying is never permissible*.[5] In this book, I argue that these interpretations are far removed from the spirit of Aquinas's writings. For one, the vocabulary and grammar of "permissibility" does not adequately capture Aquinas's mature position on lying. Even where he does deploy such language, it has a

---

[4] The scholars who have described Aquinas's position this way are legion. Noteworthy examples include Sissela Bok, Peter Kreeft, Janet Smith, and Arthur Vermeersch.
[5] For examples, see the recent work of Martin Rhonheimer, John Skalko, and Christopher Tollefsen.

precise meaning that cannot simply be mapped onto contemporary moral discourse. When we read Aquinas in his proper context, we find that one of his objectives is to minimize the sinfulness of certain kinds of lies by showing that they represent a fundamentally different kind of act from those that constitute mortal sins. At the same time, Aquinas stands apart from many contemporary moral philosophers who argue that these same lies (which he would call venial sins) are either (1) perfectly permissible and morally unproblematic or (2) not lies at all. By maintaining that they are still, in fact, lies, Aquinas's moral psychology provides the resources to explain why we should nevertheless avoid telling them.

Another way of framing this book's argument is to think of it as a response to a two-pronged challenge. The first prong assumes that the metaphysical and theological presuppositions of Aquinas's stance on lying render it obsolete in today's world. Dallas Denery, reflecting on the history of lying in the Christian West, recalls that the first crime described in the Bible is a lie. This lie, told by the devil who is the "father of lies," results in the expulsion of humanity from paradise. Yet, in the story Denery narrates, these religious presuppositions have gradually eroded in Western society. In our disenchanted, secular age (to borrow a phrase from Charles Taylor[6]), we no longer believe that "God is watching" even when we tell a white lie. As a result, humanity feels lost at sea as we seek answers to the problem of lying:

> The ground shifts, and the question of lying finds itself irrevocably separated from God and the Devil. Even as we continue to ask *Is it ever acceptable to lie?* and even as the answers we come up with appear unaltered (yes, no, sometimes, never), the framework is new. Beneath a settled and seemingly unchanged facade, everything has changed, as if, having lived too long in exile, we one day realized paradise had never existed in the first place.[7]

This is a hauntingly poetic description of our contemporary milieu, but I contend that it is not as "new" as Denery suggests. Moreover, the traditional vocabulary of moral theology is not so far removed from contemporary experience as to render it obsolete. The categories of mortal and venial sin, for example, are not found in most people's moral lexicon, yet in many ways these categories reflect moral intuitions that still resonate today as much as they did in the thirteenth century.[8] While Aquinas's

---

[6] Charles Taylor, *A Secular Age* (Cambridge, MA 2007).
[7] Dallas G. Denery II, *The Devil Wins: A History of Lying from the Garden of Eden to the Enlightenment* (Princeton, NJ 2015), 256.
[8] See McCluskey, *Thomas Aquinas on Moral Wrongdoing*, 7–10.

argument against lying is indeed shaped by his theological commitments, he does not offer a "religious argument," in the way this is often understood colloquially. For those who assume that Aquinas's medieval worldview is simply too far removed from our current understanding of language, ethics, and society, I demonstrate how his insights and those of contemporary scholars can be mutually illuminating.

The second prong of the challenge is found in arguments to the effect that Aquinas's absolutism can never satisfy our basic moral intuitions, including the commonly held assumption that it is sometimes acceptable – or even necessary – to tell a lie. As Boniface Ramsey observes:

> Perhaps the tradition that allows occasional lying and deception takes its force, rather, from an intrinsic "human" and merciful quality, for want of a better way of putting it, and from the fact that the "generous" lie is the utterly natural response to an otherwise apparently impossible situation; it is what men and women have always done and undoubtedly always will do.[9]

In contrast to this merciful and humane tradition, Ramsey claims, "there is no reconciling an absolutist position, however sympathetic it may be to the dilemmas of life […] with one that is not."[10] Perhaps he is right. The claim that an absolutist position cannot be reconciled with a non-absolutist position may be, in the end, a tautology. But if the claim is that a position like Aquinas's cannot be reconciled to the real dilemmas of everyday life, then this book offers a counterargument.

THE READERSHIP OF THIS BOOK

In addition to the readers who simply wish to learn more about Aquinas's position on lying and its contemporary relevance, there are four audiences this volume has in mind. The first group includes both critics and defenders of Aquinas who interpret him as a rigorist on lying. To these interpreters, I propose that Aquinas's rigorism is far more nuanced than it is often taken to be. Critics and defenders of Aquinas's rigorism both recognize that Aquinas does not allow for exceptions in his ban against all lies, but they also make the fundamental mistake of eliding two very different kinds of moral action. One kind of moral action is classified as mortal sin, the other venial. As my analysis unfolds, it will become clear that this distinction can hardly be overstated. The differences between

---

[9] Boniface Ramsey, "Two Traditions on Lying and Deception in the Ancient Church," *Thomist* 49 (1985): 504–533; cited at 533.
[10] Ibid., 531–532.

these kinds of "lies" are so great that they generate different answers to the question, "Is it ever permissible to tell a lie?" Some lies are clearly impermissible; for others, the language of "permissibility" is not apt to describe the nature of wrongdoing in telling the lie.[11] This difference must be taken into account.[12]

The second target audience is composed of the numerous moral philosophers and theologians who appeal to certain locutionary distinctions, such as those involved in interrogation, equivocation, and discerning meaning in a given context, to the end that many speech acts that appear to be lies are, in fact, not. In response, I argue for the importance of maintaining that such acts *do* count as lies and, in the process, demonstrate how Aquinas's *contra mentem* principle, which originates with Augustine in the fourth century, provides a more satisfying and coherent alternative to the supposedly more "humane" position, which tolerates speech that dances around the truth.

The third category includes those who agree with me that these acts count as lies, but who also argue that so long as the lies are told for benevolent ends (or at the very least, they cause no harm) they are morally permissible. To these readers I commend Aquinas's account of truthfulness as a virtue, suggesting that we should be more critical in our use of terms like "acceptable" and "permissible" when evaluating instances of lying. I ultimately argue that thinking about truthfulness in this way gives us good reasons for avoiding even so-called "harmless" lies – although at times we may find ourselves in exceptional circumstances in which we cannot avoid telling a lie without committing some worse sin.[13]

Finally, in light of the current social and political climate in Anglophone countries, there are many readers who are concerned about the status of truth in our public life. These readers comprise the fourth group, and to them I extend an invitation to join a conversation that many have probably never considered: debates in moral theology on the ethics of lying.

---

[11] Aquinas writes, "[Venial sin] is not against the law, since the one who sins venially neither does what the law forbids nor omits what the law prescribes; but he acts beside the law, by not observing the mode of reason that the law intends," *Summa theologiae* I-II.88.1 ad 1 ("Non enim est contra legem, quia venialiter peccans non facit quod lex prohibet, nec praetermittit id ad quod lex per praeceptum obligat; sed facit praeter legem, quia non observat modum rationis quem lex intendit."). See also *ST* II-II.105.1 ad 1.

[12] Christopher Tollefsen's *Lying and Christian Ethics* (New York 2014), while containing many helpful insights about Aquinas's thought on lying, only mentions the mortal–venial distinction in passing (4–5, 94).

[13] See Chapter 5, where I explain and defend this position.

In an age when politicians and public figures are raising questions about the nature of facts and objective reality, many are wondering if there is any hope for the future of public discourse. Rudy Giuliani, the personal lawyer of former US President Donald Trump, once claimed during an interview with NBC host Chuck Todd that "truth isn't truth." He later clarified that his statement was not meant "as a pontification on moral theology,"[14] but his defense belies the fact that even the extemporaneous remarks of public figures touch on some of our deepest moral, philosophical, and theological questions about the nature of truth and truthfulness.

The chapters that follow will not be of equal interest to the various audiences I have just described. Those who are primarily concerned with the crisis of truthfulness in public discourse may find the historical and exegetical chapters somewhat tedious. Likewise, those who are accustomed to the rigor and precision of contemporary analytic philosophy may find the theological and historical aspects of my argument superfluous. But one of my central claims is that the attempt to translate Aquinas's arguments against lying into the idiom of contemporary analytic philosophy has done a disservice both to Aquinas and to the discourse on lying. For this reason, the constructive arguments I make in this book are not meant to stand alone. They presuppose many features of Aquinas's position (which is admittedly my *interpretation* of his position) that cannot always be reduced to concise propositions. Where I do offer such propositions, I am assuming certain aspects of Aquinas's moral framework, and it is essential to get these details right. These are not, in other words, premises from nowhere. This remains true even in the instances where I acknowledge that I am going beyond what Aquinas says in his own writings.

THE ORGANIZATION OF THIS BOOK

One of the primary objectives of this book is to offer a definitive interpretation of Aquinas on lying. But the interpretive arguments I make cannot ultimately be separated from my normative arguments. For this reason, I begin in Chapter 1 with a Thomistic critique of the current landscape in Christian ethics on the question of lying. I consider five constructive proposals, each motivated in some way by the Christian tradition, that aim to solve a set of difficult problems regarding this perennial moral

---

[14] "Trump lawyer Rudy Giuliani defends 'truth isn't truth' remark," *BBC News*, August 19, 2018, www.bbc.com/news/world-us-canada-45252493.

problem. The purpose of this chapter is to capture the uniqueness of the discourse among Christian ethicists on the morality of lying, while underscoring some of the major problems of that discourse. The thinkers I engage, due to their theological commitments or their fidelity to magisterial Catholic teaching, have proposed solutions to the problem of lying that need to be taken seriously. But, as I argue, they are also deeply flawed. Another important feature of these proposals is that each is at odds in at least one significant way with Aquinas's position.

The proposals I engage in Chapter 1 fall into two broad categories: absolutist and soft absolutist. By absolutist I mean the position that lying is always morally impermissible, with no exceptions. The authors I engage in this category include theologian Paul Griffiths and philosophers Christopher Tollefsen and John Skalko. By soft absolutist I mean the position that lying is always impermissible, but the definition of "lying" needs to be refined such that some utterances that have traditionally been considered lies are no longer understood to be so. The authors I engage in this category include moral theologian Janet Smith and philosopher Alexander Pruss. Each category includes those who explicitly draw upon Thomistic insights to make their arguments (Smith, Tollefsen, and Skalko) as well as non-Thomistic (Griffiths and Pruss). While I do attempt to correct these authors' interpretations of Aquinas where I find them lacking, the primary aim of this chapter is to reveal the weaknesses of these authors' own positions and then in turn demonstrate why a Thomistic framework, grounded in the virtue of truthfulness, offers a superior alternative to these models.

Chapter 2, "The Ambiguous Legacy of the Eighth Commandment: 'You Shall Not Bear False Witness'," tells the story of lying in the Christian West, beginning with the biblical texts, as filtered through the outsize influence of Augustine of Hippo. Convinced that the biblical texts offer a unanimous condemnation of all lies, Augustine sets out to eradicate any doubts regarding the permissibility of falsehoods, no matter how small. He offers a litany of arguments, in multiple works, to defend his position. While he is not without critics, his stance on lying quickly becomes a touchstone within Western Christendom. As this Augustinian tradition develops, the inherent tensions and unanswered questions of Augustine's position become more and more apparent. By the Middle Ages, a consensus on the impermissibility of lying begins to emerge, and the scholastic discussion largely revolves around the eighth commandment of the Decalogue: "[Y]ou shall not bear false witness against your neighbor" (Exodus 20:16). The scholastic manuals assume, as Augustine did, that the eighth commandment prohibits all lies, but they question and quibble about whether there might be exceptions to this rule and what might constitute such an exception. When Aquinas enters this conversation as a young theologian, his writings reflect many of the same presuppositions as his interlocutors. Yet, as I demonstrate, he begins to question those who uncritically associate *lying* with the prohibition of false witness found in the eighth commandment. While nearly all scholastic theologians believe that every lie is sinful, they find it difficult to articulate why harmless or helpful lies violate the Decalogue. Inspired by Aristotle's discussion of the virtue of truthfulness in the *Nicomachean Ethics*, Aquinas begins to experiment with the idea that these "harmless" lies in fact belong in a class of their own.

What begins as an experiment soon turns into a fully developed framework. As I argue in Chapter 3, "Aquinas on the Sins of Speech," Aquinas's mature writings reflect a position on lying that stands apart from his peers and his predecessors. Rather than analyzing all lies through the lens of the Decalogue, Aquinas proposes that we think of the act of lying *per se* as a sin against the virtue of truthfulness. His definition of the lie – *locutio contra mentem*, "to speak against one's mind" – remains thoroughly Augustinian, but a lie does not rise to the level of violating the eighth commandment unless there is another element present in our moral analysis, namely, an explicit intention to harm or offend someone. When this intention is added to the falsehood, we utilize a more specific moral vocabulary: We call such actions gossip, slander, perjury, and so on. They belong with other sins of speech that violate the order of justice and charity. Lies that lack this intention cannot properly be said to violate God's law.

In Chapter 4, "Aquinas on the Virtue of *Veracitas*," I show how Aquinas gives us an account of the wrongness of lying that is not grounded in an exceptionless moral norm. A lie can never be said to be *good*. Even a lie that is told with the intention of helping someone is a morally defective action. Aquinas recognizes that the reasons for this claim will not be obvious to everyone; thus, he deploys the Aristotelian notion of *truthfulness* as a virtue, and he draws upon another classical source, Cicero, to conceptualize this virtue's relationship to the cardinal virtue of justice. By showing us the goodness of truth as a constitutive feature of human flourishing, Aquinas aims to convince his readers that we cannot coherently call an act of lying *good*. That said, the very category of venial sin tells us something about the conditions of living in a fallen world. We often face moral dilemmas in which we feel that we must choose between the lesser of two evils. As even the witness of scripture attests, many saintly people will commit heroic actions for a good end – and yet tell a lie in the process. While many would call the lie itself *good* because of the result it produces, Aquinas is no consequentialist. He cannot call the lie a good action, but he now has the conceptual resources for diminishing the sinfulness of the lie to the point of its being "forgivable." While other scholastics acknowledge the category of venial lies, Aquinas provides its parameters and is the first to set the act of lying against the virtue of truthfulness.

Chapter 5, "Lying, Asserting, and Evading: A Linguistic and Moral Analysis," summons the implicit premises that have developed thus far in the book and makes them explicit. In the first section, I elaborate my argument against equivocation as a form of lying, drawing upon Aquinas's insights to address theoretical questions that are beyond his purview. I then turn to one of the classic case studies in the ethics of lying: the "Gestapo Question," or, the dilemma of the person who is confronted by Nazis while she is hiding Jews in her basement. I offer my own answer to this dilemma, but, perhaps more importantly, I demonstrate the ways in which this particular case study both succeeds and fails to capture our most important moral intuitions about lying and truthtelling.

Taking these reflections into account, as well as those of the preceding chapters, Chapter 6, "A Thomistic Framework for the Ethics of Lying and Truthfulness," articulates the basic tenets of my Thomistic framework. Finally, as a means of illustrating the full range of the practical implications of this framework, I sketch fifteen vignettes of difficult cases in lying, followed by a brief analysis that draws on relevant features of this framework. The vignettes are adapted from a variety of sources, ranging from manuals in moral theology to popular media pieces.

In the final chapter, "A Thomistic Theory of Bullshit," I turn to the social dimensions of truth in contemporary society. I address a widespread problem that is frequently encountered but insufficiently diagnosed, namely, that disregard for truth is accepted and even expected in many contexts, yet it creates conditions for gross injustice and dehumanization. I offer an account of widespread cultural indifference to truth as structural sin, a condition I call *truth indifference*. While distinct from lying *per se*, the sin of truth indifference is no less a sin against truthfulness. I argue that social structures, like human persons, can display an inveterate resistance to the truth, and this should be understood analogously as a kind of *habit* – particularly, as a kind of *vice*. Drawing again upon the insights I have developed throughout the book, I map out the conceptual framework that must be in place before Christian ethicists can provide an adequate moral analysis of structural truth indifference. It is in this context that we most clearly see the need for truthfulness in all areas of life.

The Conclusion, of course, concludes the argument of the book, but it is not merely perfunctory. This chapter distills the key insights of Aquinas's position on lying and demonstrates the value of sustained reflection on this medieval thinker's complex understanding of the virtue of *veracitas*. Some readers may prefer to read this chapter first and then decide which of the preceding chapters merit the closest attention.

I

Lying and Contemporary Christian Ethics
A Thomistic Critique

Is lying ever justifiable or excusable? Many moral philosophers and theologians have pondered this question, including those who are generally sympathetic to Thomas Aquinas's (in)famous claim that lying is always wrong. The motivations behind the question are sensible and humane. When we consider the case of beneficent lies – lies told to save someone's life, or lies that would greatly benefit someone without harming anyone else – it seems that a desirable moral framework would find a way to excuse such utterances from an otherwise binding prohibition against lying. What if it were possible to classify certain falsehoods, such as beneficent lies, as something *other than* lies altogether? If this idea were defensible, then we could uphold an exceptionless moral norm against lying but also permit some speech acts that involve intentional false assertion. Many Christian ethicists find this approach attractive. For reasons that will become clear as the argument of this book unfolds, I believe this approach ultimately fails. As tempting as it may be, this approach solves one problem about the morality of lying while simultaneously creating a host of other problems. But it is worth asking, in this initial stage of our inquiry, *why* this approach has seduced so many Christian ethicists.

While the morality of lying is not an exclusively theological concern, history shows that Christian theologians and philosophers have been more concerned than others to preserve the notion that lying is an inherently bad moral action. At the very least, they have been more reticent to make exceptions to the prohibition against lying and instead have sought ways to redefine lying in a manner that allows for more lenience in difficult moral cases. The Christian tradition has generally taken the eighth commandment of the Decalogue (Exodus 20:16, "You shall not bear false witness against your neighbor"), along with other passages of Scripture (for example, Psalm 5:6, "You destroy those who tell lies"), to mean that lying is a violation of God's will and thus never permissible. This is not to suggest that the only reasons for prohibiting lies are theological. Immanuel Kant, the most well-known modern thinker to defend an exceptionless norm against all lies, constructs his argument on wholly secular philosophical grounds.[1] Nonetheless, the consensus among contemporary moral philosophers (and not just utilitarians or consequentialists) seems to be that at least some lies are morally permissible.[2]

Traditionally, those with Christian theological convictions hold a stricter position. Many Roman Catholics, in particular, have a special interest in preserving the norm against lying, since the official position of the Magisterium maintains that lying is always sinful. Protestant theologians have tended to share this stance and are generally hesitant to condone any form of lying, though there are notable exceptions.[3] For Catholics, the teaching of the current Catechism remains an important touchstone in the ongoing debates about the morality of lying, but the textual history of the document reveals an interesting revision. The original version of the current Catechism included the following statement: "To lie is to speak or act against the truth in order to lead into error *someone who has the right to know the truth.*"[4] As stated, the text suggests that it is acceptable to utter a willful falsehood to someone who does not have a right to the truth and that this falsehood does not constitute a lie. This approach resolves many difficult cases. In the case of the Gestapo Question, it would be permissible to say to the Nazi, "There are no Jews

---

[1] See Immanuel Kant, "On a Supposed Right to Lie from Philanthropy," trans. M. J. Gregor, in *Immanuel Kant, Practical Philosophy*, eds. A. W. Wood and M. J. Gregor (Cambridge, UK 1996). For more on Kant's position on lying, see Mahon, "Kant on Lies, Candour and Reticence." See also Christine M. Korsgaard, "The Right to Lie: Kant on Dealing with Evil," *Philosophy & Public Affairs* 15:4 (1986): 325–349.

[2] See, for example, Sissela Bok, *Lying: Moral Choice in Public and Private Life*, 2nd ed. (New York 1999) and Jennifer Saul, *Lying, Misleading, and What Is Said* (New York 2012).

[3] For example, Dietrich Bonhoeffer offers a qualified defense of lying in "What Is Meant by 'Telling the Truth'?" in *Ethics*, trans. Neville Horton Smith (New York 1995), 358–368. For more on Bonhoeffer's position on lying, see Ned O'Gorman, "'Telling the Truth:' Dietrich Bonhoeffer's Rhetorical Discourse Ethic," *Journal of Communication and Religion* 28 (2005): 224–248. See also Nancy Berlinger, "What Is Meant by Telling the Truth: Bonhoeffer on the Ethics of Disclosure," *Studies in Christian Ethics* 16:2 (2003): 80–92.

[4] *Catechism of the Catholic Church*, 1st ed. (Washington, DC 1994) § 2483. Emphasis added. The relevant text can be found at www.vatican.va/archive/ENG0015/_P8K.HTM.

in my house," because this utterance would not be a lie. The Nazi does not have the right to know the truth.[5]

The revised edition of the Catechism removes this qualification, however: "To lie is to speak or act against the truth in order to lead someone into error."[6] Although the earlier text was replaced, it is significant that the less rigorous position was at least briefly endorsed by the Magisterium – a position reflecting the fact that there have been some prominent figures in the Christian tradition who condone false assertion in certain circumstances.[7] Moral theologian Janet Smith correctly observes, "The doctrinal unity between the two editions of the Catechism is that all lying is wrong. The diversity is in whether all deliberate and voluntary acts of false assertion are immoral."[8] Those who affirm the earlier definition may hold a position that is less congruent with the most recent version of the Catechism, but one could argue that they are still within the bounds of the Catholic tradition.

There are many serious thinkers who wish to define lying in such a way as to preclude so-called beneficent lies from falling under this definition, and they present a challenge to the position I defend in this book. My position is Thomistic in the sense that it draws upon Aquinas's understanding of lying (as I interpret it), but it also goes beyond Aquinas's understanding by addressing problems that he did not address or could not have anticipated. For now, it is simply worth noting that Aquinas does not add the qualification about one's "right to know the truth" – or any other qualification regarding one's interlocutor – to his definition of the lie. By the end of this book, I hope that readers will see clearly that he was right to omit this qualification.[9] The aim of the present

---

[5] I further address this moral dilemma in the section "Equivocation and Thomistic Moral Theology."

[6] *Catechism of the Catholic Church: Revised in Accordance with the Official Latin Text Promulgated by Pope John Paul II*, 2nd ed. (Washington, DC 1997) § 2483. The relevant text can be found at www.vatican.va/archive/ccc_css/archive/catechism/p3s2c2a8.htm.

[7] See Chapter 2. See also Julius Dorszynski, *Catholic Teaching about the Morality of Falsehood* (Washington, DC 1948), 15–37.

[8] Janet E. Smith, "Fig Leaves and Falsehoods," in *First Things*, No. 214 (June/July 2011): 45–49; cited at 46.

[9] This qualifier is frequently attributed to the seventeenth-century Dutch legal scholar and philosopher Hugo Grotius. For criticisms of the Grotian qualifier, see Kenneth W. Kemp and Thomas Sullivan, "Speaking Falsely and Telling Lies," *Proceedings of the American Philosophical Association* 67 (1993): 151–170, esp. 158–159; Christopher O. Tollefsen, *Lying and Christian Ethics* (Cambridge 2014), 28–30; John Skalko, *Disordered Actions: A Moral Analysis of Lying and Homosexual Activity* (Neunkirchen-Seelscheid 2019), 99–107.

chapter, however, is of a different order. My purpose here is to capture the uniqueness of the discourse among Christian ethicists on the morality of lying while underscoring some of its major problems. These thinkers, due to their theological commitments or their fidelity to magisterial Catholic teaching, have proposed solutions to the problem of lying that are innovative and often quite clever. But none, in my judgment, has successfully constructed a framework that is philosophically consistent or theologically compelling.

In what follows, I engage a variety of proposals offered by Christian ethicists, each of which is at odds in some significant way with what I take to be Aquinas's position on the morality of lying. Each of the proponents I engage in this chapter shares a commitment to the claim that it is always wrong to tell a lie. Two of these thinkers, moral theologian Janet Smith and philosopher Alexander Pruss, propose conditions in the moral description of lying that, if applied to Aquinas's position, would reduce its scope. In other words, the list of actions that count as lies is much smaller on their account than the list of actions we would find in Aquinas's. Other thinkers argue that the scope of actions we call lies should remain fairly broad. While their descriptions of the act of lying are much closer to Aquinas's, their reasoning is unwittingly (in the case of Christopher Tollefsen and John Skalko) or wittingly (in the case of Paul Griffiths) quite different from his. I argue that all these thinkers miss the mark in their moral analyses, and I suggest that what they lack is a coherent and compelling account of truthfulness. The weakness of their moral analyses is due in part to their misreadings of Aquinas or certain Thomistic principles. A correction of these misreadings and a reconstruction of Aquinas's argument will be the tasks for the remainder of the book.

LIFE IN A FALLEN WORLD

Most Christians, regardless of how they read the opening chapters of Genesis, believe that we currently live in a world that has fallen from its original created state. In the simplest terms, this means that the sin we observe in the world, including our own sin, is not part of God's original plan for humanity. For moral theologians, this observation often adds an additional layer of complexity to one's moral analysis. In an article that has received much attention since its publication in the American journal *First Things*, moral theologian Janet Smith cautiously reconsiders the standard Thomistic position (and, by her estimation, the current position of the Catholic Church) on lying, wondering what it might mean to take full account of this Christian doctrine. Her fundamental concern is Aquinas's blanket condemnation of all intentionally false utterance. She finds his criteria for establishing what constitutes a lie to be far too strict to accommodate other important moral considerations under which an act of lying might be examined. She writes, "Aquinas's rigorism about uttering falsehoods is certainly cogent, but hard to reconcile with some of his other positions."[10] She cites, for example, Aquinas's nuanced position on killing for the sake of protecting innocent life and in turn asks, "Why shouldn't Aquinas (and the Church) permit false signification uttered in order to protect innocent life and other important goods?"[11] She is correct that, on Aquinas's account of lying, one would not be permitted to lead a would-be attacker astray (even in order to protect an innocent human being) by providing false information. She is also deft enough to avoid making the claim that lying is "permissible" in certain circumstances. Her proposal is that Aquinas's definition of lying should be modified in such a way that some forms of intentionally false utterance are compatible with the absolute prohibition of lying.

The primary weakness of Aquinas's position, Smith argues, is that it relies too heavily on the Aristotelian metaphysics of teleology, without countenancing the realities brought into existence through original sin. She concedes that Aquinas does not usually suffer from such narrow-sightedness, but in this instance, "he analyzes the question of lying with a prelapsarian understanding of the purpose of signification – an understanding that presumes the innocence of man before the Fall."[12] She notes that, in our postlapsarian world, there are many demands placed on our use of language that reach beyond the purpose of signifying truth or conveying outwardly the concepts in our minds. She rightly observes that, as a result of sin's effects in the world, certain conditions call for consolation, encouragement, prophetic speech, and verbal defiance that would not have existed in a prelapsarian world. As such, we should be open to the possibility that not all such instances should be considered lying, even when they involve untruthful utterance. She recognizes the inherent difficulty in determining precisely which false utterances should count as lies, but she counters (correctly, in my estimation) that this is no different from other important spheres of moral judgment.[13]

---

[10] Smith, "Fig Leaves and Falsehoods," 45.
[11] Ibid., 47.
[12] Ibid.
[13] Ibid., 49.

In making this critique, Smith has put her finger on the pulse not only of our contemporary ethical concerns but also of Aquinas's. She rightly points to the importance of the fall of humanity as a paradigm for Aquinas's understanding of human nature.[14] Yet, at the same time, I suggest that this is precisely where Smith's criticisms of Aquinas fail. Despite her claims to the contrary, Aquinas does account for the realities of the postlapsarian condition – she has simply failed to recognize how he does so. The Achilles's heel in her analysis of the Thomistic account of lying is that she focuses exclusively on the fact that Aquinas maintains that all lies are sinful, without considering the significance of his division of lies into mortal and venial sins.[15] The significance of this distinction is not merely that he makes it at all (which Smith entirely neglects), but also the rationale for the distinction. As we will see in Chapters 4 and 5, the category of venial sin is meant to accommodate the realities of a fallen world. When we give full weight to the mortal–venial distinction in Aquinas's account of lying, the force of Smith's criticisms is attenuated, if not dissolved entirely.

What is most striking about the nature of Smith's criticisms is that they reflect concerns with which Aquinas is broadly sympathetic. For example, Aquinas's interpretation of the episode regarding the Hebrew midwives' lie in Exodus 1:15–21 is far more lenient than that of his contemporaries. His interpretation disagrees with his predecessor, Gregory the Great, and he maintains that the midwives' lie was compatible with an eternal reward (*ST* II-II.110.4 ad 4). Yet, Smith goes well beyond Aquinas when she writes, "I believe that sound reasoning supports the notion that the preservation of harmony, justice, and truth in a postlapsarian world requires a great deal of judicious false signification, from false missives in warfare to the consolation of children and the mentally deranged."[16] Aquinas would not agree that the conditions of the postlapsarian world "require" false signification. He would be more inclined to say that in a world tainted by sin human beings are often incapable of performing morally perfect acts, either due to ignorance, time constraints, or lack of moral formation; this does not imply, however, that

---

[14] See, for example, *ST* I-II.91.6, in which Aquinas affirms that the "spark of sin" (*fomes peccati*) pervasively affects the operations of practical reason in all those who live in the postlapsarian world.
[15] See Chapter 4. On the importance of these categories in Aquinas's understanding of lying, see Dewan, "St. Thomas, Lying, and Venial Sin," 374–386.
[16] Smith, "Fig Leaves and Falsehoods," 48.

any morally imperfect act is of such a nature that it will remove the person from a first-personal relationship with God as sustained by charity. With this in mind, we can say that actions that are intentionally aimed toward a good end, which nevertheless fall short in some particular aspect, still maintain certain features of moral goodness. This does not preclude us from lamenting and repenting of the sin involved in the act, which in a perfect act would not be present.

In the kinds of cases Smith raises, what is morally praiseworthy is not the successful misleading through the utterance of falsehood. Certainly she realizes this, but at the same time she fails to make the morally relevant distinctions. She asks (rhetorically), for example, "Catholics are generally proud that many priests in the Vatican gave false passports to Jews. Should we revise our evaluation of that action?"[17] Aquinas's answer would be: well, it depends. For him, there would be no problem in praising these priests for protecting the lives of the Jews. It is important to distinguish here that it is not merely the *outcome* of their actions for which they are to be praised – Aquinas is no consequentialist. By the same token, Aquinas would qualify this assessment by adding that the falsehood they uttered belongs to the category of venial sin. Their actions would have been more perfect had they found some other means of saving the Jews that did not involve lying, but their lying was not sufficient to render the very action of saving the Jews as morally blameworthy or against the virtue of charity. Aquinas says as much when he answers a similar objection about the deception of the Hebrew midwives in the book of Exodus. His reply is: "The midwives were not rewarded for their lie but for their fear of God and their benevolence, out of which they were led to tell a lie. Thus it is written in Exodus 1, 'And because the midwives feared God, he built them houses.' But the lie that followed was not meritorious."[18] In light of the specific concerns that Smith raises, her essay's failure to engage Aquinas's treatment of such texts is a glaring omission.

Even if we wish to bracket Smith's concerns about the postlapsarian world, the questions she raises about the circumstances of our actions are valid and demand a response. The circumstances of an action are

---

[17] Ibid.
[18] *ST* II-II.110.3 ad 2: "Ad secundum dicendum quod obstetrices non sunt remuneratae pro mendacio, sed pro timore Dei et benevolentia, ex qua processit mendacium. Unde signanter dicitur Exod. I, *et quia timuerunt obstetrices Deum, aedificavit illis domos.* Mendacium vero postea sequens non fuit meritorium."

an integral component of moral description. Aquinas explains that the relationship between the object of an act and its circumstances is analogous to the relationship between a substantial form and its accidents. "In natural things," he writes, "we should observe that the complete fullness of a thing's perfection does not derive only from the substantial form that designates its species. Things derive much from supervening accidents, such as a human being who derives things from shape, color, and the like."[19] Sometimes an action's circumstances are significant enough such that the object of the action is determined (at least in part) by them. "Cutting someone with a knife" can describe the actions of a surgeon or a murderer (of course, the intention of the action is equally relevant in determining its object). Smith writes,

> Murder is the direct and voluntary killing of an innocent human being. Theft is taking something against the reasonable will of the owner, and a reasonable owner would approve of taking property to protect important goods. Therefore, properly stated, although killing and the taking of property are sometimes morally permissible, the norms against murder and theft remain absolute, without exception. Similarly, I believe that the telling of some falsehoods and other forms of false signification are compatible with the absolute prohibition of lying.[20]

Perhaps Smith does not realize that Aquinas recognizes some formal falsehoods as permissible. As we will see, he recognizes that figures of speech and hyperbole are not lies. Playacting and storytelling involve falsehoods, in the strict sense, but they are not lies. To lie is not merely to say something that is false (or even what one believes to be false); to lie is to *assert* something one believes to be false, in hopes that the listener will believe it to be true.[21] Lying requires an intention to deceive about the nature of one's thoughts. As such, it is an improper use of language as it pertains to undue matter – this is the *object* of the act. The analogical comparison to "killing" and "taking of property" does not hold.

If the object of the act is morally flawed, there are no circumstances that can change its status to a morally good act. Circumstances may help us determine an otherwise indeterminate act. Circumstances may also change an otherwise good act into a morally bad act – but not the

---

[19] ST I-II.18.3: "[I]n rebus naturalibus non invenitur tota plenitudo perfectionis quae debetur rei, ex forma substantiali, quae dat speciem; sed multum superadditur ex supervenientibus accidentibus, sicut in homine ex figura, ex colore, et huiusmodi." See *De malo* II.6 for a more detailed analysis.
[20] Smith, "Fig Leaves and Falsehoods," 47.
[21] See Chapter 5 for more details on the importance of assertion.

other way around. Aquinas writes, "The plenitude of [an action's] goodness does not consist completely in its species but also in things that are added to it by certain accidents. Such things are its due circumstances. Thus, if something for these due circumstances is lacking, it will be a bad action."[22] The requirement of due circumstances raises the bar for moral action; it does not lower it. Smith suggests, "Indeed, perhaps God is signaling that on occasion 'in particular the occasion of protecting the innocent' we are right to engage in false signification."[23] The problem here is inadequate moral description. By "false signification," Smith seems to have in mind "saying something that is false." And it is true that "saying something that is false" is not sufficient to determine whether it is a morally bad act. There are certain circumstances (for example, an actor reciting lines in movie) that warrant such actions. But the acts Smith wants to condone go beyond "saying something false" and into the territory of duplicity. Lying is a morally bad act, and there are no circumstances that can change this analysis. There are no "due circumstances" for lying, since lying is an act that pertains to undue matter.

Some of Smith's critics have argued that if we were to adopt her reasoning, then we would also have to concede that murder and theft are also permissible in certain circumstances. I disagree with these critics. While I have been critical of Smith's arguments, I believe this objection presents a misreading of Smith as well as a misreading of Aquinas. Take, for example, John Skalko's provocative counterargument:

> The argument for lying based upon an analogy with violence proves too much. If lying may be done for the sake of the common good when lives are in danger, then cannot the same rationale apply to other actions as well? If lying must be justified in order to save innocent lives for the sake of the common good, then why is not adultery, murder, or even sodomy justified in similar situations? Imagine a blackmail situation: a gang breaks into a bank and recognizes you as their old lost enemy. They insist that they will murder everyone else in the bank and leave the gun in your cold dead hands unless you kill one of the innocent bank tellers. If you can lie for the sake of the common good, then why can you not murder?[24]

---

[22] *ST* I-II.18.3: "Nam plenitudo bonitatis eius non tota consistit in sua specie, sed aliquid additur ex his quae adveniunt tanquam accidentia quaedam. Et huiusmodi sunt circumstantiae debitae. Unde si aliquid desit quod requiratur ad debitas circumstantias, erit actio mala."

[23] Smith, "Fig Leaves and Falsehoods," 46.

[24] John Skalko, "Why Did Aquinas Hold That Killing Is Sometimes Just, But Never Lying?" *Proceedings of the American Catholic Philosophical Association* 90 (2017): 227–241; cited at 234.

This is simply a bad argument. Smith's position is that sometimes it is permissible to misuse language and tell a falsehood precisely because it will bring about a good result and no one will be harmed in the process. While I believe her argument fails, it is unfair to represent her position as asserting that the common good necessarily trumps an individual's good. Even though I have criticized her for failing to take Aquinas's mortal–venial distinction into account, she at least implicitly acknowledges that the badness of lying (in its harmless varieties) is of a different order than mortal sins such as murder. In fact, this is the problem with Skalko's objection, too. He fails to consider that, for Aquinas, not all lies are equal.[25] Skalko's question, "If you can lie for the sake of the common good, then why can you not murder?" only works if all sins are equal. Or at least it only works if there is no such thing as a venial lie. The position Skalko is describing is not that of Aquinas.

Aquinas's actual position on lying is superior to Smith's for two reasons. First, it does a better job of accounting for the state of postlapsarian humanity by making a distinction between mortal and venial lies – a distinction Smith barely acknowledges. There are some lies that Aquinas calls "forgivable" (venial) and, perhaps, understandable, but Smith wants us to call them *permissible*. As John Webster writes, "In the Christian community, the speech of regenerate creatures is under repair, as thanksgiving to God and edification of neighbours are established by the moving power of the Holy Spirit."[26] This will not likely satisfy Smith's objections, but she strikes me as wanting to avoid the trap of consequentialism – a nearly impossible task given the way in which she wishes to redefine lying. Second, Aquinas's account provides much more perspicuous categories of moral action. His distinction between killing and murder, for example, mirrors his distinction between false utterance and lying. Smith's account blurs the latter two categories, to the end that the act of *lying* no longer has a clearly defined moral object. Aquinas maintains these boundaries while still accommodating the pastoral sensitivity driving Smith's concerns.

SPEAKING THE SAME LANGUAGE

In their analyses of lying, contemporary philosophers have paid a great deal of attention to the structure and uses of human language. There are many important questions about language that must be answered prior

---

[25] See the section "Disordered Speech" for a more detailed analysis of Skalko's position.
[26] John Webster, "Sins of Speech," *Studies in Christian Ethics* 28:1 (2015), 35–48; cited at 35.

to any moral analysis of lying, not least of which is the question of how to define the act of lying. In a response to Janet Smith's essay, philosopher Alexander Pruss claims that "false assertion is always wrong."[27] This may seem to suggest that Pruss is in favor of a more severe stance toward lying, but in fact his own strategy seeks to evade the harsh consequences of traditional Catholic teaching on this topic. He considers the infamous prohibition against lying as found in the first English edition of the Catholic *Catechism*: "To lie is to speak or act against the truth in order to lead into error someone who has the right to know the truth."[28] Given that this final clause regarding the "right to know the truth" was dropped in the second edition of the *Catechism*, his aim is to offer an interpretation of the Church's official (second) definition in a manner that assuages some common concerns and basic intuitions about lying.

Pruss's first move is to offer an understanding of lying that is compatible with the Church's prohibition of it. The basic principle can be formulated as such: "you may not utter an assertion which you believe to be false when understood in your interlocutor's language (i.e., the language in which your interlocutor will take your assertion to have been made), with intent to deceive."[29] What he means by this is that words are never simply *given*. When a person utters a statement, there are certain conditions that must be met in order for communication to occur. He notes that some utterances that we might traditionally be considered lies are not necessarily so once we consider how the words are received by the listener. As stated, this would seem to present a strong argument against equivocation – a stance that I share and defend in Chapter 5. Yet, surprisingly, Pruss claims that, in the classic Gestapo scenario (a Nazi at the door and Jews hiding in the basement), "[I]t is acceptable to say to the Gestapo, in a clear voice, 'No, there are no Jews in my house.'"[30] He claims that not only would this assertion be compatible with the "speak your interlocutor's language" principle and the second edition of the *Catechism* – he claims that "to say, 'Yes, there are Jews in my house,' would be to lie."[31]

---

[27] Alexander Pruss, "The Case against False Assertions," *First Things* (September 22, 2011), www.firstthings.com/web-exclusives/2011/09/the-case-against-false-assertions.
[28] Catechism of the Catholic Church, 1st ed. (English), § 2483.
[29] Pruss, "Lying and Speaking Your Interlocutor's Language," 443.
[30] Ibid., 440.
[31] Ibid., 440–441.

How can Pruss arrive at such a counterintuitive conclusion? He suggests that, for the Nazi, the term "Jew" refers, by definition, to a being who is less than human, who does not possess human dignity, and for whom justice is not required. Thus, the Nazi and the person hiding the Jews are not "speaking the same language" during this encounter. According to Pruss, it is therefore not a lie to say, "There are no Jews hiding here," because, within the strictures of the Nazi's personal language, there is no one who meets the description of "Jew" in the house:

For the Gestapo officer, the primary meaning of the word "Jew" was something like "a sub-human, cold-hearted, shameless, calculating trafficker in vices." Thus, when the Gestapo officer asked Helga, "Are there any Jews in your house?" what his question really meant in ordinary English was: "Are there any sub-human, cold-hearted, shameless, calculating traffickers in vices in your house?"[32]

This is the meaning of "Jew" that Helga must take into account when responding to the officer: "[A]fter a moment of thought during which she translated from Gestapo-speak to her own language and back, she answered with something that when translated from Gestapo-speak to ordinary English would mean: 'No, there are no sub-human, cold-hearted, shameless, calculating traffickers in vices in my house.'"[33] On this account, it would be a *lie* to answer, "They are in the basement." This understanding of lying represents a significant deviation from the traditional understanding of duplicity. This in itself does not invalidate Pruss's arguments, but it shifts the locus of debate, because we are no longer discussing a misalignment between one's own thoughts and what one speaks. But I would argue that, for one, this model sets a nearly impossible bar for moral action. It requires a kind of mind-reading that is unrealistic in most situations, and it opens new doors of casuistry that bring more obscurity than clarity to the subject of lying.

I agree with Pruss that language is defined by usage and not by dictionaries.[34] In most cases of speaking with an interlocutor, we must rely on our best knowledge of what our words are generally taken to mean, with sensitivity to our specific context. We must also assume that our interlocutor is doing the same. Pruss is unable to account for the Nazi at the door who does *not* harbor the definition given above, the Nazi who *does* speak our "language." What if this Nazi officer acknowledges the humanity of the Jews, but his conscience is hardened and he simply

[32] Ibid., 445.
[33] Ibid., 445–446.
[34] Ibid., 445.

finds it more important to follow the orders of his superiors? Pruss briefly considers this objection, but his response strains credibility: "it could be said that malice necessarily distorts one's point of view [...] so that in [the Nazi's] linguistic practice, 'Jew,' despite his explicit avowals to the contrary, necessarily takes on a meaning charged with false properties." But now we are no longer speaking our interlocutor's language – we are essentially telling him what his utterance of the word "Jew" *really* means, even though it contradicts his own conscious thoughts when he uses the word.

Even more problematically, Benedict Guevin capitalizes on Pruss's insights and adds that "the ethical context in which a communication occurs is just as important as speaking the interlocutor's language."[35] What is the "ethical context"? Guevin does not mean to suggest that Helga's intention to save the Jews makes her statement something other than a lie. Nor does he conclude that the Nazi's lack of right to the truth changes the genre of her speech act. Rather, he offers an idiosyncratic argument proposing that her actions did not occur within the context of "human communication." I quote Guevin in full:

Now let us consider the broader ethical context in which Helga "lied" to the Gestapo. For Aquinas, a lie is evil because it is contrary to reason, destroying the rational ordering of human communication and is, therefore, an offense against the virtue of justice. But is there human communication present when the Gestapo asks Helga if she is hiding Jews in her house? Certainly there is, but only in the limited sense that human beings (Helga and the Gestapo) are speaking to each other. Is this human communication as Aquinas understood it? I think not, especially if we recall that for him truthful human communication fosters the mutual trust needed to live together in society. What passed as "human communication" in Nazi Germany can hardly be seen as fostering mutual trust. In fact, I would argue that the Gestapo's interrogation of Helga itself constitutes an act of genocide if, on the basis of her "truthful" response to them, they were to capture the Jews and kill them. In light of the broader context in which Helga "lied" to the Gestapo, we can conclude that what she said did not violate the virtue of truthfulness and was, therefore, not a lie.[36]

It is hard to see this argument as anything but circular. It builds into the notion of "communication" the very notion of what ought to be the aim of communication, namely, the fostering of truth. Guevin is suggesting that when this aim is absent, so is authentic communication. The only thing that saves this from obliterating the very possibility of lying

---

[35] Benedict M. Guevin, "When a Lie Is Not a Lie: The Importance of Ethical Context," *Thomist* 66 (2002): 267–274; cited at 267.
[36] Ibid., 272–273.

is the fact that Guevin considers the entire historical landscape of Nazi Germany to be an "ethical context." As such, "The ethical context in which she willingly deceived the Gestapo is part of the morally objective dimension of her action, objectified by the practical reason."[37] Her context may be a morally objective dimension of her action, but Guevin has failed to demonstrate why it does not constitute human communication.

A UNIVERSAL MORAL NORM

Many ethicists have argued that lying is always wrong because it violates a universal moral norm. Some Thomists have defended this view and have argued that Aquinas grounds his opposition to lying on this principle. Christopher Tollefsen, a Catholic philosopher and ethicist, has written a book-length defense of this argument, *Lying and Christian Ethics*, which (like my own project) draws heavily from Aquinas while also extending his analysis to address contemporary questions. Under close examination, however, his arguments diverge significantly from Aquinas's, and, in my judgment, his constructive account is less than persuasive. Tollefsen finds the wrongness of lying, not in its opposition to the virtue of truthfulness, but rather in its opposition to the "basic goods" of personal integrity and sociality.[38] If this proposal succeeds, then there is a universal moral norm against lying, and it must therefore never be done. The nature of the lie or the purpose for which it is told is irrelevant; all lies share the same feature which makes them wrong, namely, that they are opposed to fundamental, basic goods of human society.

My first objection to Tollefsen's proposal, insofar as it claims to be Thomistic, is that it contains an inadequate analysis of the virtue of truthfulness. This is not a minor omission. For Aquinas, the virtue of truthfulness does not merely supplement his analysis of lying; it sets the very structure within which his analysis occurs. In Tollefsen's account, this virtue only appears as a secondary consideration in order to "clarify" what Aquinas might have meant in his analysis of lying in Question 110 of the *secunda secundae*. He expresses puzzlement, even embarrassment,

---

[37] Ibid., 273. Guevin is drawing here on principles articulated by Martin Rhonheimer in *Natural Law and Practical Reason: A Thomist View of Moral Autonomy*, trans. Gerald Malsbary (New York 2000), 452–483.
[38] Tollefsen also includes the goods of *truth* and *religion* among the goods to which lying is opposed, but he does not believe that these are as fundamental or universally recognizable as the goods of *sociality* and *integrity*. See *Lying and Christian Ethics*, 126.

at Aquinas's claim that speech "naturally" signifies intellectual acts. In his endeavor to explain this away, he misses the intrinsic connection between Aquinas's claim about the *naturalness* of truthfulness and the *virtue* of truthfulness in *ST* II-II.109. He laments that Aquinas appears to be repeating a version of the "perverted faculty" argument (which I address below), and he develops his own defense that does not rely on this specious claim.

In his attempt to read between the lines and fill in the gaps in Aquinas's account, Tollefsen develops a "basic goods" approach to the fundamental impermissibility of lying. This move reflects Tollefsen's commitment to the "New Natural Law" school of moral philosophy, which seeks to apply a broadly Thomistic account of practical reason to contemporary moral issues without relying on any specific metaphysical framework. On this account, basic goods are "basic underived aspects of human well-being and fulfillment, such as life and health, knowledge, friendship and so on."[39] He approaches the prohibition against lying from a law- or norm-based perspective, which ignores the placement of Aquinas's analysis of lying within his treatise on the virtues rather than the treatise on law. The argument that lying is against the basic goods of integrity and sociality is far weaker than Aquinas's own understanding of the virtue of truthfulness, precisely because Tollefsen wants this claim about basic goods to do something Aquinas himself does not attempt: to claim that all lies are impermissible because they violate an exceptionless moral norm. Tollefsen's framework does not allow for gradations of sin among various types of lies. There is simply an exceptionless moral norm against all lying. Aquinas, on the contrary, designates some lies as venially sinful (but not "impermissible," insofar as they are not prohibited by the law) and others as mortal (which are strictly impermissible).

Like Smith's reading, Tollefsen's account also misses the nuances of the mortal–venial distinction in its assessment of the moral gravity of lying. He does not only miss the nuances – he misses the distinction entirely. I find it inexplicable that a monograph-length, Thomistic argument against lying could fail to acknowledge the distinction between mortal and venial sin. The fact that Tollefsen is a philosopher and not a theologian is not sufficient to explain this omission. Elsewhere in the book, he acknowledges that his arguments freely move "between philosophy and theology."[40] Neither can the omission be explained because Tollefsen is trying to develop his own constructive account and is merely borrowing

---

[39] Tollefsen, *Lying and Christian Ethics*, 109.
[40] Ibid., 101.

a few key concepts from Aquinas. He frequently ascribes central aspects of his own view to Aquinas himself, for example, when he describes the malice of lying as a "deliberate sundering of [one's] integrity and thus is always wrong." He goes on to say, "And this thought appears to be present in Aquinas's treatment as well."[41] Yet, he wanders even farther from Aquinas when he claims:

> It is, then, this twofold contrariety to human good in manifestation of the world and self to others through signs that is, for Aquinas, "unnatural" – contrary to reason – and "undue" – inordinately related to genuine human goods. The argument is not based on any idea of the thwarting or perverting of the natural function of something, whether speech or tongue. It is grounded in human good and a sound sense of what is chosen in this particular choice: to assert what is contrary to one's own mind.[42]

Tollefsen seems momentarily to have forgotten (perhaps intentionally, given his reservations) *ST* II-II.110.3, in which Aquinas claims that "words are by nature signs of one's thoughts" and therefore "it is unnatural and undue that anyone should signify with words that which is not in one's mind."

The problem with Tollefsen's position is not that it poorly represents Aquinas's own position. Rather, the problem is that it attempts to use Aquinas's arguments to defend a rigorist position that is indefensible. This is due in part to the fact that the basic goods approach cannot accommodate degrees of *malum* in the act of lying. It also cannot resolve difficult cases, such as the Nazi-at-the-door scenario, which I engage at length in Chapter 5. In the end, any proposal that seeks to locate the wrongness of lying in an exceptionless moral norm will be laden with insurmountable difficulties. Moreover, it neglects the very foundation of Aquinas's argument against lying, namely, that truthfulness is a virtue.

DISORDERED SPEECH

The claim that lying is opposed to basic goods of human society is not the only basis for the view that there is an exceptionless moral norm prohibiting it. Some ethicists, including some Thomists, share Tollefsen's absolutist position on lying, but they instead ground the prohibition in the lie's perversion of the human faculty of language. While they do not deny that the use of language is an inherently social practice, they choose to emphasize

[41] Ibid., 54.
[42] Ibid., 56.

the role of language as a natural human faculty. In other words, they first propose a metaphysical account of human nature, one that is broadly Aristotelian and Thomistic, and then develop an account of the purpose or *telos* of language that is grounded in human nature. If it can be shown that lying is opposed to this *telos*, then it ought never be done, and it follows that there must be an exceptionless moral norm against lying.

Christopher Tollefsen and other New Natural Law theorists are not sympathetic to this argument, even if some support for it can be found in Aquinas. For example, Aquinas claims that "spoken words are by nature signs of one's thoughts,"[43] and he uses this claim to support his argument that it is never good to tell a lie.[44] In *Lying and Christian Ethics*, Tollefsen laments that Aquinas's argument here

> looks very much like a version of a perverted faculty argument, an argument that holds that the "natural function" of something should not be thwarted deliberately. Such arguments are hardly compelling in their most common setting, which concerns the use of bodily organs, such as sex organs. That the natural function of an organ *is* such and such does not provide a *reason* for agents to respect that function, at least, not absent some account of the relation of the function to a good that is preserved or promoted by that function. Thus, on their own, natural-function arguments are empty of their normative significance.[45]

---

[43] *ST* II-II.110.3: "Est enim actus cadens super indebitam materiam, cum enim *voces sint signa naturaliter intellectuum*, innaturale est et indebitum quod aliquis voce significet id quod non habet in mente" (italics added to indicate translated portion). Aquinas refers to words as "signa intellectuum" twenty-two times throughout his works, but, curiously, this is the only instance in which he adds the qualifier "naturaliter." A more literal translation might read, "Spoken words are naturally signs of the intellect," where *intellectuum* is Aquinas's standard term for the higher cognitive faculty. Given the context of this passage, however, he is simply trying to convey the notion that words are verbal signifiers of one's thoughts.

[44] Aquinas is drawing here on Aristotle's view that words are signs of one's thoughts, although Aristotle specifically states that spoken words are signs of the "passions of the soul": Ἔστι μὲν οὖν τὰ ἐν τῇ φωνῇ τῶν ἐν τῇ ψυχῇ παθημάτων σύμβολα ("spoken words are symbols of the soul's passions"), *Peri Hermeneias* I.1. It is worth noting that Aristotle does not deploy this principle to argue against lying. Rather, Aristotle's objections to lying (*Nicomachean Ethics* IV.7) are framed within a spectrum that includes boasting and false humility, both of which extend beyond the mean of virtue. Thus, Aquinas, in typical fashion, is drawing upon Aristotle in order to go beyond what the Philosopher says himself. For an insightful analysis of Aristotle's position on lying, see Jane S. Zembaty, "Aristotle on Lying," *Journal of the History of Philosophy* 31:1 (1993): 7–29. Zembaty concludes (correctly, in my judgment) that, while Aristotle holds a generally negative view of lying, for him some lies are morally acceptable "when they harm no one, involve no undeserved disrespect, and stem from excellence and self-sufficiency rather than some deficiency of character" (29).

[45] Tollefsen, *Lying and Christian Ethics*, 45.

Tollefsen is articulating a version of the "Is–Ought" fallacy, made famous by the eighteenth-century British philosopher David Hume.[46] If Aquinas's argument against lying is grounded in the natural purpose of language, then he has mistakenly derived an "ought" from an "is." To make matters even worse, Tollefsen explains,

> The argument that Aquinas seems to be giving in this passage is made more problematic by its seeming focus on the natural purpose of *language*, for language is an artifact, something made by human beings to serve their purposes; this is something St. Thomas is quite aware of. And there is no principled reason why an artifact made to serve one purpose might not have several purposes.[47]

Thus, not only has Aquinas incorrectly inferred a morally normative claim directly from a feature of the natural world; he seems to have momentarily forgotten that language is not even a "natural" phenomenon at all – it is an *artifact*, a human creation. Tollefsen still finds Aquinas's analysis of lying to be persuasive overall, but he rejects this specific line of argument as an embarrassing flaw. To rescue Aquinas, Tollefsen draws our attention away from language and toward the basic goods of *society* and *personal integrity*.

Such attacks have not deterred certain thinkers from deploying some version of the perverted faculty argument (hereafter "PFA"). John Skalko, in *Disordered Actions: A Moral Analysis of Lying and Homosexual Activity*,[48] argues that not only does Aquinas ground his position on the morality of lying in PFA but also that this strategy is philosophically defensible. The title of Skalko's book will strike many contemporary readers as an arbitrary juxtaposition of two discrete topics of ethical inquiry, but given the author's commitment to PFA, the volume functions as a coherent whole. Since lying and homosexual activity both involve the frustration of

---

[46] The *locus classicus* of the "Is–Ought" fallacy can be found in David Hume, *A Treatise Concerning Human Nature*, eds. David Fate Norton and Mary J. Norton (New York 2000), 3.1.1. Hume observes that moral philosophers, when describing a state of affairs (the way things are), often slip imperceptibly into normative statements: "For as this *ought*, or *ought not*, expresses some new relation or affirmation, 'tis necessary that it shou'd be observ'd and explain'd; and at the same time that a reason should be given, for what seems altogether inconceivable, how this new relation can be a deduction from others, which are entirely different from it." Hume scholars in fact debate the correct reading of this text, which has been interpreted variously to support noncognitivism, to refute naturalistic moral arguments, or simply to criticize what Hume considered intellectual laziness. Nonetheless, Hume became associated with the so-called "Is–Ought" fallacy, which now functions as a sort of lightning rod among moral philosophers.

[47] Tollefsen, *Lying and Christian Ethics*, 45.

[48] John Skalko, *Disordered Actions: A Moral Analysis of Lying and Homosexual Activity* (Neunkirchen-Seelscheid 2019).

a natural human faculty, they are immoral for the same fundamental reason. This claim, of course, stands or falls on the cogency of PFA. Skalko's arguments are more nuanced than most defenders' of PFA, and he does not make the mistake of asserting that all violations of a natural function are morally bad.[49] The basis of his argument, which he approvingly refers to as "Aquinas's perverted faculty argument," is as follows: "[A]ny action not ordered to its due end is a disordered action. The natural end of an action is its due end."[50] While there are several more premises and qualifications involved in Skalko's argument,[51] it ultimately amounts to the claim that a universal norm against lying can be generated from the observation that lying frustrates the natural end of a human faculty.

Skalko addresses Tollefsen's criticisms, first by noting that "lying is not opposed to the faculty of language as such, but rather to a particular instantiation of language, namely, assertions."[52] I am in full agreement with Skalko on this point. This important distinction also mitigates Tollefsen's criticisms to a certain extent.[53] I also share Skalko's emphasis on the importance of human nature for understanding the morality of lying, but we disagree on the normative significance generated by the faculty of assertion.[54] He writes,

In asserting, one is engaging in an act (asserting) that has its own natural end of conveying the truth to another. But in telling a lie one is using this type of action (an assertion) for an end contrary to what it is naturally ordered towards. In other words, one is engaging in an action that has a natural end of its own, and then deliberately and at the same time frustrating that end from happening. One is engaging in an action with its own natural order to an end, and then superimposing on this action an end contrary to its natural end.[55]

[49] Ibid., 169–186.
[50] Ibid., 319.
[51] For Skalko's reconstruction of PFA that addresses the shortcomings of its prominent advocates, see ibid., 258–263.
[52] Ibid., 167. Skalko makes a similar move in his analysis of homosexuality, arguing that it is not opposed to the function of the sex organs themselves, but rather it is opposed to that which makes them distinctly *sexual*, namely, the purpose of reproduction (and by extension, education of offspring). See pp. 217–218.
[53] Skalko offers a thorough response to Tollefsen and the New Natural Law school in *Disordered Actions*, 147–156.
[54] See my essay, "Speaking Truthfully: A Thomistic Perspective on the Peculiar Origins of Human Language," in *The Evolution of Wisdom*, eds. Celia Deane-Drummond and Agustín Fuentes (Lanham, MD 2017), 109–126, where I argue that the naturalness of language is morally significant but does not generate moral norms *ipso facto*. For a constructive account of trust and its role in human societies, grounded in the idea of social personalism, see Thomas O. Buford, *Trust, Our Second Nature: Crisis, Reconciliation, and the Personal* (Lanham, MD 2009).
[55] Skalko, *Disordered Actions*, 166.

For Skalko, this is why lying is an intrinsically disordered act, and such acts are never morally permissible. According to this logic, lying is analogous to using a condom during sexual intercourse: It is an act that deliberately frustrates a natural faculty. Regardless of one's subjective intention (to save another person's life, to prevent an unwanted pregnancy, etc.), such acts are always wrong.[56] Thus, Skalko's and Tollefsen's positions can be described as absolutist, and they share a commitment to a universal norm against lying. Yet, they greatly disagree about the basis of this universal norm. Indeed, the feature of Aquinas's argument that Tollefsen finds embarrassing is the feature that Skalko finds most compelling. In the end, I find the proposals of both authors to be misguided.

One of the central convictions of this book is that the wrongness of lying is not to be found in its violation of a universal moral norm. To be clear, this is not because I reject the idea of universal norms, nor do I think that we should create "exceptions" to the norm against lying. Rather, I reject the PFA against lying for two reasons. First, I believe that it ultimately fails as a philosophical argument. The strongest versions of PFA, including Skalko's, rely on the notion that a human faculty can be "frustrated," but proponents have never successfully articulated what it means to frustrate a faculty's end. Skalko frequently notes that frustrating differs from merely "not using" a faculty (the former is morally blameworthy; the latter is not), but it remains unclear how this does not simply amount to some different use of the faculty's power. The argument is especially dubious when applied to faculties other than the faculty of reproduction. What would it mean to frustrate the faculty of sight, for example?[57] Second, I believe that Aquinas's position on lying rests not on PFA but rather on a more promising foundation.[58] In short, Aquinas argues that lying can be considered not only as an action but as a vice – more precisely, a vice against the virtue of truthfulness. Truthfulness is a virtue related to justice, but it is not identical to it. When we consider the nature of truthfulness, we find that it is incoherent to describe any lie as

---

[56] Ibid., 19–21.
[57] I wish to thank my student, Adrian McCaffery, OP, for this insight. I have benefited greatly from his (yet unpublished) work on the perverted faculty argument.
[58] Skalko acknowledges that his detailed presentation of Aquinas's argument against lying is not explicitly in Aquinas (185). There is nothing wrong with this, and the same could be said of my own presentation of Aquinas's argument against lying found in this book. But it should be noted that both Skalko and I are extending Aquinas's analysis and attempting to make his implicit premises explicit. Ultimately, the reader will have to judge whose reconstruction is most compelling.

a morally good action. To understand the full force of these claims, we will need to situate them within a broader structure of the virtues and the moral law, which will be done in the chapters that follow.

SPEAKING TRINITARIAN

Some Christian ethicists would object to all the preceding proposals on the grounds that they make their arguments on wholly secular terms. In other words, the wrongness of lying – more precisely, the wrongness of *all* lying – can only be discerned through the lens of theological anthropology (the study of human nature) and hamartiology (the study of sin). Some even accuse Aquinas of falling short in this regard. In his book, *Lying: An Augustinian Theology of Duplicity*, Catholic theologian Paul Griffiths offers a striking Augustinian critique of Aquinas's position on lying.[59] Griffiths's position could be classified as an "extreme absolutist" position, insofar as he believes not only that lying is always impermissible, but that *all* lies are mortally sinful. He criticizes Aquinas for being a "less than fully Christian thinker" on the morality of lying precisely because he introduces a distinction between mortal and venial lies.[60] Griffiths claims, incorrectly in my judgment, that Aquinas makes lies primarily about harm and injustice, and as a result, this places the locus of moral analysis within the realm of social ethics. He argues that starting with justice "ensures that Aquinas's discussion of the particularities of the lie will consider its wrongness principally in terms of its relation to and effects upon someone other than the liar – and will therefore move in the sphere of (what we might call) interpersonal and social ethics."[61] For Griffiths (who takes himself to be following Augustine), the fundamental wrongness of lying is personal rather than social: All lies break the bond between a person's thought and word, and therefore they sever the bonds of charity. "The contrast with Augustine's position is dramatic," he explains. "For Augustine, duplicitous speech is a rupture of the divine image, a recursively incoherent act best characterized as a refusal of the divine gift by attempted expropriation. It is sin's very paradigm. In Aquinas's terms, this would be an offense against love, and thus a mortal sin."[62] The human faculty of speech is a divine gift, and any sin

---

[59] Paul J. Griffiths, *Lying: An Augustinian Theology of Duplicity* (Grand Rapids, MI 2004).
[60] Ibid., 183.
[61] Ibid., 174.
[62] Ibid., 183.

against this gift is mortal. Here, we find echoes of the PFA, but Griffiths's version is adamantly theological.

While Griffiths acknowledges that Aquinas is closer to Augustine (and to Griffiths's own position) than any other Christian writer on the subject of lying,[63] he still detects a fundamental failure in Aquinas's position. For Augustine, a lie is a rupture of the divine image; for Aquinas, it is principally a sin against justice.[64] This makes Aquinas's position less Trinitarian, less theological, which *ipso facto* means that it is inferior. There are two problems with this claim. First, the claim that Augustine grounds his prohibition of lying on his anthropology of the *imago Dei* is dubious. As Matthew Puffer has decisively shown, Augustine does not develop this notion until his very late work, *De trinitate*, and it is virtually absent in his discussions on lying prior to this work.[65] Augustine develops his position based on his reading of the biblical texts, and he offers an assortment of reasons for the impermissibility of lying.[66] The second problem with this claim is that Aquinas does not relate all lying to the realm of justice simpliciter (that is, other-regarding concerns). In his exposition of Aquinas, Griffiths frequently collapses the virtue of truthfulness into the virtue of justice, but this is a mistake. As I will explain in subsequent chapters, the virtue of truthfulness is *annexed* to the virtue of justice, but they are not the same. Griffiths would likely respond that this distinction is irrelevant for his purposes; both virtues are concerned with human interpersonal relationships. But this is not quite right, either. The virtue of *veracitas* (truthfulness) does indeed pertain to humanity, but it does not generate claims of justice, precisely because it does not have the nature of *debt*. If *all* lies truly violated interpersonal relationships, then all lies would be mortal sins, as Griffiths claims. Griffiths would still contend that Aquinas mislocates the failure of lying by placing it outside the human–divine relationship. But this is also false, because all mortal sins are sins against charity.

Griffiths's departure from Augustine (and by extension, Aquinas) is most evident in his analysis of Augustine's eightfold hierarchy of lies in *De mendacio*, 25.[67] Augustine places lies concerning religious doctrine at the top of his hierarchy. These are the most sinful lies a person can

---

[63] Ibid., 174.
[64] Ibid., 184.
[65] Matthew Puffer, "Retracing Augustine's Ethics."
[66] See Feehan, "The Morality of Lying in St. Augustine."
[67] See Table 2.1.

utter, he maintains.⁶⁸ The remaining types of lies are listed in order of descending gravity. Yet, Griffiths singles out the category found, not at the top, but in the middle: lies told for the mere pleasure of lying. Griffiths writes,

> [T]hese classifications are intended mostly to show that although lies can be told in order to bring about good results, this has nothing to do with what makes them lies, with the deliberate duplicity that, recall, is the evil proper to lying. That evil is most clearly evident in the fourth kind of lie, the pure or unmixed lie: the fact that this lie is told only for the pleasure of telling it is what makes it pure.⁶⁹

Griffiths is correct that the principles dictating the way in which these lies are placed within the hierarchy are distinct from the principles that make lying sinful as such. But it does not follow that the evil of lying is "most clearly evident" in lies told for the mere pleasure of lying. This is true, perhaps, in a trivial sense, namely, that these lies are unadorned by any additional motives. But the evil is not "most clearly evident" in the sense that such actions display the highest degree of sinfulness one can achieve by lying. If that were the case, they would be the most sinful lies, and they would be at the top of the hierarchy rather than in the middle.

Apart from my exegetical concerns, Griffiths's position is untenable as a framework for the ethics of lying. This is not merely because it is "unrealistic." Most people, it is true, would find it preposterous to suggest that a lie told out of flattery (or to save someone's life for that matter) is of equal moral gravity with slander. But it also fails to do justice to scripture. It cannot explain why the Hebrew midwives, or Rahab, or Judith are not depicted as performing grave evils when they tell *officiosum* lies. In this regard, Augustine is more sensitive than Griffiths to the contours of biblical theology. Griffiths's view also fails to do justice to the Christian tradition. While Aquinas's position (as with Augustine's) is stricter than that of many other influential figures in the Christian tradition, his at least incorporates the concerns and intuitions of those who hold that lying is sometimes justified, even if his answers are different than theirs. Griffith's position, however, leaves no room for such incorporation, which leaves one to wonder whose position is "insufficiently Christian."

---

⁶⁸ Griffiths expresses confusion at Aquinas's claim that a lie's sinfulness can depend on its topic (*Lying*, 180), yet he expresses no reservations at Augustine's ranking of lies according to topic here.
⁶⁹ Ibid., 38.

In this chapter, I have given critical analyses of five proposals regarding the morality of lying that are at odds in at least one significant way with Aquinas's position. Each of these proposals reflects a commitment, either explicitly or implicitly, to some central tenets of Christian doctrine. But they mislocate the wrongness of lying in an act of injustice, a failure to speak the "language" of one's interlocutor, a violation of a universal moral norm, a perversion of the faculty of language, or a rupture in the *imago Dei*. What each proposal lacks, and what each proposal fails to recognize in Aquinas's thought, is a thick account of the virtue of *veracitas*, or truthfulness. An account that is grounded in this virtue will also have the corollary feature of giving an account of the *purposes* of human language that is not reducible to its "natural" function. For human beings, the use of language is constitutive of our growth in virtue, and the virtuous person will also strive to be a truthful person. As the argument of the book unfolds, it will become clear that this insight is what enables Aquinas's creative application of the mortal–venial distinction to the problem of lying. As we will see in Chapter 2, this mode of analysis eluded the biblical interpreters and moralists in the early period of Christianity, which resulted in an ambiguous legacy on the morality of lying. Aquinas and his medieval contemporaries struggled to reconcile the biblical texts, the patristic commentaries, and their own moral intuitions about lying. The resemblance between their concerns and the concerns of the contemporary authors I have engaged in this chapter is remarkable, and close attention to these concerns will put us in a better position to understand Aquinas's response to these problems.

2

The Ambiguous Legacy of the Eighth Commandment
"You Shall Not Bear False Witness"

Thomas Aquinas believes that every lie is a sin. Many people, if they are familiar at all with Aquinas's position on lying, are only aware of this feature of his argument. This is doubtless because virtually every reference work in moral philosophy and theology counts Aquinas, alongside Augustine and Immanuel Kant, as representative of the strict absolutist school, which maintains that there are no exceptions to the prohibition against lying.[1] But there is more to the story. In fact, the three most famous figures of the so-called strict absolutist school – Augustine, Aquinas, and Kant – reflect three distinct understandings of what it means to lie and why such an action is morally bad. While Aquinas inherits much from the Augustinian tradition on lying, he reshapes this tradition to suit his own purposes. Moreover, Aquinas's mature position on lying stands in stark contrast with the position that Kant would articulate nearly five centuries later. The fact that each of these three figures believed in an exceptionless prohibition against lying tells us very little about their respective views on the nature of language, the ethics of interpersonal communication, or the moral status of truth. To claim that their views constitute a uniform stance on lying would be as vapid as it would be to claim that their views on killing constitute a uniform stance on murder.

---

[1] For a typical example of this sort of conflation, see Ronald Preston's entry in *A New Dictionary of Christian Ethics*, eds. James F. Childress and John Macquarrie (London 1986), 363. Preston writes, "Centuries later [Augustine] was to be followed by Kant, who wrote against the supposed right of telling lies from benevolent motives." Similarly, James Mahon writes, "Like several prominent moral philosophers before him, such as St Augustine and St Thomas Aquinas, Kant held that it is never morally permissible to tell a lie," in "Kant on Lies, Candour and Reticence," *Kantian Review* 7 (2003): 102–133; cited at 102.

The purpose of the present chapter is to describe the historical and cultural context of Aquinas's thought on lying. To do this, the chapter focuses entirely on his sources and interlocutors. As a result, the uniqueness of his position will come into greater focus, laying the necessary groundwork for the more constructive chapters that follow. While the focus here is historical and interpretive, the overarching objective of Chapters 2 and 3 is to bring out the distinctive and, at times, puzzling features of Aquinas's position, and this will inevitably raise more questions than answers. These new questions will be addressed in due course, but it is important that we begin this study by stepping into Aquinas's own world and considering the questions that were most important to him and his contemporaries. In the process, we will discover nuances and distinctions that are frequently overlooked when we mistakenly assume that we, as moderns, can plunge right into the normative questions and draw on Aquinas as a convenient resource for moral reflection. The method I am proposing here instead allows Aquinas to set the agenda, even if we ultimately decide that we must go beyond what Aquinas says in order to address our contemporary concerns.

In the present chapter, I briefly trace the development of the church's teachings on lying as Aquinas inherited them. I begin with his most important and well-known theological sources, the Bible and the writings of Augustine, but I also draw attention to the array of conflicting positions within the Christian tradition, of which Aquinas was certainly aware. Moving into the Middle Ages, I articulate the reception of these earlier texts and the nuances that begin to emerge under the rigors of the scholastic method. This is the environment in which Aquinas operates, and while his writing is always indebted to the scholastic training he received under Albert the Great and the Dominicans, he is not afraid to stand apart from his contemporaries when he finds it necessary. As we shall see, there are two main features of Aquinas's position that render it unique. First, his development of the mortal–venial sin distinction pushes the analysis of lying into new territory with an unprecedented degree of precision. Second, the fact that his most extensive discussion of lying appears within an analysis of the virtue of truthfulness sets him apart from nearly every other author who has written on the subject, either before or after him. Why contemporary commentators have overlooked these two features of Aquinas's analysis of lying remains a mystery. But in order to understand why Aquinas engaged this question the way he did, we must first understand what came before him.

BIBLICAL AND PATRISTIC SOURCES

For Aquinas and his forebears, the Bible is the most important resource for assessing the moral status of lies. Yet, anyone familiar with relevant biblical texts knows that the Bible does not offer a coherent, systematic analysis of lying. Some might argue that the Bible does not offer a coherent, systematic analysis of any ethical subject. But lying stands apart from other immoral actions that are frequently addressed in the Bible, such as murder or avarice, insofar as it is rarely addressed as a discrete subject of moral scrutiny. When lying does appear in the biblical texts, it frequently takes the form of a character telling a lie within a narrative (e.g., Abraham telling Abimelech that Sarah is his sister, in Genesis 20). Often such lies are narrated without any commentary from the biblical author, much to the frustration of theologians and readers of scripture throughout the centuries.[2] One notable exception to this pattern is the story of Ananias and his wife, Sapphira, in Acts 5. Ananias had sold a piece of property and (as was the custom of his community) brings the proceeds before the apostles – except he secretly holds back a portion for himself. After Peter offers the rebuke, "You have not lied to men but to God" (Acts 5:4), Ananias is struck dead. In other instances, biblical characters tell lies in order to cover up more heinous actions, but due to their ancillary nature these lies receive less narrative attention than the primary sins.[3] Some biblical characters tell lies with no repercussions, presumably because the lie was told for a good end. Rahab, who lies to the Canaanite soldiers in order to protect Joshua's spies (Josh. 2:4–6), is depicted as noble and is later eulogized in the New Testament (Hebrews 11:31, James 2:25). This legacy of ambiguity is a source of difficulty for the early church fathers and theologians of the Middle Ages.

---

[2] See Evelin Sullivan, "The Bible: A Casebook," in *The Concise Book of Lying* (New York 2001), 3–28.

[3] For example, in Gen. 37:31–34, after Joseph's brothers sell him to a caravan of Ishmaelites, they report his "death" to their father, Jacob, by showing him Joseph's bloodstained robe (which they had dipped in goat's blood). The brothers' presentation of the robe is a curious blend of lying and what Aquinas calls "dissimulation"; that is, they do not say outright that an animal has killed Joseph. Rather, they simply say, "This we have found" (37:32), and they show Jacob the robe. As Robert Alter has observed, "The brothers are careful to let the contrived object, 'this [*zot*],' do their lying for them – it goes before them literally and syntactically – and of course they appropriately refer to Joseph as 'your son', not by name nor as their brother. Jacob now has his prop, and from here on he can improvise his own part: 'He recognized it [*vayakirah*], and he said: "It is my son's tunic! A vicious beast has devoured him, / Joseph is torn to shreds!"' (Gen. 37:33)," *The Art of Biblical Narrative* (New York 2011), 25.

The writings of the patristic period reflect a variety of perspectives on the subject of lying. While the majority of writers in this period held the position that lying is never permissible under any circumstances, there are a significant number who find no problem with falsehoods that are told for a good end. The most notable figures representing this latter strand include Clement of Alexandria, Origen, John Chrysostom, Hilary of Poitiers, Ambrose, and John Cassian.[4] It should be noted that, with the exception of Cassian, their affirmations of certain falsehoods are only made in passing, without any attempt to offer a detailed conceptual analysis of lying. Some of these affirmations are known through somewhat dubious anecdotes, such as the story of Athanasius, who was being pursued by Roman persecutors under the authority of the emperor Julian. Some of the pursuers stumbled upon Athanasius without recognizing who he was. When they asked him, "Is Athanasius nearby?" he replied, "He is not far." They continued on their way, without realizing they had just spoken with the man they were pursuing.[5]

This anecdote illustrates a form of equivocation, or as the casuists would later call it, "broad mental reservation." As Alasdair MacIntyre notes, "Whether one thinks this is a pointless anecdote or not reveals something fundamental about one's attitude to lying."[6] The question of whether such utterances count as lying remains a subject for debate, even among the church fathers. But some patristic authors offer a bolder, yet still qualified, endorsement of falsehoods that cannot even claim the label of equivocation. In his treatise, *On the Priesthood*, Chrysostom recounts how he leads his friend, Basil, into receiving Holy Orders under the pretense that both of them were to be ordained to the priesthood. Chrysostom tells Basil that he is also going to be ordained, because he

---

[4] See Julius Dorszynski, *Catholic Teaching about the Morality of Falsehood* (Washington, DC 1948), 16–18; Boniface Ramsey, "Two Traditions on Lying and Deception in the Ancient Church," *Thomist* 49 (1985): 504–533; Marcia Colish, "Rethinking Lying in the Twelfth Century," in *Virtue and Ethics in the Twelfth Century*, eds. István Bejczy and Richard Newhauser (Boston 2005), 155–173.

[5] The origins of this story are uncertain, but it is recounted by a number of authors, both ancient and contemporary. For example, see Alasdair MacIntyre, "Truthfulness, Lies, and Moral Philosophers," in *The Tanner Lectures on Human Values*, vol. 17, ed. Grethe B. Peterson (Salt Lake City 1994), 309–369; cited at 336. MacIntyre is quoting from F. A. M. Forbes, *St. Athanasius* (London 1919), 102. This story is also referenced in Kenneth W. Kemp and Thomas Sullivan, "Speaking Falsely and Telling Lies," *Proceedings of the American Philosophical Association* 67 (1993): 151–170; cited at 156. Kemp and Sullivan are quoting from Herbert Thurston and Donald Attwater, *Butler's Lives of the Saints* (Christian Classics 1990), II, 215.

[6] MacIntyre, "Truthfulness, Lies, and Moral Philosophers," 336.

knows that Basil will be reluctant otherwise. When the time for ordination comes, Chrysostom hides himself, and Basil is the only one who receives the sacrament. Chrysostom defends himself, explaining, "This was for the advantage both of yourself who were deceived and of those to whom I betrayed you by my deception."[7] He elaborates further:

> But if it is not always harmful; if it is made bad or good by the intentions of those who use it, stop accusing me of deception, and prove that I used this means for an evil end. For while this proof is lacking, it remains the duty of those who want to be fair, so far from finding fault and criticizing, rather to give their approval to the deceiver. A timely deception used with a right purpose is such an advantage that a lot of men have been called to account on many occasions for failing to deceive.[8]

Chrysostom goes on to provide examples of doctors using deception in treating their patients, for the purpose of healing them. The idea of benevolent deception as "medicine" is a common metaphor among the Eastern fathers. Origen writes, "The man who finds it necessary to lie, should diligently see to it that he uses the lie as a condiment and medicine."[9] Virtually all of these affirming remarks are offered anecdotally or in brief comments on passages of scripture. Not until the writings of John Cassian, a disciple of Chrysostom, do we find any systematic analysis in support of lying. Cassian dedicates fifteen chapters of his *Collationes* to this subject, but he concludes that lying can only be chosen when it is clearly the lesser of two evils: "When then any grave danger hangs on confession of the truth, then we must take to lying as a refuge, yet in such a way as to be, for our salvation, troubled by the guilt of a humbled conscience."[10] Thus, in the early Christian tradition, even the most notable supporter of the notion that lying is sometimes permissible finds the practice to be morally problematic.

AUGUSTINE ON LYING AND BEARING FALSE WITNESS

Despite the diverse opinions of the church fathers on this topic, the patristic legacy on lying is dominated by the writings of Augustine of Hippo. No other figure even comes close to Augustine's influence on the development of Christian theology (at least in the West), and his position on lying is no exception. Up until the fourth century, it remains an open question as to

---

[7] St. John Chrysostom, *On the Priesthood*, trans. Graham Neville (Crestwood, NY 1977), I.8.
[8] Ibid.
[9] Origen, *Stromatum*, 6 (J.-P. Migne, *Patrologiae Graeca* [PG] 29, col. 102). Cited in Dorszynski, *Catholic Teaching*, 17.
[10] John Cassian, *Collationes*, 17, c. 17 (PG 49, col. 1062). Cited in Dorszynski, *Catholic Teaching*, 18.

whether it might be permissible to tell lies on occasion. Yet, his absolutist position – that it is never permissible to lie – largely wins the day. As a young bishop, he first begins to articulate his views in a series of letters to the more senior and well-known Jerome. Augustine is troubled by Jerome's suggestion that the scriptures teach the idea that "pretense is useful and should be adopted on occasion."[11] Augustine writes a letter addressed to Jerome, which was widely circulated, in which he singles out Jerome's interpretation of Galatians 2:11–14, concerning Paul's rebuke of Peter for maintaining certain Jewish customs (but only when other Jews were watching him). Jerome finds Paul's rebuke rather curious, since Paul was prone to such practices himself. He cites Acts 18:18, 21:23–6, and 16:3, showing that Paul participated in Jewish religious rites, including Nazarite vows, almsgiving, and circumcision. Rather than assuming that Paul is simply a hypocrite for rebuking Peter's similar behavior, Jerome concludes that there must have been a secret agreement between the two of them. In other words, Paul's rebuke of Peter was only a ruse. As Jason Myers explains, "[F]or Jerome, the conflict between Peter and Paul is not really a conflict between them, for Peter knew what was right and Paul himself had participated in similar actions. Rather, the conflict was to bring about harmony in the group, and Paul's confrontation was not really a confrontation of Peter, but of those whom Peter represented."[12] Jerome's exegetical and hermeneutical commitments trumped whatever concern he might have had about the possibility that the Bible could condone a falsehood.

Augustine would have none of it. As Roger Ray describes, "In Jerome's exegesis Augustine saw no less than the potential collapse of biblical authority and thus of the Gospel itself."[13] In a letter dripping with dramatic irony, Augustine laments, "To find a defense of falsehoods [in your commentary on Galatians], whether by such a person as yourself or perhaps by someone else (if it is someone else's writing), distresses me, I must confess, until my mind can be changed on this matter – if that is even possible."[14] After expressing his incredulity that Jerome could

---

[11] Jerome, *St. Jerome's Commentaries on Galatians, Titus, and Philemon*, trans. Thomas P. Scheck (Notre Dame, IN 2010), 98–99.
[12] Jason A. Myers, "Law, Lies and Letter Writing: An Analysis of Jerome and Augustine on the Antioch Incident (Galatians 2:11–14)," *Scottish Journal of Theology* 66:2 (2013), 131.
[13] Roger D. Ray, "Christian Conscience and Pagan Rhetoric: Augustine's Treatises on Lying," *Studia Patristica* 22 (1987): 2321–2325; cited at 2323.
[14] Letter 28.3. "Ibi patrocinium mendacii susceptum esse vel abs te tali viro, vel a quopiam, si alius illa scripsit, fateor, non mediocriter doleo, donec refellantur (si forte refelli possunt), ea quae me movent." *S. Aurelii Augustini Opera Omnia*, in *Patrologiae Cursus*

maintain such a position, Augustine writes a follow-up letter calling on him to retract this opinion in writing.[15] At least in these letters, Augustine is less concerned about the morality of lying as such as he is about the possibility of sacred scripture containing a lie: "It is one question whether at any time a good person has a duty to deceive, yet it is a different question whether it could have been the duty of an author of holy scripture to deceive. In fact, it is not merely a different question – it is not a question at all."[16] While Augustine's motives for writing the letters were most likely somewhat mixed (and needless to say, Jerome did not appreciate this unsolicited rebuttal), we find in these texts the beginnings of Augustine's mature position on lying, namely, that it is never permitted, regardless of circumstances.[17]

Around the same time these volleys were being exchanged between Jerome and Augustine, the latter set to work on a treatise on the subject of lying.[18] Augustine's *De Mendacio*, written in 395, articulates the (in)famous Augustinian definition of a lie:

Thus, a person lies who **has one thing in mind yet expresses something else with words** (or any kind of sign). This is why it said that the liar has a "double heart," or, in other words, a double thought: the one, concerning that which he either knows or thinks to be true, but does not make known; the other, which he makes known, while knowing or thinking it to be false.[19]

Completus Series Latina, vol. 33, ed. J.-P. Migne (Paris 1865). Hereafter, all texts found in *Patrologiae Latina* are cited in "PL," followed by the volume number. Unless otherwise stated, English translations of Augustine's writings are my own.

[15] Letter 40.7, in *S. Aurelii Augustini Opera Omnia* (PL 33).

[16] Letter 28.3. "Alia quippe quaestio est, sitne aliquando mentiri viri boni; et alia quaestio est, utrum scriptorem sanctarum Scripturarum mentiri oportuerit: imo vero non alia, sed nulla quaestio est."

[17] Looking forward, Aquinas will reference this dispute in his Galatians commentary, noting that the text of Gal. 2:14 was the occasion for "no small controversy" between Jerome and Augustine (*In Gal.* 2:14 § 86). He goes into great detail regarding the nature of their disagreement, but he ultimately (and unsurprisingly) sides with Augustine (§ 88). *Super epistolam ad Galatas lectura*, ed. Raphael Cai, *Super epistolas S. Pauli lectura*, 8th rev. edn, 2 vols. (Turin 1953), vol. 1, pp. 563–649.

[18] Ray suggests that, while it is likely that Augustine's correspondence with Jerome served as the catalyst for the first treatise on lying, there was more at stake: "Beyond the foreground of strictly theological controversy there is, I believe, a conflict between Christian conscience and the utilitarian ethic of the pagan rhetorical schools," in "Christian Conscience and Pagan Rhetoric," 322.

[19] *De mendacio*, 3: "Quapropter ille mentitur, qui **aliud habet in animo, et aliud verbis** vel quibuslibet significationibus enuntiat. Unde etiam duplex cor dicitur esse mentientis, id est, duplex cogitatio: una rei eius quam veram esse vel scit vel putat, et non profert; altera eius rei quam pro ista profert sciens falsam esse vel putans" (in PL 40). Emphasis mine.

This text will become the *locus classicus* on lying in the Christian tradition, through the Middle Ages and beyond. While Augustine has much more to say about the morality of lying, it is worth noting that his formal definition of the act does not contain anything about the person on the receiving end of the lie – it is merely a formal description of duplicity. Nor is this definition concerned with the material falsehood of the utterance. One can utter an objectively false statement ("Paris is the capital of Germany") without lying, so long as she herself believes the statement to be true. Likewise, she can utter an objectively true statement ("Paris is the capital of France") while still being guilty of lying, provided that she believes this statement to be false. The principle at work here is what I will refer to as the *contra mentem* principle: to lie is to speak that which is opposed to one's mind.[20] This principle is the foundation of Augustine's negative stance toward lying, and it is one that Aquinas will endorse and develop in his own writings on the subject.

Another conspicuous feature of this definition is that it says nothing about the speaker's intention to deceive. Granted, Augustine at times appears to suggest that such an intent is a necessary condition for lying, such as in this frequently cited text from *De mendacio*: "But no one doubts that it is a lie when a person willingly declares a falsehood for the purpose of deceiving: thus, a false statement declared with an intention to deceive [*voluntate ad fallendum*] is a manifest lie."[21] But Augustine only indicates that a false utterance with intent to deceive is a *sufficient* condition for determining that a lie has been told: "Yet it is another question whether this alone is a lie."[22] There is at least a possibility that lies need not meet the above conditions. And given what

---

[20] The precise term *contra mentem* is introduced in the literature on lying by Raymond de Peñafort in his *Summa de casibus poenitentiae* (1224–1226): "Mentiri est contra mentem ire et hoc secundum ethimologiam vocabuli" ("Lying 'goes against the mind,'" in accordance with the etymology of the term"), *Summa S. Raymundi de Peniafort, cum glossis Joannis de Friburgo, secunda editio auctior et correctior* (Avignon 1715), I, tit. 10, 1.

[21] *De mendacio*, 5. "Nemo autem dubitat mentiri eum qui volens falsum enuntiat causa fallendi: quapropter enuntiationem falsam cum voluntate ad fallendum prolatam, manifestum est esse mendacium." I translate *voluntate ad fallendum* as "intention to deceive," following William E. Mann in his essay, "To Catch a Heretic – Augustine on Lying," *Faith & Philosophy* 20:4 (October 2003): 479–495. On the difference between "desires" and "intentions," Mann writes, "Our desires come to us unbidden (but not necessarily unwelcome). We generally have no more direct voluntary control over them than we do over our ordinary beliefs. Just as my beliefs can be inconsistent, my desires can conflict with each other: the satisfaction of one can logically preclude the satisfaction of others. In contrast, many intentions are arrived at voluntarily" (483).

[22] *De mendacio*, 5.

he says in these treatises, it is clear that intent to deceive is not a necessary feature. Still, it would be misleading to claim, as some interpreters have, that deception is extraneous to Augustine's definition of the lie. It is crucial to distinguish between two senses of "deception" in this context: (1) intending to mislead another person regarding the actual state of affairs in the world and (2) intending to mislead another person regarding the contents of one's thoughts. On Augustine's account, the first kind of deception – while often present when a lie is told – is not a strictly necessary criterion for lying, whereas the second kind of deception is always necessary.[23] This distinction is sometimes lost on Augustine's interpreters, but its importance will become clear as my analysis unfolds.

Augustine is well aware that his position reflects a minority report within the Christian tradition. As Boniface Ramsey puts it, Augustine "must introduce his position into already occupied territory."[24] He notes that the question of whether it might be permissible to tell a lie for a good reason – say, to save someone's life – is "a question of which even the most learned persons tire themselves trying to resolve."[25] This awareness partly explains the fragmented approach he takes in defending his arguments. First, he is sensitive to scripture's legacy of ambiguity on the question of lying. He does not himself find scripture to be ambiguous on this matter, but he acknowledges that some passages are less clear than others, and he recognizes that the interpretations of his peers often differ from his own.[26] For Augustine, the primary biblical text in support of his position is the precept of the Decalogue that prohibits false witness, the eighth commandment (or ninth commandment, in Protestant and other traditions): "You shall not bear false witness against your neighbor." One might reasonably object that the wording of this commandment suggests something much narrower than a condemnation of

---

[23] Thomas D. Feehan, "Augustine on Lying and Deception," *Augustinian Studies* 19 (1988): 131–139; see 135–136 for the author's analysis of this distinction.
[24] Ramsey, "Two Traditions," 531.
[25] *Contra mendacium*, 33 (in PL 40).
[26] For a helpful list of all the biblical passages Augustine addresses in relation to lying, including specific references to where these are discussed by Augustine, see Gregor Müller, OSB, *Die Wahrhaftigkeitspflicht und die Problematik der Lüge: Ein Längsschnitt durch die Moraltheologie und Ethik unter besonderer Berücksichtigung der Tugendlehre des Thomas von Aquin und der modernen Lösungsversuche* (Freiburg 1962), 61–62. See also Thomas D. Feehan, "Augustine's Own Examples of Lying," *Augustinian Studies* 22 (1991): 165–190; 171–172 describes Augustine's examples from scripture, and 178–180 outlines Augustine's responses to objections based on these scripture passages.

all lying as such.[27] Augustine is quick to explain that "false witness" covers a broader spectrum of action than might appear at first glance: "'You shall not bear false witness.' Under this general term all lying is included: for whoever declares anything bears witness to one's own mind."[28] For those who remain unconvinced by this broad reading of the commandment, he points to the myriad references throughout scripture that cast a condemnatory judgment upon all falsehoods (Ps. 5:7, Wis. 1:11, Matt. 5:37, Eph. 4:25, etc.). Augustine's rhetorical strategy is to build a cumulative case against lying by pointing to the vast number of biblical passages that condemn the practice, even if none of these passages in isolation offers clear warrant for the position that lying is always wrong.

The difficulty of Augustine's strategy, of course, is the fact that there are also a number of biblical passages that appear to condone lying (as noted above). Yet, this is also where we find Augustine displaying his cleverness. In his later treatise, *Contra mendacium*, he confronts these texts and explains that each of the problematic passages falls into one of two categories: (1) what appears to be a lie is, in fact, not, or (2) it is not lying *per se* that is condoned, but rather some concomitant action that is indeed praiseworthy.[29] While his exegetical moves are often plausible, at other times they strain credibility. Consider his analysis of Genesis 20, for example, in which Abraham tells King Abimelech that his wife, Sarah, is his sister out of fear that the king will kill him and take his wife. Augustine defends Abraham, explaining, "He did not say, 'She is not my wife.' Rather, he said, 'She is my sister,' because she was in truth so nearly related, that she might be called a 'sister' without lying."[30] Augustine finds

---

[27] In Jewish rabbinic traditions, the commandment is interpreted in a narrower, legal sense. This discrepancy of interpretation between Jewish and Christian traditions has been acknowledged at least since the thirteenth century, seen in Nicholas of Lyra's comment on Exodus 20 in his *Postillae perpetuae in universam S. Scripturam*. As Patrick Miller explains, "The primary context of the commandment against false testimony is from the beginning and in virtually all its references the administration of justice, but the starting point is a false or empty word, harmful or potentially so, uttered about a neighbor in the community even outside the court but most definitely inside the court. At issue ultimately is slander that leads to a court case (e.g., Deut. 22:13–19)," *The Ten Commandments* (Louisville, KY 2009), 348. See also Cornelius Houtman, *Exodus* (Leuven 2000), 247–248, and, for further commentary on a similar elaboration of the commandment in Lev. 19:16, see Jacob Milgrom, *Leviticus 17–22* (New York 2000), 1645.

[28] *De mendacio*, 6. "*Falsum testimonium ne dicas*; quo genere complectitur omne mendacium: quisquis enim aliquid enuntiat, testimonium perhibet animo suo."

[29] *Contra mendacium*, 31.

[30] Ibid., 23.

such utterances defensible on the grounds that *withholding the truth* (as opposed to *lying*) is permissible: "It is not a lie when the truth is hidden through silence, but rather when a falsehood is declared through speech."[31] This interpretation of Abraham's actions is not entirely without merit, given that Abraham's own post hoc justification for his actions flows in a similar vein: "Besides she is indeed my sister, the daughter of my father but not the daughter of my mother; and she became my wife" (Gen. 20:12). What is remarkable, however, is that Augustine classifies Abraham's actions as an instance of withholding the truth rather than an act lying. He correctly observes that Abraham did not utter the statement "Sarah is my wife," but he curiously describes Abraham's utterance, "She is my sister," as partially holding back the truth. While it certainly does hold back the fact that Sarah is Abraham's wife, it does more than that. It also asserts that the term "sister" designates the kind of relationship shared by Abraham and Sarah – a term that would normally indicate that the two are *not* married. Thus, even if Augustine is correct that concealing the truth is permissible in certain circumstances, it is not obvious that this principle can support his exegesis of this passage.[32] We might wonder why he does not simply acknowledge that Abraham told a lie in

---

[31] Ibid. "Non est ergo mendacium cum silendo absconditur verum, sed cum loquendo promitur falsum."

[32] It is worth noting how Aquinas handles this passage centuries later. Aquinas never explicitly disagrees with Augustine in his writings, and he defers (at least ostensibly) to Augustine's judgment that Abraham did not tell a lie. Yet, unlike Augustine, Aquinas couches Abraham's claim that she is his sister within a special category of "prophetic speech." He borrows this category from Augustine, in *De mendacio*, 7: "Whence we may believe in regard of those persons of the prophetical times who are set forth as authoritative, that in all that is written of them they acted and spoke prophetically" (cited by Aquinas in *ST* II-II.110.3 ad 3). Ironically, Augustine himself does not use this special category to defend Abraham's actions. Aquinas interpolates this text alongside Augustine's actual defense of Abraham, which is based solely on the fact that Abraham "held back" the truth and did not tell a lie. Aquinas seems uncomfortable with this assessment and thus supplements one Augustinian text with another. As I argue in Chapter 5, Abraham's utterance is an equivocation of the word "sister," and as such counts as a lie within the Thomistic framework I develop. Aquinas's discomfort with the Augustinian interpretation of Abraham's utterance is reflective of certain medieval developments around the problem of lying – and the case of Abraham, specifically. Emily Corran offers an excellent analysis of Augustine's exegesis on this passage as found in the writings of Hugh of St. Victor, Peter the Chanter, and Stephen Langton in the late twelfth century. She explains that all three of these authors agree with Augustine that lying is wrong, but they are less willing to endorse his statement that Abraham justly hid the truth. Thus, they develop an account of dishonesty that is in some ways stricter than Augustine's own position. See "Hiding the Truth: Exegetical Discussions of Abraham's Lie from Hugh of St. Victor to Stephen Langton," *Historical Research*, 87:235 (Feb 2014): 1–17.

this instance. There are two factors that likely prevent him from taking this route. The first is that Augustine's interpretive milieu, shared by all of the church fathers, presupposes that the patriarchs of the Old Testament were paragons of virtue. A second and related factor is Augustine's (correct) observation that the biblical account offers no explicit condemnation of Abraham's actions. In Augustine's estimation, these provide sufficient reasons for describing Abraham's utterance in Genesis 20 as truthful.

When interpreting other passages of scripture, however, Augustine is willing to admit that biblical characters tell lies. Such is the case with the Hebrew midwives, who defied the king of Egypt's command to kill the newborn sons of the Hebrew women. When the king hears that the midwives have been allowing the male babies to live, he asks them why they have ignored his command. Their response: "Because the Hebrew women are not like the Egyptian women; for they are vigorous and are delivered before the midwife comes to them" (Ex. 1:19). This is presumably a falsehood, yet the text declares, "And because the midwives feared God he gave them families" (1:21).[33] Augustine is quick to point out that the text nowhere praises the midwives for lying. Their fear of God is displayed, not in the lie they told, but in their disobedience of the king's unjust command. The fact that they are praised at all is significant – Augustine implies that, had the midwives told a different kind of lie (say, a lie that was intended to harm someone else or a lie regarding a religious truth), then even their otherwise noble intention to save the Hebrew children would not be enough to render their actions morally praiseworthy. This is where we begin to see the subtlety of Augustine's position. While he is a rigorist about lying – he insists, after all, that the midwives told a lie – he also displays a pastoral sensitivity to the exigencies of life. Even if he is unwilling to condone the benevolent lie, he is eager to recognize the good intention behind it: "For a sin is more grievous when it is done with the intention of harming than when it is done with the intention of helping."[34] On Augustine's analysis, God *rewards* the act of saving the Hebrew children by disobeying the king's command, and, on the basis of their good intentions, God *forgives* the minor lie that is told in the process.

---

[33] In the Latin translations used by Augustine and Aquinas, the text states that God gave the Hebrew midwives "spiritual houses" as a reward: "Deus aedificavit illis domos spirituales," cited in *ST* II-II.110.4 ad 4 and *Contra mendacium*, 33.

[34] *Contra mendacium*, 32. "Gravius est enim peccatum quod animo nocentis, quam quod animo subvenientis efficitur." Augustine provides a similar explanation of the midwives' lie in his remarks on Psalm 5:6 ("You destroy those who speak lies"). See *Enarrationes in Psalmos*, 5, § 7 (in PL 36).

The reason God forgives the lie of the Hebrew midwives reflects Augustine's conviction that not all lies are equally grievous. In *De mendacio*, he provides an eightfold schema of lies, descending in order of moral gravity (see Table 2.1).[35] At the top of the list are lies in matters of religious doctrine. The second category includes lies that hurt someone yet profit no one. The third includes lies that profit someone at the expense of another. Lies that are told merely out of a lust for lying (what Augustine calls "pure" lies) comprise the fourth category. In the fifth place are lies that are told out of flattery, or an inordinate desire to please the listener. The sixth category includes lies that help someone financially yet harm no one else. The seventh includes lies that save or benefit someone without harming anyone else. At the bottom, in the eighth place, are lies that harm no one yet preserve someone from defilement of the body. While each of these presents a distinct kind of action that is morally prohibited, this eightfold list also forms a functional spectrum of lying. "In these eight kinds," Augustine explains, "a person sins less when telling a lie in proportion as he or she ascends to the eighth: more, in proportion as he or she descends to the first."[36] This eightfold list will preoccupy Augustine's medieval interpreters as they develop their own analyses of lying. Aquinas also borrows Augustine's list in a slightly modified form, but he offers an ever further degree of specification, namely, that all lies can be classified as either mortal or venial sins. While Augustine never makes this distinction explicitly in his treatises on lying,[37] he does suggest (as in the case of the midwives) that some lies are insignificant enough so as to be immediately forgiven depending upon the circumstances, even if they are not committed without some degree of sin. It is this observation that Aquinas makes explicit in his own analysis when he classifies certain lies as venially sinful. Indeed, the term "venial" simply means "able to be forgiven" or "pardonable."[38] Thus, certain lies, while still never permissible, are in a sense forgivable.

---

[35] *De mendacio*, 25.
[36] Ibid., 42. "In his autem octo generibus tanto quisque minus peccat cum mentitur, quanto emergit ad octavum; tanto amplius, quanto devergit ad primum."
[37] Although one could argue that Augustine's parenthetical remark following the first five categories, "All these being completely renounced and rejected, a sixth kind follows [...]," (*De mendacio*, 25) signifies a conceptual break between categories 1–5 and 6–8. The specific difference is found in the benevolent intentions behind the lies that fall within categories 6–8, which is lacking in the lies of categories 1–5.
[38] As Aquinas explains, "Dicendum, quod veniale dicitur a venia" ("It should be noted that the forgivable is said to be 'venial.'"), *De malo* 7.1. See also *ST* I-II 88.2.

TABLE 2.1 *Augustine's hierarchy of lies*

Type of Lie	Example
1. Lies regarding religious doctrine	"Jesus did not really rise from the dead."
2. Lies that profit no one yet injure someone	"Yes, I witnessed this man commit the murder."
3. Lies that profit one and injure another	"The previous results were due to an administrative error. It appears that Marcus actually won the race instead of Javier."
4. Lies told out of a mere lust for lying	Practically any lie, no matter how mundane the subject matter.
5. Jocose lies	"Hey, I just saw a Porsche get totaled in the parking lot. Isn't that your car?"
6. Lies that profit someone by saving money	"This bottle of wine doesn't have a price tag on it, but the sign said that it was $5.99."
7. Lies that profit someone by saving from death	"There are no Jews hiding in the basement."
8. Lies that save a person from unlawful defilement of the body	"I have an STD."

Yet even with this further specification of lies, I have not addressed Augustine's answer to what is perhaps the most fundamental question one could ask about lying: Why is lying wrong *per se*? That is, in cases where no obvious harm is done, why is lying morally impermissible? Augustine frequently invokes the Pauline principle that we cannot do evil in order that good may come about (Romans 3:8), but this argument already presupposes that all lying is evil. I have described Augustine's commitment to the position that scripture condemns lying universally, but more needs to be said. Augustine is too sophisticated a thinker to assert scripture's authority on a moral matter without even considering why scripture might contain a particular moral command in the first place. He suggests in several places[39] that lying harms the soul, and he deploys this principle in order to argue that it is better to allow one's (or another's) body to be defiled through another person's evil actions than to harm one's own soul through the act of lying. But again, this argument presupposes that lying in itself is harmful to the soul. Contemporary interpreters of Augustine have largely appealed to works outside of his two treatises on lying in order to illuminate the philosophical and theological

[39] See, for example, *De mendacio*, 9 ff.

commitments that undergird his assertion that lying is harmful to one's soul. Some have pointed to Augustine's theological anthropology, found in works like *De Trinitate*, as the basis for the claim that duplicitous speech is inherently sinful.[40] This approach is not without textual support. Augustine sometimes makes explicit connections between God, the source of all truth, and the truthfulness of human speech. He writes, for example, "Nobody should regard anything as one's own, except perhaps a lie. For all truth comes from the one who says, 'I am the truth' [John 14:6]."[41] In addition to cryptic remarks such as this, he also indicates that human language, as an extension of human nature, was created by God with a specific purpose, of which lying is a violation: "Surely words were not instituted so that people could deceive each other with them, but so that each person could make his or her thoughts known to each other. Using words for the purpose of deceiving, and not for what they were instituted, is a sin."[42] Thus, the *contra mentem* principle is grounded in a particular understanding of the *purpose* of language. Language performs a social function, but humans are social creatures, and so lying is harmful to the soul of the liar. Of course, the question of language's purpose is closely intertwined with questions about what language *does* and how it has developed. But for now, I simply want to underscore the fact that Augustine's arguments against lying are grounded in even more fundamental presuppositions about God, human nature, and language – presuppositions that he appears less concerned to defend than his more pragmatic arguments against lying in everyday circumstances.

The historical legacy of Augustine's position on lying is as contentious as it is polarizing. It has boasted many supporters and even more detractors, yet the question of what constitutes the most authentically Augustinian position on lying remains disputed. Contemporary theologians have interpreted Augustine's stance on lying in contradictory ways and deployed it for very different purposes. Some theologians, such as Paul Griffiths and David Decosimo, make similar exegetical moves yet arrive at incompatible

---

[40] The most extensive and compelling example of such analyses can be found in Paul J. Griffiths's monograph, *Lying: An Augustinian Theology of Duplicity* (Grand Rapids, MI 2004). I engaged Griffiths' interpretation and defense of Augustine in Chapter 1. See also Matthew Puffer, "Retracing Augustine's Ethics: Lying, Necessity, and the Image of God," *Journal of Religious Ethics* 44:4 (2016): 685–720.
[41] *De doctrina christiana*, Preface, 17 (in PL 34).
[42] *Enchiridion de fide, spe et charitate*, 22 (in PL 40). "Et utique verba propterea sunt instituta non per quae se homines invicem fallant sed per quae in alterius quisque notitiam cogitationes suas perferat. Verbis ergo uti ad fallaciam, non ad quod instituta sunt, peccatum est."

conclusions. Griffiths argues that, when we consider Augustine's position on lying in light of his broader theological anthropology, we are led to the stronger conclusion that lying always constitutes *mortal* sin. It is not merely the case that all lies are sins – all lies, no matter how small, are the kind of sin that severs one's relationship with God.[43] Decosimo also draws upon Augustine's notion of the self in order to extend Augustine's original arguments against lying. Yet, unlike Griffiths, he contends that this synthetic interpretation leads to the conclusion that Augustine would "regard certain instances of public lying as permissible and even obligatory."[44] It is not my intention to intervene in this debate. But it is worth noting that Augustine's arguments against lying continue to attract scholarly attention, and his more recent interpreters have sought to plumb the depths of his anthropology in order to amplify and defend an Augustinian understanding of the lie and its impermissibility.

MEDIEVAL INTERPRETATIONS

The medieval inheritance of Augustine's position on lying reflects a different story. The scholastic theologians who turn their attention to the subject of lying invariably give Augustine pride of place in their analyses.[45]

---

[43] Griffiths writes, "For Augustine, duplicitous speech is a rupture of the divine image, a recursively incoherent act best characterized as a refusal of the divine gift by attempted expropriation. It is sin's very paradigm. In Aquinas's terms, this would be an offense against love, and thus a mortal sin," *Lying*, 183.

[44] David Decosimo, "Just Lies: Finding Augustine's Ethics of Public Lying in His Treatments of Lying and Killing," *Journal of Religious Ethics* 38:4 (2010): 661–697; cited at 661. Decosimo points to the "agent (*auctor*) – instrument (*minister*)" distinction, found in *De civitate Dei* and elsewhere, to argue that, just as Augustine endorses certain instances of state-sponsored killing, there are instances in which Augustine would endorse state-sponsored lying. On Augustine's understanding of human action, it is possible for a person to *perform* an action without being the primary *agent* of that action. For example, when the state (justly) executes someone for a capital crime, it is not the executioner but rather God who is the agent of the killing. The human person is only an instrument of God's will. By analogy, in conditions of warfare, an agent of the state might tell a lie or perform some other act of deception in order to thwart the enemy. In such cases, the person telling the lie is not in fact guilty of lying, because she is not the agent of the action. On Decosimo's view, the Augustinian position does not necessarily rule out all instances of lying – in fact, it might demand lying on certain occasions. To be fair, Decosimo asserts that his arguments are in fact compatible with Griffiths's interpretation of Augustine. I will set this question aside, since it is peripheral to the concerns of the present volume.

[45] See Müller, *Die Wahrhaftigkeitspflicht und die Problematik der Lüge*, Chapter 3 ("Die Wahrhaftigkeitspflicht nach der Lehre der vor- und frühscholastiker"), especially Müller's summary remarks on pp. 94–98.

This does not mean, however, that they are unaware of competing voices within the tradition.[46] But given Augustine's preeminence among theological authorities, it should come as no surprise that the medieval manuals of theology take his position on lying as a starting point for their own discourse on the topic. Unlike Augustine's contemporary interpreters, many of whom rely more heavily on Augustine's theological anthropology than his actual writings on lying, the theologians of the Middle Ages develop four particular insights that they find in Augustine: (1) the definition of the lie as an utterance at odds with one's own mind, (2) the conviction that scripture universally condemns all lying, and, more specifically, that the eighth commandment of the Decalogue prohibits any intentional utterance of a falsehood, (3) affirmation that it is permissible at times to hold back the truth rather than reveal it, and (4) the conviction that lying is a violation of the purposes of human speech, as instituted by God.

The primary vehicles for bringing Augustine into the medieval conversation are Peter Lombard's *Sentences* and Gratian's compilation of

---

[46] In her essay, "Rethinking Lying in the Twelfth Century," Marcia Colish offers an extensive survey and analysis of texts that challenge the notion of an Augustinian consensus on lying, either in the patristic era or in the high Middle Ages. I have already noted the competing strands on lying in the patristic period, but Colish overstates her argument that an alternative tradition (exemplified by Ambrose's references to lying) constitutes a major challenge to the Augustinian consensus in the Middle Ages. Ironically, she entirely neglects the medieval author whose writings would have best supported her argument: Raymond de Peñafort (see below). The examples she provides of medieval scholastics supposedly disagreeing with Augustine do not amount to much. For instance, she contends that some medieval thinkers "introduce qualifications [to Augustine's position] that suggest the availability of alternative approaches to the subject" (165). To support this claim, she cites Gratian, who "adds to his analysis the factor of ignorance which may lessen or heighten the culpability of the liar or perjuror" (Ibid.). But this is no different from Augustine's principle that a liar's culpability decreases as she descends through the eightfold classification of lies. Moreover, she cites Lombard's division of lies into mortal and venial sins as if it were an innovation, yet the text to which she refers (*Sententiarum* III.38.2.2) is merely a restatement of Augustine's classification of lies. She also marshals texts from authors such as Hugh of St. Victor and William of Auxerre, who dismiss the category of "jocose lies" as harmless, yet it should be noted that in doing so they never explicitly disagree with Augustine. They may very well think that they are agreeing with him, given the opacity of his remarks on jocose lies. She also incorrectly states that Aquinas holds that "the jocose lie is no lie at all" (p. 170), when he explicitly says that it is a lie in *ST* II-II.110.2 and 110.3 ad 6. She makes a stronger case when referencing the works of Pseudo-Peter of Poitiers, Gandulph of Bologna, Alexander of Hales, and John of Rupella, who remove not only the category of the jocose lie but also the officious lie. But the fact that these lesser-known figures silently remove an Augustinian category – and, as she admits, they do not appeal to any alternative authorities – only serves to underscore Augustine's influence in the Middle Ages rather than undermine it.

canon law, the *Decretum*, both of which summarize the Augustinian position and quote liberally from his writings.[47] Gratian cites Augustine's definition of a lie as "a false signification with the purpose of deceiving"[48] and also includes the eightfold classification of lies.[49] He notes Augustine's principle that it is sometimes permissible to hide the truth and, indeed, sometimes necessary to hide the truth rather than tell a lie, even if for a noble cause.[50] Peter Lombard cites much of the same material but also makes some important modifications of his own. Most significantly, he places his analysis of lying in the *Sentences* within his broader exposition of the Decalogue. Thus, his comments on this subject fall under the rubric of the eighth commandment's precept against bearing false witness. This method will set the precedent for nearly every scholastic theologian going forward, as nearly every theological discussion of lying in the Middle Ages is cast in relation to the eighth commandment.[51] The second contribution Lombard makes is to draw attention to a lesser-known classification of lies – one that also originates from Augustine. This is not the eightfold list from *De mendacio*, but rather a simple, threefold division found in Augustine's brief remarks on Psalm 5:6, "[Y]ou destroy those who speak lies." Augustine describes these categories as (1) lies told to help someone else, (2) lies told in jest, and (3) malicious lies. The first and second, while still lies,

---

[47] See Peter Lombard, *Sententiarum libri quatuor* III.38 (in PL 192) and Gratian, *Decretum magistri Gratiani*, in *Corpus iuris canonici*, eds. E. Richer and Emil A. Friedberg, 2nd ed. (Leipzig 1879; repr. Graz: Akademische Druck U. Verlagsanstalt, 1959), vol. 1, Pt. 2, causa xxii. On the broader significance of these two texts within the scholastic project, see R. W. Southern, *The Making of the Middle Ages* (New Haven, CT 1953), 205–210. Southern explains, "The *Sentences* and the *Decretum* were books of the schools, but they looked out on to the world. In every way, their appearance was a work of conciliation: conciliation between the discordant testimonies of the past, conciliation between the accumulated riches of the past and the sharp questionings of the present, conciliation between the dialectical and authoritarian tendencies of their age" (206).

[48] *Decretum*, Pt. 2, causa xxii, q. ii, c. v. "Est enim mendacium (ut Augustinus ait) 'falsa significatio cum voluntate fallendi.'"

[49] Ibid., c. viii.

[50] Ibid., c. xiv. "Ne quis arbitretur perfectum et spiritualem hominem pro ista temporali vita, morte cuius sua vel alterius non occiditur a anima, debere mentiri, sed quoniam aliud est mentiri, aliud verum occultare" ("No one should think that the perfect and spiritual person ought to lie to save his own soul or another's; it is one thing to lie and another thing to hide the truth").

[51] Another, less common, format includes treatises on the seven deadly sins, in which "sins of the tongue" were grouped together with sins pertaining to that which enters and leaves the mouth (e.g., gluttony). See Richard G. Newhauser, *The Treatises on Vices and Virtues in Latin and the Vernacular* (Turnhout, Belgium 1993), 193–197.

are very minor faults. Indeed, the second category includes lies that do not even have the effect of deceiving the listener, "because the person to whom it is told is aware that it is told in jest."[52] Lombard's third contribution is to clarify the meaning of the Augustinian definition of lying, "a false signification with the purpose of deceiving." Lombard cites the standard definition from *De mendacio*, but he adds a remark from the *Enchiridion*, "For this evil is unique to liars, that they have one thing hidden in their hearts and another ready on their tongues,"[53] in order to underscore the fact that the feature of "deception" is first and foremost a deception about the contents of the speaker's mind. Lombard's own definition of the lie is "to speak against that which a person has in his or her mind, whether what is said is true or not,"[54] thus reinforcing the *contra mentem* principle.

These texts of Gratian and Lombard are of utmost importance for understanding Augustine's influence on the debates about lying in the Middle Ages, for the simple reason that most scholastic authors did not engage Augustine's writings on lying directly. As Dallas Denery observes, "Scholastic writers did not so much follow Augustine as borrow some of his statements to serve as the basic building blocks for their own analyses of mendacity. As a result, they often sound Augustinian even as they diverge, often radically, from Augustine's own opinions."[55] Denery suggests that most of what the scholastics knew of Augustine's position on lying was taken from the excerpts they read in collections such as Lombard's *Sentences*. He overstates, in my judgment, the extent to which it might have made a difference had the scholastics read Augustine's treatises more deeply. While it is true that Augustine's collected remarks need to be read in context and that his treatises offer a number of important qualifications and nuances, the fact is that his analysis leaves many questions unanswered. Gareth Matthews claims, for example, that Augustine "never provides what he considers a

---

[52] Lombard, *Sententarium* III.38, c. 1 (in PL 192; col. 833). "Est et aliud mendacii genus quod fit joco, quod non fallit. Scit enim cui dicitur, causa joci dic." He will go on to mention the eightfold list later in c. 1, with the introduction, "It is also known that there are eight kinds of lying ..."

[53] Ibid., c. 2 (col. 834), citing *Enchiridion*, 18. "Hoc enim malum est proprium mentientis, aliud habere clausem in corde, aliud promptum in lingua."

[54] Ibid., c. 3 (in PL 192; col. 834). "Mentiri vero est loqui contra hoc quod animo sentit quis, sive illud verum sit, sive non."

[55] Dallas G. Denery II, *The Devil Wins: A History of Lying from the Garden of Eden to the Enlightenment* (Princeton, NJ 2015), 119.

satisfactory analysis of what it is to tell a lie."[56] Equally important is the question of what makes lying inherently wrong. As Joseph Boyle notes, Augustine flirts with theological positivism, or the idea that "[W]hat is decisive is the simple fact that God has told us that lying is always wrong."[57] While Augustine asserts that the liar always harms her own soul when she utters a lie, he never clearly identifies the nature of this harm. The closest he comes to offering a unifying principle that explains the moral badness of all lies is found, not in his two treatises on lying, but in his brief argument in the *Enchiridion* that lying violates the purpose of language as God instituted it.[58] Boyle suggests that Augustine probably thought that there was a general wrong-making feature in all lies, but that he failed to identify it clearly or show why it makes all lies wrong.[59] Thus, the greatest difficulty facing the scholastic theologians as they confront the problem of lying is not their inadequate exposure to Augustine's writings, but rather the remaining conceptual challenges that have yet to be adequately addressed. Among these, the most important are the questions, "What is the common feature of all lies that make them sinful?" and, assuming that this question is answered in part by the claim that lying is a violation of the purpose of speech, then what do we mean by this claim?

The scholastics of the twelfth and early thirteenth centuries wrestle with these questions, even though they generally refrain from pointing out inadequacies in Augustine's position. While they tend to follow Augustine's lead, they often make subtle distinctions of their own when necessary. Hugh of St. Victor, for example, follows Augustine quite closely, and while he follows Lombard and his contemporaries in placing his discussion of lying within the broader context of the Decalogue, he

---

[56] Gareth B. Matthews, *Augustine* (Malden, MA 2005), 132. As a counterpoint, Feehan suggests (correctly, in my judgment) that Augustine does settle on the criteria for lying, namely, that the intention to deceive (in the sense of deceiving about one's own beliefs) is a necessary condition and, when combined with the intention to impart a falsehood, a sufficient condition. Feehan, "Augustine on Lying and Deception," 138.

[57] Joseph Boyle, "The Absolute Prohibition of Lying and the Origins of the Casuistry of Mental Reservation: Augustinian Arguments and Thomistic Developments," *American Journal of Jurisprudence* 44:1 (1999): 43–65; cited at 52. Again, Feehan offers a counterpoint. He detects eight distinct arguments that Augustine develops in support of his position that lying is always sinful. Of course, whether these arguments are successful is an entirely different question, but there seems to be more at work than the mere assertion that God has commanded us not to lie. Feehan, "The Morality of Lying in St. Augustine," *Augustinian Studies* 21 (1990): 67–81.

[58] *Enchiridion*, 22.

[59] Boyle, "The Absolute Prohibition of Lying," 53.

also marks a distinction between bearing false witness and lying *per se*. For Hugh, bearing false witness goes beyond the mere act of lying to the point of defending one's falsehood against the truth.[60] Other scholastics bend Augustine's position in more creative ways. William of Auxerre concurs with Augustine's definition of the lie ("a false statement declared with a will to deceive"), but only *in genere*. This allows for other kinds of actions to count as lies, even if they do not meet the formal definition. Analysis of such actions must account for the motive, circumstance, and the person telling the lie.[61] His classifications are somewhat obscure and the upshot of these additions is not obvious. By the same token, William proposes the idea that some utterances that *do* meet the formal definition of a lie might not in fact be sinful. The example he gives is remarkably mundane: He imagines a teacher in a classroom declaring something she does not believe to be true, not with the purpose of misleading her students, but rather as an academic exercise in order to arrive at the truth.[62] One could imagine how we might read Augustine to accommodate such instances,[63] but the fact that William so hesitantly raises this counterexample is indicative of just how reluctant the scholastics are to contradict Augustine's authority.

Unlike the patristic writers, whose divergent opinions on the permissibility of lying were readily acknowledged, the canonists and theologians of the medieval period are in broad agreement about the sinfulness of all lies – even if the culpability of lying admits of degrees. The only relevant examples that approach something like a divergent voice are those suggesting that certain forms of equivocation may fall outside the scope of lying *per se* and are thus permissible at times. In a later gloss on

---

[60] Hugh of St. Victor, *De sacramentis christianae fidei* I.12 (in PL 176; col. 357): "Falsitatis testimonium est cum quis alterius mendacio de veritate testimonium perhibet. Qui non solum mentiendo reus efficitur sed quia etiam ipsum mendacium contra veritate patroncinari conatur" ("False witness occurs when one asserts a falsehood about another's true testimony. Such a person is not only guilty of lying but also of attempting to sustain the lie, over against the truth").

[61] William of Auxerre, *Summa aurea* III.45, c. 1, in *Magistri Guillelmi Altissiodorensis, Summa Aurea*, vol. 3, ed. Jean Ribaillier, Spicilegium Bonaventurianum (Paris 1980).

[62] Ibid., III.45, c. 2.

[63] We do not have to imagine, in fact. Augustine provides a nearly identical example in one of his earlier writings, *De magistro* 13.41 (in PL 32), only to explain that such acts are not lies. William of Auxerre seems to think that he is pushing the boundaries of the Augustinian position by positing this example, even though the example itself is thoroughly Augustinian. This lends further support to the thesis that the scholastics only consulted select Augustinian texts, as collected in the medieval theological textbooks, when writing on the subject of lying.

Gratian's *Decretum*, the author of the gloss raises the question of how one is supposed to answer a person who asks about the whereabouts of a fugitive he is pursuing. Assuming that silence would indicate the presence of the fugitive, and a confession of the fugitive's whereabouts would amount to cooperation in murder, what should one do? The glossator recommends the equivocation: *non est hic, id est, non comedit hic* ("He is not here," that is, "He is not eating here"), playing on the ambiguity of the Latin *est*, which can mean "being" or "eating."[64] While the likelihood of success in this approach seems dubious at best, the important point is that equivocation is seen as a way *around* the sin of lying rather than an *exception* to the prohibition of lying (recall Athanasius's "he is not far" episode). Raymond de Peñafort, in his *Summa de casibus poenitentiae*, takes a similar tack, while simultaneously reminding the reader that Augustine would not allow a lie to be told to the pursuer. He acknowledges that other doctors of the church (most likely referring to the Eastern fathers) say that "in such a case one must lie."[65] He does not endorse this opinion, however. Instead, he commends silence, or, if there is a concern that this would reveal the fugitive, then diversion or equivocation is an option. Finally, and inexplicably, he offers another way out of the dilemma as a last resort: "Or simply say that one ought to make a denial and assert that he is not present; if indeed one's conscience prompts him to speak thus, then thus one should speak; then one is not speaking against his conscience, but is following it rather, and one shall not sin in any way."[66] As more and more authors in the late Middle Ages and the modern period will go on to endorse practices such as equivocation and mental reservation, this text will be drawn upon frequently. But for now, it should be noted that Raymond displays no awareness that he is signaling a major break from the Augustinian consensus.

Bonaventure, like his contemporary, Aquinas, addresses the morality of lying both in sermons and in theological treatises. In his sermon on the eighth commandment, Bonaventure first observes that lies that harm

---

[64] *Decretum Gratiani*, C. 22, q. 2, c. 14, gloss, casus (CIC, Rome, 2), cited in Julius A. Dorszynski, *Catholic Teaching about the Morality of Falsehood* (Washington, DC 1948), 24.

[65] Raymond de Peñafort, *Summa de casibus poenitentiae*, 1, tit. 10, 4, p. 100: "Et ita dicunt simpliciter plerique doctors. Alii dicunt in tali casu mentiendum esse." Cited in Dorszynski, *Catholic Teaching*, 25.

[66] Ibid., p. 101: "Vel dic simpliciter, quod debet negare, et asserere eum non esse ibi, sit amen sua conscientia dictat sibi quod ita debeat dicere, tunc non dicet contra conscientiam, imo sequitur eam, et nullo modo peccabit." Cited in Dorszynski, *Catholic Teaching*, 25.

one's neighbor are prohibited by this particular commandment. But then he adds that we are also to understand by this commandment that "every lie is evil."[67] To support this claim, he simply recounts the Augustinian prohibition against lying. Having recently preached a sermon on the seventh commandment in which he gives examples of someone taking things belonging to another in times of necessity (a frequent medieval motif), he feels the need to clarify that the ban on lying cannot admit of exceptions. Unlike property ownership, which is changeable (and thus God is able to "excuse" theft), the "nobility of truth" is immutable, and thus, it is not possible even for God to declare a lie to be sinless.[68] While Bonaventure strikes a confident tone in his sermon, his theological treatises offer a more candid assessment of the theoretical difficulties surrounding the subject of lying. In his *Sentences* commentary, he openly admits that Augustine's reasoning behind the claim that all lies are sins is "difficult to determine."[69] He speculates that Augustine's definition of the lie only applies to malicious lies.[70] To help clarify matters, he adds his own division of lies, arguing that the most complete lies are those that combine falsehood with an intent to deceive (as in Augustine's classical formulation), followed by those only with an intent to deceive (yet technically "true" insofar as they do not violate the *contra mentem* principle), and last, those that utter a falsehood without an intent to deceive. The second category could possibly entail a strong indictment of equivocation, but Bonaventure does not pursue this line of thought.

The theologians of the high Middle Ages are famous for their lively and, at times, arcane debates on assorted philosophical and theological topics. They often register profound disagreements on matters related to the freedom of the will, the nature of the soul, the role of analogical language in theology, and many other topics. Yet, their writings reflect widespread consensus in other areas, such as the validity of natural law and the real presence of Christ in the Eucharist. The medieval analyses of

---

[67] Bonaventure, *Collationes de decem praeceptis*, VII.3, in *Opera omnia*, 5 (Quaracchi, Italy 1891).

[68] Ibid., VII.5.

[69] Bonaventure, *Commentarius in IV Libros Sententiarum* III.38, a. 1, q. 2, in *Opera Omnia* 1–4 (Quaracchi, Italy 1882–1889): "Et hoc Augustinus dicit expresse et nititur multipliciter probare; et in hoc communiter concordant doctors. Sed rationem huius difficile est assignare, et ad hoc possumus niti diversimode" ("Augustine says this explicitly and tries to prove it in many ways; and the doctors generally agree. Yet, his reasoning is difficult to determine, and it is possible to be understood in different ways").

[70] Ibid., III.38, a. 1, q. 2.

lying do not fit neatly into either of these categories. The theologians of the high Middle Ages do not generally express deep disagreements with one another about the permissibility of lying, but neither do they assume that all the complex theoretical questions have been settled. The milieu could be accurately described as a climate of shared puzzlement. Their reverence for the Decalogue and their esteem for Augustine's theological insights lead them to revisit and wrestle with the relationship between lying and bearing false witness, as well as many related sins of speech. The scholastics were both fascinated and perplexed by the demands of the eighth commandment. As Lesley Smith observes,

> In comparison with the commandments which instantiate the debt to thought and to deed, only this single precept represents the debt to word. In the paradoxical world of medieval exegesis, this has a particular logic. Sins against the Word are so important, and so ubiquitous, that they can only be dealt with in one commandment; more than one would suggest that there might be more than one interpretation of how the divine gift of language should be rightly used. In contrast, the *interpretation* of the commandment against false witness was fissiparous – indeed, it had to be, so as to encompass all the ways that false speaking might find its way into the world.[71]

Almost without exception, the scholastic theologians of the twelfth and early thirteenth centuries follow the same recipe when addressing the subject of lying: formally, their analyses fall within the Decalogue's precept against false witness; materially, their analyses take Augustine's position as normative, even as they express puzzlement at some of its features. As we will see in Chapter 3, Aquinas also takes Augustine's position as normative, but he is far bolder than his contemporaries in his constructive analysis, and he does not hesitate to correct the received tradition when his analysis demands it.

---

[71] Lesley Smith, *The Ten Commandments: Interpreting the Bible in the Medieval World* (Boston, MA 2014), 173.

3

Aquinas on the Sins of Speech

As we saw in Chapter 2, the medieval scholastic debates on lying were dominated by the influence of Augustine. Augustine's position on lying is exceedingly complex, and it is compounded by the fact that he offers several discrete arguments against lying. He also acknowledges several different categories of lies, all of which are not equally sinful.[1] There is no question that Augustine believes all lies are sinful in some sense. Yet, when he offers an argument against lying, it is not always clear if the specific argument is intended to demonstrate the impermissibility of all lies, or only certain kinds. In the Middle Ages, Aquinas's contemporaries attempt to streamline and clarify the Augustinian position. They generally take the line that the eighth commandment prohibits all lying but then qualify this claim by noting that some lies are, in fact, only venially sinful. Aquinas agrees that a lie can never be entirely without sin, but, as I demonstrate in the first section of this chapter, he is more cautious about associating this principle with a precept of the Decalogue. His mature position is that the eighth commandment prohibits malicious speech acts, all of which are mortally sinful, but he then brackets the act of *lying* as a special moral problem. Even in his earlier commentary on Lombard's *Sentences*, we see the influence of Aristotle leading him to reconsider the nature of lying and what, precisely, makes it a morally bad action.

As we will see, the way Aquinas reads his sources will ultimately lead him to decouple the act of lying from the eighth commandment. By the

---

[1] See Feehan, "The Morality of Lying in St. Augustine," *Augustinian Studies* 21 (1990): 67–81.

time he writes the *Summa theologiae*,[2] he comes to the conclusions that (1) the moral domain of this precept pertains to sins of speech that exhibit an explicit intention to harm one's neighbor and (2) that the species of "lying" – in its purest, Augustinian formulation – does not fall into this category. The kinds of actions that directly violate the eighth commandment (and, by extension, the norms of particular justice) include insult (*contumelia*), slander (*detractione*), gossip (*susurratione*), mockery (*derisione*), and cursing (*maledictione*) (*ST* II-II.72–76). Of course, any kind of lie that is told with the intention of harming one's neighbor would also violate the norms of justice, as well as the eighth commandment. Aquinas, along with the other scholastics who draw upon Augustine, classifies these as pernicious (*perniciosum*) lies. But the species of lying *per se*, defined as speech that is opposed to one's mind, does not necessarily include the intention to harm anyone. Otherwise, we would not have the category of the "useful" or beneficent lie, which even Augustine recognized.

THE EIGHTH COMMANDMENT AND THE PROHIBITION OF LYING

In his earliest writing on lying, Thomas Aquinas follows his contemporaries insofar as his analysis is framed by the precepts of the Decalogue. In his commentary on the *Sentences*, he explains that all lies violate the eighth commandment, but they can do so in different ways. When Lombard writes, "Not every lie is forbidden by this precept," Aquinas explains that this is meant to demarcate the kinds of lies that are directly opposed to the commandment.[3] Pernicious lies, he says, are a direct violation of the commandment, in that they are destructive and "against one's neighbor." Other kinds of lies, such as useful lies and jokes, also violate the eighth commandment, but only indirectly.[4] Generally, Aquinas's

---

[2] Aquinas wrote his *Sentences* commentary approximately during the years 1254–1266 CE and the *Summa theologiae* from around 1266 until shortly before his death in 1274 CE.

[3] Thomas Aquinas, *Scriptum super Sententiis* III, Dist. 38, expos.: "Nec omne mendacium isto praecepto prohiberi videtur. Intelligendum est directe sicut contrarium praecepto" ("'Nor does it seem that every lie is prohibited by this precept'. This should be understood to refer to those directly contrary to the precept"). Quotations from the *Sentences* commentary are from *Scriptum super Sententia magistri Petri Lombardi*, Vol. 3, ed. M. F. Moos, OP (Paris 1933).

[4] *In Sent*. III, Dist. 38, a. 4, ad 5. "Ad quintum dicendum, quod divino praecepto prohibetur aliquid dupliciter. Uno modo directe, quod contra praeceptum dicitur; et sic prohibetur mendacium perniciosum, quod ex ipsa forma praecepti patet: non loqueris contra proximum tuum falsum testimonium. Alio modo indirecte, quod praeter praeceptum

commentary on Book III, Distinction 38 of Lombard's *Sentences* mirrors that of his contemporaries. He affirms that the Augustinian formulation (*falsa significatio vocis cum intentione fallendi*) is a fitting definition of the lie,[5] and he argues for the fittingness of the threefold division into useful, jocose, and pernicious lies, as well as the eightfold division (see Table 2.1).[6] Nothing thus far is indicative of a scholar who is attempting to break the mold.

There are a few places in the *Sentences* commentary where we find Aquinas engaging aspects of lying that do not appear in any of his other works. One of these includes a comment on Lombard's curious remark that useful lies and jocose lies are venial for the "imperfect" but mortal for the "perfect." Lombard has in mind here those who have taken religious vows. In his response to an objection, Aquinas explains that this cannot mean that the exact same act counts as a mortal sin for one person yet venial for another, unless the former is acting directly in opposition to his or her vows. If any person (not just a religious) tells a lie that is generically venial, yet he knowingly speaks against his conscience, or intends to cause scandal, then this could amount to a mortal sin. In other words, Aquinas interprets Lombard's words as an exhortation to the religious, rather than as a fundamental distinction between their actions and those of the laity.[7] The "useful" [*officiosum*] lie, no matter who utters

---

dicitur; et sic mendacium jocosum et officiosum, sicut et alia peccata venialia, praecepto divino prohibentur" ("In reply to the fifth: Something can be forbidden by a divine precept in two ways. In the first way, directly, which is said to be *contrary* to the precept. Thus, a pernicious lie is prohibited, which can be understood from the form of the precept, 'You shall not bear false witness against your neighbor.' In another way, indirectly, which is said to be *beside* the precept. It is in this latter way that officious and jocose lies are prohibited by a divine precept, as with other venial sins").

[5] *In Sent.* III, Dist. 38, a. 1, cor.
[6] *In Sent.* III, Dist. 38, a. 2, cor. Aquinas explains that the eightfold division can be reduced into the threefold in a. 2, ad 4.
[7] *In Sent.* III, Dist. 38, a. 4, ad 4: "Et ideo dicendum, quod nec mendacium nec aliquod peccatum quod ex genere suo peccatum mortale non est, perfectis viris mortale peccatum fit, nisi sit contra eorum votum. Sed per accidens potest eis mortale fieri sicut et aliis, ut si fiat contra conscientiam, quamvis errantem, vel ratione scandali, vel alicujus hujusmodi. Quod vero dicitur in littera, quod mendacium officiosum perfectis viris est damnabile, intelligendum est comparative: quia in eodem genere peccati magis peccat perfectus quam imperfectus, quamvis uterque venialiter vel mortaliter. Non tamen haec circumstantia aggravans aggravat in infinitum, ut quod uni est veniale, alteri mortale fiat" ("It must be said that a lie (or any other sin that is not mortally sinful in its genus) will, for the perfect, become a mortal sin, unless it is done against his own will. But it can be made mortal for others, as well, if it is done against one's conscience (even an erring conscience), or because of scandal, or something similar. But what is said in the text,

it, designates a specific kind of action, with its own nature or *ratio*. He explains further that, even though the useful lie has more of the manner [*ratio*] of a lie than a jocose lie, insofar as it more clearly asserts a falsehood, the jocose lie is worse from a moral standpoint. In other words, the useful lie has less of an evil *ratio* joined to it.[8] This leads to another observation that is unique to the *Sentences* commentary. Aquinas responds to an objector who wonders if it might belong to a person's job to lie, such as a public figure. He explains that the *ratio* of the useful lie is still sinful, and thus even this kind of lie can never be completely free from sin.[9] The emphasis on the *ratio* of lying and specific kinds of lies will remain an important focus in Aquinas's writings on the subject, and he will go on to develop these insights extensively in the *Summa theologiae*.

Aquinas's remarks on lying in the *Sentences* commentary also display a novel feature that will become a trademark of Aquinas's legacy: his use of Aristotle. The writings of Aristotle were widely unavailable in the West until the thirteenth century. By the mid-thirteenth century, Aristotle's works on logic, metaphysics, and ethics became centerpieces in the scholastic curricula at the universities in Paris and Oxford. Under the influence of his mentor, Albert the Great, Aquinas reads these works eagerly and seeks to incorporate their insights into his own writing.[10]

---

namely, that an officious lie is a damnable sin for the perfect, is to be understood relatively. This is because the sinfulness is greater when committed by the perfect than when the same sin is committed by the imperfect, although they both sin mortally (or venially). However, this additional weightiness cannot be extrapolated to every situation, and it remains true that what is venial for one person may be mortal for another").

[8] *In Sent.* III, Dist. 38, a. 5, ad 3: "Ad tertium dicendum, quod quamvis mendacium officiosum habeat plus de ratione mendacii quam jocosum, inquantum habet plus de assertione; tamen officiosum habet minus de malo ratione utilitatis adjunctae; et ideo est minus peccatum" ("To the third: Although an officious lie has more of the nature of the lie than a jocose lie does (insofar as it more clearly asserts), an officious lie is by nature less evil, because of its utility, and therefore it is a lesser sin").

[9] *In Sent.* III, Dist. 38, a. 3, ad 7. Interestingly, the objector's position reflects the argument made by Decosimo in "Just Lies," cited above. It should be noted, however, that Decosimo couches his argument within an Augustinian framework.

[10] While Albert's influence on Aquinas is significant, the latter departs from the former's opinion in several instances. On the subject of lying, for example, Albert does not interpret Aristotle's remark in *NE* IV.7 that lying is "base and blameworthy" to mean that lying *per se* is always wrong. See Albertus Magnus, *Super Ethica* 4.14 n. 339, in *Alberti Magni Opera omnia* (Editio Coloniensis), ed. B. Geyer et al. (Münster 1951) 14, 288. On the ways in which Albert's thought bears on Aquinas's position on lying, see Carla Casagrande and Silvana Vecchio, *Les péchés de la langue: Discipline et éthique de la parole dans la culture medieval* (Paris 1991), 117–121 and 154–158. For a more general overview of Albert's moral philosophy, see Stanley B. Cunningham, *Reclaiming Moral Agency: The Moral Philosophy of Albert the Great* (Washington, DC 2008).

Aquinas is one of many scholastic theologians who draws upon Aristotle to make his arguments. "The Philosopher" (Aquinas's preferred title for Aristotle) is not an obvious interlocutor on the subject of lying, however, for the simple reason that he has very little to say about it. The only place where he addresses this topic is *Nicomachean Ethics* IV.7, and even there it is clear that he is considering a very narrow conception of lying. In this text, Aristotle is describing social life and the necessary habits that a man must have in order strike the mean of virtue and foster meaningful interpersonal relationships. He writes,

> The boastful man, then, is thought to be apt to claim the things that bring repute, when he has not got them, or to claim more of them than he has, and the mock-modest man on the other hand to disclaim what he has or belittle it, while the man who observes the mean is one who calls a thing by its own name, being truthful both in life and in word, owning to what he has, and neither more nor less.[11]

Aristotle is not concerned here with questions about the sinfulness of lying or whether it might be permissible to lie to someone who is looking for the fugitive hiding in one's basement. He is concerned with the way we speak about ourselves and present ourselves to others. And while there is a mean of virtue between boastfulness and mock modesty, Aristotle explains that the virtuous person is inclined to understate the truth about himself: "But those who use understatement with moderation and understate about matters that do not very much force themselves on our notice seem attractive. And it is the boaster that seems to be opposed to the truthful man; for he is the worse character."[12] Thus, for Aristotle, the truthful person is not necessarily the person who never speaks against one's own mind, but rather the person who maintains a clear, honest assessment of herself and presents herself to the world accordingly.[13]

---

[11] Aristotle, *Nicomachean Ethics* IV.7, 1127a13–1127a32, trans. W. D. Ross, in *The Complete Works of Aristotle*, ed. Jonathan Barnes (New York 1991).

[12] Ibid., 1127b23–1127b32.

[13] While Aquinas's adaption of Aristotle is somewhat loose in this instance, there is no doubt that Aristotle profoundly shaped Aquinas's understanding of virtue. For more on the Aristotelian underpinnings of Aquinas's virtue theory, see Nicholas Austin, SJ, *Aquinas on Virtue: A Causal Reading* (Washington, DC 2017). See also Kevin Flannery, SJ, *Acts Amid Precepts: The Aristotelian Logical Structure of Thomas Aquinas's Moral Theory* (Washington, DC 2001). For a helpful corrective against interpretations of Aquinas that tend to reduce his moral theory to Aristotle's, see Eleonore Stump, "The Non-Aristotelian Character of Aquinas's Ethics: Aquinas on the Passions," *Faith & Philosophy* 28:1 (2011): 29–43. David Decosimo offers a different perspective on the Aristotelian character of Aquinas's ethics in *Ethics as a Work of Charity: Thomas*

Given what we have seen about the medieval discussions of lying, we might wonder how Aquinas could possibly integrate Aristotle's thought into the Augustine-dominated conversation. In the question on whether Lombard's (i.e., Augustine's) division of lies is fitting, Aquinas considers the objection that, according to Aristotle, the proper division of lies is a twofold distinction between boasting (*jactantiam*) and mock-modesty (*ironiam*). In his response to the objection, Aquinas explains that Aristotle is considering lying from a different, albeit complementary, perspective, according to the mean of virtue.[14] This division, he argues, can stand alongside the other Augustinian divisions that are already widely accepted. This may strike us as somewhat forced, but regardless, Aquinas has now brought Aristotle into the conversation.[15] But what to do about the fact that Aristotle claims that the virtuous person inclines toward less regarding the truth about himself? Would this not require a person at times to speak falsely, *contra mentem*, about her own abilities and accomplishments? Aquinas must be creative here. He surmises that this must really mean that a person should often be silent about one's own accomplishments, even though this is not quite what Aristotle says.[16] As we will see, Aquinas eventually finds a way to integrate Aristotle more fluidly into his analysis of lying. Indeed, the influence of Aristotle will serve

---

Aquinas and Pagan Virtue (Stanford, CA 2014). Decosimo would likely consider Stump's account to be another example of "hyper-Augustinianism," and Stump would likely consider Decosimo's account to be insufficiently Augustinian. While some of Stump's and Decosimo's particular claims may be irreconcilable, I believe their central theses are ultimately compatible: namely, that true virtue is infused by God and is aimed at beatitude as its final end, but that there is nonetheless a way to describe acquired ("pagan") virtue as *real* virtue, whose perfection and end is found in natural happiness. The coexistence of the acquired and infused virtues in an individual (i.e., whether this is possible and how they might relate to each another) is a contested matter among Thomists, but I will not wade into that debate here.

[14] *In Sent.* III, Dist. 38, a. 2, ad 6.

[15] Kevin Flannery offers a fairly persuasive argument that a consideration of truth and lies *as such*, not just about oneself, is present in embryo in NE IV.7 as its core idea, and that Aquinas gets Aristotle right on this point. I am not convinced, however, by his claim that, for Aristotle, "the idea that lying is intrinsically evil is fundamentally determinative" (139), although he may be correct that Aquinas reads him this way. See "Being Truthful with (or Lying to) Others about Oneself," in *Aquinas and the Nicomachean Ethics*, ed. Tobias Hoffman, Jörn Müller, and Matthias Perkams (New York 2013), 129–145. For an alternative interpretation of Aristotle on this point, see Jane S. Zembaty, "Aristotle on Lying," *Journal of the History of Philosophy* 31:1 (1993): 7–29; also R. A. Gauthier and J. Y. Jolif, *L'Éthique à Nicomaque*, 4 vols., 2nd ed. (Leuven 2002), at I,1: 275–276.

[16] *In Sent.* III, Dist. 38, a. 3, ad 3.

as an impetus for Aquinas's departure from the traditional discourse on lying. But for now, I simply note the ways in which he is already beginning to nudge the discussion into new territory.

While Aquinas's most well-known arguments against lying are found in his magnum opus, the *Summa theologiae*, there are two additional, mature works that provide greater insight into the conceptual moves that we will find him making in the *Summa*. The first of these, the *Collationes in decem preceptis*, which were likely given as sermons in their original form, illustrate some key tenets of Aquinas's thought on the Decalogue. More importantly for our purposes, they demonstrate his mature interpretation of the eighth commandment and its relationship to the act of lying. As I will argue, we begin to see in this text the ways in which Aquinas departs from the medieval mainstream on this relationship. The exact date of this text is uncertain, but it was most likely written either just before or just after Aquinas composed the *secunda secundae pars*, the second part of the second part of the *Summa*.[17] Any apparent differences in what Aquinas claims in these two texts should probably be attributed to differences in genre rather than development in his thought. If for no other reason, the *Collationes* are worthy of our attention because they articulate some important themes that we might otherwise overlook when reading the *Summa*.

Aquinas begins his *Collationes* not with the Decalogue itself, but with the twofold love commandment given by Christ in Matthew 22:37–40: "You shall love the Lord your God with all your heart, and with all your soul, and with all your mind. This is the great and first commandment. And the second is like it, You shall love your neighbor as yourself. On these two commandments depend all the law and the prophets."[18] As he explains, "The entire law of Christ depends upon charity; and charity depends on two precepts, one of which is the love of God, and the other being love of neighbor."[19] These two precepts are mirrored in the two tables of the Decalogue, and the commandment against bearing

---

[17] According to Jean-Pierre Torrell, the *secunda secundae* was written in Paris in 1271–1272, whereas *In prec.* was written in Italy in 1261–1268 or 1273. See Torrell, "Les *Collationes in decem preceptis* de saint Thomas d'Aquin. Edition critique avec introduction et notes," *Revue des Sciences philosophiques et théologiques* 69 (1985): 5–40 and 227–263; cited at 15.

[18] *In prec.* V.

[19] *In prec.* XI: "Sicut iam dictum est tota lex Christi pendet a caritate; caritas autem pendet a duobus preceptis quorum unum est de dilectione Dei, reliquum de dilectione proximi; et de istis duobus iam dictum est."

false witness falls within the second table, which pertains to sins against one's neighbor.[20] He describes two contexts within which it is possible to violate this commandment: either in a court of law or in ordinary conversation.[21] The fact that Aquinas directs our attention to the legal context should not surprise us. Nearly every medieval discussion of the eighth commandment's prohibition of lying is appended by a discussion of perjury, typically defined as a lie confirmed by an oath.[22] But Aquinas does not have perjury *per se* in mind here.[23] He articulates three ways this commandment is violated in the context of the courtroom: (1) when a person is brought to court under a false accusation, (2) when a witness provides false testimony, or (3) when a judge delivers an unjust sentence.[24] While the first two instances will likely involve perjury, Aquinas is first and foremost concerned about the harm brought against the person who is falsely accused in court. This is the primary and paradigmatic mode in which the eighth commandment is violated.

In extrajudicial contexts, there are several additional ways to violate this commandment. The first way is by slander, in which a person willfully seeks to harm another person's reputation.[25] The second is by a sort of "passive detraction," in which one willingly listens to other slanderers yet does nothing to prevent the harmful claims from being perpetrated. The third way is through gossip, in which one repeats whatever he or she hears without regard to the truth of the statement or to the potential damage that it might do.[26] The fourth is through flattery,[27] and the fifth is through grumbling,[28] particularly against those who exercise

---

[20] *In prec.* XVIII. In the *Summa*, Aquinas explicitly states that the precepts of the second table of the Decalogue are arranged in descending order of their moral gravity (*ST* I-II.100.6).

[21] *In prec.* XXVIII: "Hoc autem potest esse dupliciter uel in iudicio uel in communi locutione" ("This can be done in two ways: either in the courtroom or in everyday conversation").

[22] Cf. Lombard, *Sententiarum* III.39, c. 1 (in PL 192; col. 835): "Perjurium est mendacium juramento firmatum" ("Perjury is a lie confirmed by an oath").

[23] Aquinas makes a few brief remarks about perjury in the *Collationes*, but they are in reference to the second commandment, "You shall not take the name of the Lord your God in vain," not the eighth commandment. See *In prec.* XIII.

[24] *In prec.* XXVIII.

[25] See also *ST* II-II.73.

[26] See also *ST* II-II.74.

[27] See also *ST* II-II.115.

[28] Historically, the sin of grumbling has been of special concern to those in religious orders. St. Benedict's *Rule*, for example, condemns grumbling as particularly corrosive to the common good of the monastery. See St. Benedict, *The Rule of St. Benedict* (New York 2008), 34.5–7 and 40.9. I am grateful to Evan Bednarz for this reference.

authority over us.[29] As with the first grouping of sins occurring within a judicial context, what is noteworthy about this list is that falsehood (either formal or material) is not an essential feature of any of these malfeasances. Rather, it is the undue harm that is inflicted on one's neighbor through the use of words that constitutes a violation of the commandment, "Do not bear false witness against your neighbor." Thus, whether we are considering sins of speech in a court of law or in everyday interactions, the emphasis falls on the *against neighbor* clause of the commandment rather on the truth or falsity of one's speech.

Aquinas does, however, believe that the commandment bears upon lying *simpliciter* in some way. Citing Ecclesiasticus 7:14 ("Refuse to utter any lie"), he declares that the eighth commandment condemns all lies.[30] Again, we are given another list – this time, to articulate why we should never tell a lie. His arguments echo Augustine's (although Aquinas never mentions him by name), with their blend of theological reasoning and pragmatic focus. For example, in his first argument, he makes the sobering assertion that lying makes one like the devil. Citing John 8:44, he reminds his listeners that the devil is "a liar and the father of lies," yet, in contrast to this, "others are those who speak the truth, and they are the children of God, who is truth."[31] The gift of speech is a manifestation of human nature, as humans were created in the image of God, who is Truth itself. The second reason lying is prohibited is that it contributes to the ruin of society. "Humans are naturally communal," Aquinas avers, "but this could not be possible if they do not speak the truth to one another."[32] The third reason is that those who lie will eventually lose their reputation for the truth. The fourth reason, according to Aquinas, is that a liar "kills" his own soul. By this he means that lying is a mortal sin; yet, he adds the qualification that lies can be either mortal or venial.[33] This qualification reinforces the crucial distinction in Aquinas's interpretation of the eighth commandment, namely, that not all instances of lying fall under the rubric of "bearing false witness against one's neighbor." Thus, only those lies that most fully meet the criteria of

---

[29] Interestingly, the sin of grumblers (*murmuratores*) has no corollary among the sins of speech listed in the *Summa*.
[30] *In prec.* XXIX. "'Non loqueris,' etc. [Ex. 20:16]. In hac prohibitione prohibetur omne mendacium" ("In this prohibition all lies are prohibited").
[31] Ibid.
[32] Ibid. "Homines enim naturaliter simul uiuunt, quod esse non posset si sibi uerum non dicerent."
[33] Ibid. "Unde aduertas quod ipsorum est mortale et ueniale" ("From this we see that they are mortal and venial").

the eighth commandment are counted as mortal sins, whereas other types of lies that fall short of these criteria remain venial.[34] While not every lie explicitly violates a precept of the Decalogue, the eighth commandment – when understood rightly – teaches us that lying can never be *good*.

If the *Collationes* approach lying from the perspective of divine precepts and mortal sin, Lecture 15 of the *Ethics* commentary is its secular counterpart. This is not to say that Aquinas is attempting to argue against the moral permissibility of lying, sans theological apparatus. Rather, what we find in the commentary is a discussion of an entirely different domain of action. While Aristotle's original text in *NE* IV.7 is only concerned with the virtue of truthfulness, which is opposed by the vices of boasting and mock-modesty, Aquinas takes the opportunity to consider the inordinateness of duplicitous speech more broadly. Nonetheless, we should be mindful that none of the examples Aquinas considers, whether Aristotle's or his own, are what he would classify as a mortal sin. Lest there be any mistake about this important delineation, he clarifies,

We are not, however, considering the person who speaks truthfully in judicial testimony, for example, someone who confesses the truth when questioned by a judge; nor the person who speaks the truth in any matter in which justice or injustice is at stake. This would pertain to another virtue, namely, justice. Rather, we are considering the truthful person who manifests the truth in his life and in his speech, in such things that do not properly distinguish between justice and injustice.[35]

---

[34] While I will continue to refer to and develop the mortal-venial distinction as it relates to lying, a basic overview of Aquinas's understanding of this distinction can be found in ST I-II.85–89. The fundamental premise is that mortal sins violate a precept of divine law, are incompatible with the virtue of charity, and thereby sever one's immediate relationship with God; venial sins, while not conducive to one's final end in God, are nevertheless compatible with a person's continuance in the state of grace, or charity. Aquinas provides a more detailed analysis of this distinction in *De malo* VII.1–12. For more on the nature of venial sin and the important ways in which it differs from mortal sin, see A. J. McNicholl, OP, "The Ultimate End of Venial Sin," *Thomist* 2 (1940): 373–409; P. DeLetter, SJ, "Venial Sin and Its Final Goal," *Thomist* 16:1 (1953): 32–70; Jordan Aumann, OP, "The Theology of Venial Sin," *Proceedings of the Catholic Theological Society of America* 10 (1955): 74–94; T.C. O'Brien, "Appendix 3: Venial Sin (1ae2ae 89)," in *Summa theologiae*, Vol. 27 (New York 1974), 118–124; Michel Labourdette, OP, *Grand cours de théologie morale, 4: Vices et péchés* (Ia-IIae, qu. 71–89) (Paris 2017), 257–282; Steven J. Jensen, *Sin: A Thomistic Psychology* (Washington, DC 2018), 66–83.

[35] Thomas Aquinas, *Sententia libri Ethicorum*, IV.7 § 838, in *S. Thomae Aquinatis opera omnia ut sunt in indice thomistico*, ed. Roberto Busa, vol. 4 (Stuttgart-Bad Cannstatt: Friedrich Frommann-Holzboog, 1980): "Non autem intendimus nunc de eo qui veritatem loquitur in confessionibus iudiciorum, puta cum aliquis interrogatus a iudice confitetur quod verum est; neque etiam de eo qui verum dicit in quibuscumque pertinentibus ad iustitiam vel iniustitiam; haec enim pertinent ad aliam virtutem, scilicet ad iustitiam. Sed de illo veridico intendimus qui verum dicit et vita et sermone in talibus, quae non habent differentiam iustitiae et iniustitiae."

If justice and injustice are not at stake in acts of truthfulness, then what exactly is at stake? According to Aristotle, the virtuous person avoids speaking falsely about himself because falsehood in itself is base and blameworthy.[36] It is the mark of a virtuous person that he will speak truthfully even with nothing is at stake, simply because his "character is such."[37] The truthful person loves truth, and he has acquired a habit, a stable disposition, to speak truthfully even when it does not matter; *a fortiori*, he will be all the more inclined to speak the truth when a matter of justice is at stake.[38] But in everyday, mundane conversation, the virtue of truth guides one to represent himself accurately – no more or no less than what he actually is – among his peers. Given the scope and aims of the *Nicomachean Ethics*, Aristotle is more concerned here with truthfulness as a character trait rather than specific acts of truthtelling. As Aquinas comments, the virtuous person is truthful "not only in his speech but also in the way he lives, insofar as his outward conduct, as well as his speech, conforms to his nature."[39] This does not necessarily mean that he will never utter a falsehood, but rather that his manner of life is informed by the acquired habit of truthfulness.

Yet, as we might expect from a scholastic theologian, Aquinas cannot resist the temptation to extend Aristotle's argument into a more precise analysis of human action. He writes, "Signs were instituted so that they might represent things as they are. Thus, if someone lies and represents a thing other than as it is, he is acting inordinately and viciously. But if he speaks the truth, he is acting orderly and virtuously."[40] It is this disorder, regardless of any harm that might be caused, that disinclines the virtuous person to speak falsely, whether about his own abilities or about any matter whatever.[41] Whereas in the earlier *Sentences* commentary we

[36] NE IV.7, 1127a13–1127a32.
[37] Ibid., 1127a33–1127b9.
[38] For a sound defense of this interpretation, see Flannery, "Being Truthful," 133 ff.
[39] *In Eth.* IV.7 § 835: "Est enim verax inquantum de se confitetur ea quae sunt; et hoc non solum sermone, sed etiam vita; inquantum scilicet exterior sua conversatio conformis est suae conditioni, sicut et sua locutio."
[40] *In Eth.* IV.7 § 837: "Ad hoc enim signa sunt instituta quod repraesentent res secundum quod sunt. Et ideo si aliquis repraesentat rem aliter quam sit, mentiendo, inordinate agit et vitiose. Qui autem verum dicit, ordinate agit et virtuose."
[41] *In Eth.* IV.7 § 839: "Et hoc ideo quia abhorret mendacium secundum se tamquam quoddam turpe, et non solum secundum quod cedit in nocumentum alterius" ("This is because he abhors the lie as something disgraceful in itself and not only insofar as it causes harm to another"). We also find Aquinas making this elision of "truth about one's abilities" and "truth about one's thoughts" in *De veritate*, written between the *Sentences* commentary and the *Summa*. He writes, "[D]icitur de homine, propter hoc quod electivus est verorum

witnessed Aquinas smuggling Aristotle into an Augustinian analysis, now we find the reverse: Aquinas is appealing to an Augustinian principle about the purpose of human signification in order to reinforce Aristotle's encomium to truthfulness.[42] Aquinas will have more to say about the disorder of duplicitous speech. What is most important, however, is that he has been able to disentangle his analysis of lying *per se*, which is understood as an inordinate use of language, from his analysis of malicious speech acts that contradict both the virtue of justice and a divine precept. The *Sentences* commentary, like the commentaries of Aquinas's peers, is unable to probe the nuances of this distinction, given the limitations of its genre and the fact that in this work Aquinas is still developing his understanding of the problem of lying. However, by addressing these two different aspects (indeed, two different *kinds*) of lying in his later works, the *Collationes* on the Ten Commandments and the *Ethics* commentary, he is in a better position to offer discrete analyses of these moral acts. When we turn to the *Summa*, we find this distinction fully developed and deployed with a new degree of precision. The result is an innovative framework for thinking about lying that is unlike any other author's in the Middle Ages.

THE VIRTUE OF JUSTICE AND ITS POTENTIAL PARTS

If a reader of Aquinas wishes to learn about his mature position on lying as it is found in the *Summa theologiae*, she can learn nearly as much from the organizational structure of the *secunda secundae* as she can from the actual content of the articles. The *secunda pars*, divided into two volumes, is organized in the form of several treatises on topics such as habits, sin, law, and grace. While the first volume, the *prima secundae*, offers a cursory overview of the virtues in the treatise on habits (I-II.49–70), the second volume, the *secunda secundae*, dedicates an entire set of questions to each of the major virtues (II-II.1–170). Of these, the virtue of justice receives the lengthiest analysis (II-II.57–122). For Aquinas, the virtue of justice is "a habit according to which a person, with a constant

---

vel facit existimationem de se vel de aliis veram vel falsam per ea quae dicit vel facit. Voces autem eodem modo recipiunt veritatis praedicationem, sicut intellectus quos significant," *Quaestiones disputatae de veritate* I.3, in *S. Thomae Aquinatis opera omnia ut sunt in indice thomistico*, ed. Roberto Busa, vol. 3 (Stuttgart-Bad Cannstatt 1980).

[42] Flannery, "Being Truthful," 139. While one could argue that Aquinas simply has in mind Aristotle's claim in *Peri Hermeneias* I.1 that words are signs of the "passions of the soul," his language more closely echoes Augustine's remarks on signs in *De doct.*, Book II.

and perpetual will, renders to each that which is his or her right."[43] The virtue of justice is the habit that perfects the will (II-II.58.4), and its actions establish equality by ensuring that each person's right [*ius*] is respected (II-II.57.1).[44] Virtues receive their species from their objects, and the proper object of justice is our interaction with other persons (II-II.58.1). Justice is therefore unique among the cardinal virtues for its other-regarding perspective. In our relationships to our broader communities and to the common good, justice is considered a general virtue (II-II.58.5), but as it describes our relationships with individuals, it is a particular virtue (II-II.58.7), especially as it pertains to the realm of communication and social interaction [*ad communicationem vitae*] (II-II.58.8 sc). As human experience bears out, there are many ways in which justice can be violated. Aquinas categorizes these injustices broadly into those that inflict harm on one's body (II-II.64–65), one's possessions (II-II.66), and one's honor (II-II.67–76).

In each analysis of the virtues in the *secunda secundae*, Aquinas includes, in addition to a detailed discussion of the virtue itself and its opposing vices, a discussion of the "potential parts" of the virtue, as well as a description of the precept(s) of the Decalogue that pertain to it. Since there are many moral and intellectual virtues that do not meet the formal criteria of a cardinal virtue (justice, prudence, temperance, fortitude)[45] or a theological virtue (faith, hope, charity), these additional virtues are included by annexing them to the virtue they most closely resemble. These are the potential parts of the virtue. It would be easy to assume that an annexed virtue is of lesser importance than the virtue to which it is annexed, but this would be a mistake. While many of the annexed virtues are of relatively lesser status, this is not necessarily so. Indeed, the virtue that Aquinas describes as the "preeminent" [*praecipua*] moral

---

[43] *ST* II-II.58.1: "[I]ustitia est habitus secundum quem aliquis constanti et perpetua voluntate ius suum unicuique tribuit."
[44] The notion of "equality" is of course hotly contested in our own day, as is the modern notion of "natural rights." As Jean Porter explains, Aquinas is drawing upon "what we might call two traditions of equality, namely, the classical tradition of natural law and natural right, which takes equality of status to be one of the touchstones of the pristine law of nature, and a Christian scriptural tradition, which insists on the fundamental equality of all men and women as bearers of the divine image and, at least potentially, participants in a shared friendship with God," *Justice as a Virtue: A Thomistic Perspective* (Grand Rapids, MI 2016), 121. For a reliable guide to the development of natural rights in the late Middle Ages, see Brian Tierney, *The Idea of Natural Rights: Studies on Natural Rights, Natural Law, and Church Law 1150–1625* (Grand Rapids, MI 1997).
[45] For the rationale in limiting the cardinal virtues to these four, see *ST* I-II.61.2–3.

virtue is the virtue of *religio*, which is annexed to the virtue of justice.[46] This peculiar virtue, quite foreign to the discourse of contemporary virtue ethics, directs human beings to worship and give reverence to God the creator. *Religio* is a potential part of justice because it falls short of a formal criterion for the virtue of justice proper, namely that the virtue of *religio* describes what we owe to God, who is not our "equal" in any sense. Even though we can rightfully say that humans owe a "debt" to their creator, it would be impossible for this debt to be "fulfilled" in any meaningful sense of the word; thus, *religio* cannot establish *equality* between us and the person, or being, to whom it is directed, which is one of the hallmarks of the virtue of justice. But the fact that *religio* falls short of a cardinal virtue from a purely logical standpoint does not lessen its importance for the moral life, according to Aquinas. In addition to *religio*, the virtues of piety, observance, honor, and obedience are annexed to justice for the reason that they fall short of the aspect of equality (II-II.80.1).[47]

Other virtues fall short of the virtue of justice, but for a different reason, namely, that they fall short of the aspect of due (*debitum*). In other words, they do not pertain to a *legal* due, in the robust sense, which is the domain of justice proper.[48] Nevertheless, they still describe a *moral* due, which a person owes in respect of the dignity of the virtue. These are virtues that belong to moral rectitude, but they do not generate the sort of strict obligation that can be directly governed by law (II-II.80.1). In fact some of these virtues (friendship and liberality) cannot even be said to be *necessary* for moral rectitude, although they are conducive to it. Other virtues that are necessary for moral rectitude include gratitude,

---

[46] *ST* II-II.81.6 "Ergo religio est praecipua inter virtutes morales" ("Therefore, religion is preeminent among the moral virtues").

[47] John Bowlin, *Tolerance among the Virtues* (Princeton, NJ 2016) offers an excellent constructive account of a virtue (in this case, the virtue of tolerance) that is annexed to justice. Bowlin's account goes beyond Aquinas's, but it faithfully extends Aquinas's thought and convincingly demonstrates its contemporary relevance.

[48] An important point of clarification is in order. When Aquinas says that justice directs one's actions that fulfill a "legal" due (II-II.80.1), he is not limiting this to general, or legal, justice. He also means to include particular justice, which is co-divided into commutative and distributive justice (II-II.61.1), under the rubric of "legal" debt. Both general and particular justice are considered aspects of the virtue of justice proper, and thus, any of their acts are concerned with legal due. Each of the virtues Aquinas annexes to justice, however, is annexed to *particular* justice, with the sole exception of *epieikeia*, which he annexes to general justice (II-II.80.1 ad 5), since *epieikeia* is the virtue by which a person sets aside, when necessary, the letter of the law for the sake of the common good (II-II.120.1).

vindication, and the virtue that most pertains to our present interests: the virtue of truthfulness (*veracitas*). If the reader wishes to find the *Summa*'s exposition on lying, this is where she will find it, within the Questions on the virtue of truthfulness and its opposing vices (II-II.109–113).

It is worth pausing momentarily to consider the origins of this list of virtues annexed to justice. While it is not an entirely original creation, Aquinas's exact list is unlike any of his peers'. The virtues catalogued here are largely modeled after Cicero's principles of the "laws of nature" in *De inventione* II.53 – and Aquinas is not even the first scholastic theologian to co-opt Cicero's list[49] – but he nevertheless tailors these "potential parts" of justice for his own purposes.[50] The final product is a hybrid of Cicero, Macrobius, Andronicus, Aristotle, and other anonymous sources (II-II.80.1). This is noteworthy for at least two reasons. First, it indicates a number of conflicting voices, any of which could be recognized as a legitimate authority, yet without any obvious means of reconciling them. Article 1 of Question 80 does not contain a *sed contra*, which would normally give Aquinas the opportunity to cite an authority that lends support to his own position. This omission seems to suggest that there is no definitive authority as to which virtues should be annexed to justice. This leads to the second reason, which is the fact that the list that Aquinas finally settles on is uniquely his own. This list includes all of Cicero's virtues, but it also adds one from Macrobius (friendliness), one from an anonymous source (obedience), one from Andronicus (liberality), and one from Aristotle (*epieikeia*). Indeed, it becomes quite clear that the authorities mentioned in the Objections are carefully chosen for the express purpose of including a specific set of virtues in Aquinas's final inventory. He recognizes, for example, that Cicero does not name the virtues of liberality and friendship because they do not have the aspect of due (*ratione debiti*) in them (II-II.80.1),

---

[49] In the twelfth century, Peter Abelard draws upon Cicero's *De inventione* in his list of virtues related to justice, nearly 150 years before Aquinas. See Odon Lottin, "Le concept de justice chez les théologiens du moyen âge avant l'introduction d'Aristote," *Revue Thomiste* 44 (1938): 511–521; cited at 511.

[50] Cicero does not use the language of "annexed to" or "potential parts" of the virtue of justice. Rather, the first principles of justice "proceed from nature, then certain rules of conduct became customary by reason of their advantage" (*Inv.* II.53). This claim that the principles of justice proceed from nature leads him to elaborate: "The law of nature [*naturae ius*] is that which is not born of opinion, but implanted in us by a kind of innate instinct [*quaedam in natura vis insevit*]: it includes religion, duty, gratitude, revenge, reverence and truth" (Ibid.), in Cicero, *On Invention; Best Kind of Orator; Topics*, Loeb Classical Library 386, trans. H. M. Hubbell (Cambridge, MA 1940), 1–346.

but nevertheless, Aquinas wishes to include them, since they pertain to our relationships with others and are conducive to moral rectitude. Thus, Aquinas's list of virtues annexed to justice is neither *sui generis* nor the slavish reproduction of some classical construction. He has given himself the freedom to say what he wants to say, while still situating his claims within a recognized tradition.

Given this freedom, there is still no reason to expect that Aquinas's analysis of lying should fall under the virtue of truthfulness, as annexed to justice. In fact, one could even argue that a more faithful rendering of his sources would lead him *not* to introduce a broad discussion of lying in this section of the *secunda secundae*. We have already noted that Aquinas is aware that Aristotle's virtue of truthfulness has a rather restricted frame of reference; it is the mean between the vices of boasting and mock-modesty. But the same can be said of Cicero's virtue of truthfulness. Aquinas recognizes as much when he cites the Ciceronian definition of truthfulness as "the faithfulness by which one acts as he speaks," particularly in the context of keeping one's promises, but he informs us, "[T]ruthfulness contains much more, as will be made clear in what follows" (II-II.80.1 ad 3).[51] If Aquinas is merely concerned to include the virtue of truthfulness as a virtue annexed to justice (following Cicero) and to provide a virtue that strikes the mean between the vices of boasting and mock-modesty (following Aristotle), he could do just that. This is precisely what he does with the virtue of friendliness, for example, which follows immediately after, in II-II.114. That is, Aquinas describes the virtue of friendliness in and of itself, followed by a brief discussion of its two opposing vices: flattery (II-II.115) and quarreling (II-II.116). But when Aquinas turns to the vices opposed to the virtue of truthfulness, he lists lying (II-II.110) and hypocrisy (II-II.111) before mentioning the Aristotelian vices of boasting and mock-modesty.[52] Clearly, Aquinas has

---

[51] *ST* II-II.80.1 ad 3: "Fides autem, per quam fiunt dicta, includitur in veritate, quantum ad observantiam promissorum. Veritas autem in plus se habet, ut infra patebit."

[52] Contemporary moral philosopher Christian Miller addresses a similar set of taxonomical problems in his work on the virtue of honesty. He develops a "Widespread Character approach," which can accommodate an account of vice that is not limited to the excess or deficiency of a virtue. By the same token, the vices opposed to a virtue need not be opposed to one another. One upshot of this approach is that there is no vice that is an "excess" of honesty or truthfulness. There can be multiple, overlapping vices opposed to a virtue. While the correct exegesis of Aquinas is peripheral to Miller's concerns, it is worth noting that this approach is consistent with Aquinas's classification of the vices opposed to truthfulness, and it can also illuminate the creative ways in which Aquinas extends Aristotle's analysis of truthfulness. See Miller, *Honesty*, 166–177.

his own agenda, shaped by his particular understanding of the virtue of truthfulness, which is neither Ciceronian nor Aristotelian, even if he is indebted to both thinkers in significant ways. At the very least, we can see that Aquinas is deliberate in his placement of lying within the *secunda secundae*. He is not merely following tradition here; his structuring of the potential parts of justice, including the vice of lying and the virtue of truthfulness, has no precedent.

We might wonder then: Where else *could* Aquinas's analysis of lying fall within the *Summa*? We might surmise that it falls where it does simply for lack of a better alternative. But there is actually a rather obvious candidate, especially for readers familiar with medieval manuals of theology. Elsewhere in the *secunda secundae*, Aquinas describes extrajudicial sins of speech (II-II.72–76), and there is plenty of reason one might expect to find an analysis of lying there – not least because Aquinas tells us these sins are direct violations of the eighth commandment, and all of Aquinas's contemporaries endorse the view that lying is the paradigmatic example of that which the commandment prohibits. He could have included lying among these sins of speech while still listing truthfulness as a virtue annexed to justice in II-II.109, with its opposing vices of boasting and mock-modesty. But he does not, and we must ask ourselves why. As far as I can tell, no contemporary scholar has bothered to consider – let alone offer an explanation for – why the vice of lying is not included among the extrajudicial sins of speech catalogued in II-II.72–76. But its omission here tells us something about what Aquinas thinks about the sin of lying. What this "something" is will become clear in due course. While the precise location of Aquinas's analysis of lying within the *Summa* might seem like a topic only of interest to historians or scholars of Aquinas, what we find is that the placement of these articles is no less important than their content.[53] Aquinas's decision to place the virtue of truthfulness (and its opposing vices) among the virtues annexed to justice is itself an innovation, and, if it is a sound decision, then it has major implications for the way we should think about lying as a moral problem.

---

[53] For more on the broader development and organization of the *secunda secundae*, see Jean-Pierre Torrell, OP, *Aquinas's* Summa: *Background, Structure, & Reception*, trans. Benedict M. Guevin, OSB (Washington, DC 2005), 27–48. For more on the structure and organization of the virtue of justice and its potential parts within the *secunda secundae*, see Porter, *Justice as a Virtue*, 49–50, 127–131. For more on Aquinas's inclusion of the social virtues of friendliness and truthfulness among the potential parts of justice, see Kevin White, "The Virtues of Man the *Animal Sociale*: *Affabilitas* and *Veritas* in Aquinas," *Thomist* 57:4 (1993): 641–653.

SINS OF SPEECH

The unique location of the sin of lying within the *Summa* becomes even more apparent once we consider how the reader would go about answering the following question: "What are the sins that violate the eighth commandment, 'Do not bear false witness against your neighbor?'" The trajectory launched by this question takes us in a very different direction. Here, we are not guided to the virtue of truthfulness, but rather the virtue of justice proper. More specifically, we are guided to a specific list of injustices that inflict harm on another person by injuring or insulting her honor. The term "honor" does not have quite the same resonance in our own day as it did in Aquinas's, but these are sins that broadly constitute forms of verbal abuse. The term "honor" is simply meant to distinguish the mode in which a person inflicts harm, in contrast to bodily injury or loss of physical goods. While the formal structure of the *secunda secundae* is not modeled directly after the Ten Commandments, Aquinas does provide the reader with the resources for connecting each of the commandments with the corresponding virtues, gifts, and vices that illuminate their relationship. As he explains in the *Prologue*, if one wishes to understand the commandment "do not commit adultery," one should examine the particular sin of adultery, and in order to understand the sin, one should also understand the opposing virtue. So what is the particular sin prohibited by the commandment, "do not bear false witness against your neighbor"? Aquinas answers that injuries inflicted through speech (*nocumenta ad locutionem*), such as slander, are to be understood as prohibited by the precept against bearing false witness, as such actions are directly opposed to justice.[54]

We must keep in mind that, for Aquinas, an act of injustice is necessarily a sin against charity (II-II.59.4), and a sin against charity is a mortal sin (I-II.88.2). Here we find the interconnection between justice, charity, and law: Aquinas states that any species of mortal sin is also a transgression of a divine precept (II-II.79.2).[55] Concerning the sin of perjury, for

---

[54] II-II.122.6 ad 2: "Quae [nocumenta] autem pertinet ad locutionem, sicut detractiones, blasphemiae, et si qua huiusmodi, intelliguntur prohiberi falso testimonio, quod directius iustitiae contrariatur" ("Injuries that pertain to speech, such as slander, blasphemy, and other such things are understood to be prohibited as false testimony, which is directly opposed to justice").

[55] For Aquinas, the term "precept of the law" denotes a dictate of practical reason that proceeds from the eternal law, which is unchanging and an expression of divine providence (I-II.91.1). Thus, any moral precept – whether known through the natural law, divine law, or human law (assuming it is just) – can be understood as a precept of the

example, Aquinas cites a precept from the book of Leviticus: "Every sin that is contrary to a divine precept is a mortal sin. But perjury is contrary to a divine precept, as it is written in Lev. 19: 'You shall not swear falsely by my name.' Therefore it is a mortal sin."[56] And we should be mindful that charity and justice are not simply two ways of describing the same thing, although they are closely related. It is not the case, for Aquinas, that charity is a religious synonym for justice. Charity describes a person's final end and directs all her actions to God (II-II.23.6), including those actions pertaining to relations among persons, which is the domain of justice. The overlap between these two virtues, as well as the potential for confusion, is found in the fact that both virtues reside in the will (II-II.58.4; II-II.24.1). The will, which Aquinas calls the *rational appetite* (I.82.5), is the power of deliberate choice – it guides our actions through the use of reason, but it is neither a neutral intellectual capacity nor an impulse in the way we might describe the animal passions.[57] The virtues

---

law insofar as it originates in the eternal law. Unlike the ceremonial and judicial precepts of the Old Law, which were given to Israel in the context of a particular time and place, the moral precepts "are efficacious due to the dictates of natural reason, even if they had never been stated in the law" (I-II.100.11). When he uses the term "divine precept," he means to designate a precept that has been directly promulgated by God (as recorded in scripture). This would certainly include the precepts of the Decalogue, but additionally it might include commands that were given to specific people in specific contexts. For example, God's command to Hosea to take a prostitute for a wife (Hos. 1:2) was a divine precept (II-II.154.2 ad 2). To act against a divine precept expresses contempt for God, the lawgiver, and is thus a mortal sin (II-II.105.2).

[56] II-II.98.3 sc: "Sed contra, omne peccatum quod contrariatur praecepto divino est peccatum mortale. Sed periurium contrariatur praecepto divino, dicitur enim Levit. XIX, non periurabis in nomine meo. Ergo est peccatum mortale." While this precept may sound very similar to the second commandment, "you shall not take the name of the Lord your God in vain" (Ex. 20:7), the specific passage Aquinas quotes (Lev. 19:12) belongs to the "holiness code" in Leviticus, which outlines God's covenantal relationship with the people of Israel and includes numerous ceremonial and ethical guidelines. The prohibition against swearing falsely by God's name, since it is given directly by God, is a divine precept. The similarity to the second commandment, however, is hardly incidental; rather, it underscores Aquinas's claim that all the moral precepts of the Old Law are ultimately reducible to the ten precepts of the Decalogue (I-II.100.3). Elsewhere, Aquinas states unequivocally that the second commandment forbids perjury (I-II.100.11). His decision to cite the Leviticus text in II-II.98.3 sc instead of the Decalogue most likely reflects the particular point he wishes to make here, which is concerned specifically with perjury.

[57] For three excellent analyses of Aquinas on the will's role in moral action, see Michael Sherwin, OP, *By Knowledge & by Love: Charity and Knowledge in the Moral Theology of St. Thomas Aquinas* (Washington, DC 2005) 18–62; Daniel Westberg, *Right Practical Reason: Aristotle, Action, and Prudence in Aquinas* (New York 1994), 43–175; and Stephen L. Brock, *Action and Conduct: Thomas Aquinas and the Theory of Action* (Edinburgh 1998), 137–196.

of justice and charity reside in and perfect the will, and each plays a role in directing the other moral virtues to a common end: "just as charity can be called a general virtue, insofar as it orders the acts of all the virtues to the divine good, so can legal justice, insofar as it orders the acts of all the virtues to the common good" (II-II.58.6). The point here is not to create a strict divide between the natural and supernatural dimensions of human existence, but rather to distinguish two discrete, yet overlapping, ends of virtue.[58]

Wherever a precept of the law is transgressed, there is an action that is either against charity or against justice (or both). While not every sin against charity is a sin against justice (a person might blaspheme God without intending to harm another person, for example), every sin against justice is also a sin against charity. The virtuous person who possesses justice and charity loves the law ("Oh how I love thy law! It is my meditation all the day," Ps. 119:97) and willfully recognizes its precepts as binding. Charity recognizes the law as a gift from God, but this same disposition also belongs to legal, or general, justice, which recognizes the need for equitable social arrangements in order for communities to flourish. Aquinas writes, "Just as it belongs to the nature of legal justice to consider precepts as generating something that is due, so it belongs to the nature of transgression to consider precepts with contempt."[59] As he elaborates in his *Romans* commentary, "Legal justice, which sums up every virtue, is directed toward the observance of precepts of the law, which concerns the *ratio* of obedience. But legal injustice, which is the sum of all malice, as it is written in [Aristotle's] *Ethics*, Bk. V, is directed toward the transgression of precepts of the law, which concerns the *ratio* of disobedience."[60] While legal justice, as the name suggests, is concerned with the kind of actions that fall under the domain of legal authority, this does not mean that it is only concerned with the actual, positive law that happens to be codified in individual's community. Neither does it

---

[58] For more on the relationship between justice and charity as virtues of the will, see Jean Porter, *Justice as a Virtue*, 54–58 and 163–169.

[59] *ST* II-II.79.2: "[S]icut enim ad propriam rationem iustitiae legalis pertinet attendere debitum praecepti, ita ad propriam rationem transgressionis pertinet attendere contemptum praecepti."

[60] *In Rom.* 5:19 § 447: "[Q]uia iustitia legalis, quae est omnis virtus, attenditur in observatione praeceptorum legis, quod pertinet ad rationem obedientiae. Iniustitia autem legalis, quae est omnis malitia ut dicitur V Ethicorum, attenditur in transgressione mandatorum legis, quae pertinet ad rationem inobedientiae," *Super epistolam ad Romanos* lectura, ed. Raphael Cai, *Super epistolas S. Pauli lectura*, 8th rev. edn, 2 vols. (Turin 1953), vol. 1, pp. 1–230.

mean that a person commits a sin when she transgresses an *unjust* law. Aquinas is a defender of the principle *lex iniusta non est lex* ("An unjust law is no law at all"). Traditionally attributed to Augustine, and given renewed attention in the twentieth century by Martin Luther King, Jr.,[61] this principle maintains that civil laws only bind the conscience insofar as they are in accord with natural law (I-II.96.4). Nonetheless, the person who possesses the virtue of justice will recognize her legal due to other persons, whether or not the written laws in her community adequately articulate this due.

It is this understanding of justice and the nature of legal due that frames Aquinas's analysis of the sins of speech. While a person's general stance and attitude toward the common good is a feature of general justice, the actual, on-the-ground interactions of daily life belong to particular justice. These interactions bring with them a legal due, insofar as we can describe what we *owe* other persons. After considering harms such as murder, assault, and robbery, Aquinas turns to vices that consist in words that hurt our neighbor (II-II.67 pr.). These fall into two broad categories: judicial and extrajudicial harmful speech. While most people do not spend much of their daily lives in the courtroom, either in our own day or in Aquinas's, there are two reasons he prioritizes sins of speech that occur within the context of judicial proceedings. The first is that, since these are sins that clearly violate a legal debt, there is no more obvious place in which a person's legal debt is made manifest than an environment that is under the direct supervision of a judge, who is a minister of the law.[62] The second reason is that Aquinas, as he reminds us in II-II.122.6 and the *Collationes*, thinks of injustices in relation to the precepts of the second table of the Decalogue, which tell us how we ought to treat our neighbors. And the precept of the Decalogue that directs one's *speech* toward one's neighbor is articulated in the language of the courtroom: "You shall not bear false witness against your

---

[61] King writes, "A just law is a man made code that squares with the moral law or the law of God. An unjust law is a code that is out of harmony with the moral law. To put it in the terms of St. Thomas Aquinas: An unjust law is a human law that is not rooted in eternal law and natural law. Any law that uplifts human personality is just. Any law that degrades human personality is unjust. All segregation statutes are unjust because segregation distorts the soul and damages the personality," in Martin Luther King, Jr., "Letter from a Birmingham Jail," *Why We Can't Wait* (Boston 2011), 106.

[62] For a contemporary articulation of judicial authority informed by Thomistic insights, see Jean Porter, *Ministers of the Law: A Natural Law Theory of Legal Authority* (Grand Rapids, MI 2010), 262–272.

neighbor." For Aquinas, these reasons are sufficient to make false testimony in the courtroom the paradigmatic sin of speech.

While Aquinas does not deny that the eighth commandment bears upon several additional sins of speech, including lying, he also grants that this relationship is not entirely obvious. There is an important epistemological insight to be gleaned from his articulation of the precepts of the Decalogue, namely, that sometimes we need a little help in order to understand why certain actions are commanded or proscribed. As he explains,

> Now of these [moral precepts of the law] there are three grades. Some are so certain and so manifest that they do not need to be promulgated, such as the commandments to love God and our neighbor and others like these [...], which are really the ends of the moral precepts. Concerning these it is not possible to err in one's judgment. Then there are some precepts that are more specific, and yet even the average person is able to grasp them easily. Although, in some cases, human judgment concerning these precepts can become corrupted, and for this reason they need to be promulgated. These are the precepts of the Decalogue. Finally, there are precepts whose reasons are not readily apparent to everyone, but only to the wise: these are the moral precepts added to the Decalogue, given by God and handed down to the people by Moses and Aaron.[63]

While each precept of the Decalogue explicitly commands or prohibits certain actions, there are also corollary precepts that are less obvious.[64] The eighth commandment forbids false testimony, Aquinas explains,

---

[63] *ST* I-II.100.11: "Horum autem triplex est gradus. Nam quaedam sunt certissima, et adeo manifesta quod editione non indigent; sicut mandata de dilectione Dei et proximi, et alia huiusmodi, ut supra dictum est, quae sunt quasi fines praeceptorum, unde in eis nullus potest errare secundum iudicium rationis. Quaedam vero sunt magis determinata, quorum rationem statim quilibet, etiam popularis, potest de facili videre; et tamen quia in paucioribus circa huiusmodi contingit iudicium humanum perverti, huiusmodi editione indigent, et haec sunt praecepta Decalogi. Quaedam vero sunt quorum ratio non est adeo cuilibet manifesta, sed solum sapientibus, et ista sunt praecepta moralia superaddita Decalogo, tradita a Deo populo per Moysen et Aaron."

[64] Stephen Brock, in his magisterial exposition of Aquinas's theory of natural law, *The Light That Binds: A Study in Thomas Aquinas's Metaphysics of Natural Law* (Eugene, OR 2020), explains why the goodness of truthful speech does not necessarily give rise to a primary precept of the natural law: "The *universal* prohibition of lying does not seem to be primary either, or even secondary (involving only a little reasoning)" (p. 131, fn. 81). He notes, furthermore, that "while the Decalogue forbids false testimony, the universal prohibition of lying requires instruction from the wise. This is so even though truthfulness is 'naturally loved' and even though lying is 'unnatural.' We naturally understand that veracity is generally good and that mendacity is generally bad, but it is not so obvious to us that there is never a truly good reason to lie. What Thomas says even suggests that instruction is needed in order to see that, besides false testimony, other lies can also be grievously sinful or violations of strict duty" (223).

but there are additional moral precepts *added* to this commandment, given their proximity to false testimony. Among these are the precepts against false judicial sentences (Ex. 23:2), against lying (Ex. 23:7), and against slander (Lev. 19:16) (I-II.100.11). The sins prohibited by these additional precepts describe varying degrees of harm as well as varying degrees of moral culpability. But "the wise" (in this case, Moses and Aaron) have shown us that these precepts are morally binding, even if they are less obvious than the paradigmatic precepts found in the Decalogue.

Beginning with Question 67 of the *secunda secundae*, Aquinas articulates a series of vices opposed to commutative justice, beginning with injuries inflicted by words that are uttered in a judicial context. These injustices can be committed by any party involved in the judicial proceedings, including judges, prosecutors, defendants, witnesses, and attorneys. The demands of justice determine the role of each participant, in regards to what he or she may declare in court. The judge, for example, is bound to make judgments only on the basis of what is proven in court, rather than on the basis of private opinion (II-II.67.2), and he cannot condemn a person who has not been rightfully accused (II-II.67.3).[65] The words of the judge are, of course, disproportionate in their power and significance when compared with other participants in the courtroom. Unlike the words of witnesses or defendants, which *assert* a party's guilt or innocence as a matter of fact, those of the judge efficaciously *declare* a party guilty or innocent, i.e., that she is guilty or innocent under the law and must either bear punishment or be acquitted.[66] The judge's words carry a certain creative power, even if his declaration happens to be materially false. We might (anachronistically) call such declarations *performative utterances*, a term coined by J. L. Austin to describe a category of speech acts in which "the issuing of the utterance is the performance of an action."[67] When a judge declares an innocent party to be guilty, this is

---

[65] For a helpful overview of Aquinas's requirements for judges, see Charles Nemeth, *Aquinas in the Courtroom: Lawyers, Judges, and Judicial Conduct* (Westport, CT 2001), 127–143.

[66] See *ST* II-II.76.1 for Aquinas's remarks on the threefold relation of *speaking* to the *thing spoken*, especially by way of cause (*per modem causae*) in the imperative mood.

[67] J. L. Austin, *How to Do Things with Words* (Cambridge, MA 1962), 5–6. Austin's conception of illocutionary acts (of which performative utterances are a subcategory) was further developed by his student, John Searle, in *Speech Acts: An Essay in the Philosophy of Language* (New York 1969) and has been refined and debated by philosophers of language ever since.

not merely false testimony; it is a false *judgment*, which is an even greater injustice. Thus, the judge bears a profound responsibility as an *interpres iustitiae* ("interpreter of justice," II-II.67.3), and the moral gravity of a false condemnation from a judge is greater than that of false testimony uttered by a witness.

The other parties in the courtroom are nevertheless capable of committing injustices with their words – or, in some cases, by their silence. When a rightful accusation is made against a person, however, this exposure of the crime is for the benefit of the common good (II-II.68.3). But the person who willfully provides false testimony "sins both against the accused person as well as the commonwealth, and he is punished accordingly."[68] By "accordingly," Aquinas means that the accuser is subject to the same punishment to which he (potentially) subjected the accused. Here Aquinas follows Deuteronomy 19:18–19, which states, "the judges shall inquire diligently, and if the witness is a false witness and has accused his brother falsely, then you shall do to him as he had meant to do to his brother." This is not merely a matter of personal justice but a means of creating stability within the community. As the text of Deuteronomy continues, "so you shall purge the evil from the midst of you. And the rest shall hear, and fear, and shall never again commit any such evil among you" (19:19b–20). The false accuser does more than simply harm a person's reputation or honor – his words have a direct and immediate effect on the accused's material conditions. If the accusation serves as the basis for a judge's sentence, then the defendant will be fined, imprisoned, or possibly put to death. False testimony is first and foremost a matter of justice, and this justice pertains even more directly to a person's well-being than the mere utterance of harmful words.

These observations set the tone for Aquinas's remarks on the remaining sins of speech that can be committed within a judicial context. Depending on the circumstances, it can be a sin to remain silent in the courtroom. Defendants, for example, are not only prohibited from providing false testimony but also (in certain cases) from hiding the facts that might lead to one's own conviction:

> Thus the accused has a duty to tell the truth to the judge, who demands the truth from him according to the form of the law. If he refuses to tell the truth that he is obliged to tell, or if he denies it by telling a lie, he commits a mortal sin. If, however, the judge demands something of the accused that is not in accordance

---

[68] *ST* II-II.68.4: "Ad secundum dicendum quod ille qui male accusat peccat et contra personam accusati, et contra rempublicam."

with the order of justice, then the accused is not bound to respond, but may rather make an appeal or resort to some other licit means of evasion (which does not include lying).[69]

The qualification about making appeals, or simply evading the truth, is not to be overlooked, as it underscores two important principles operating in Aquinas's ethics of truthtelling. The first and broader principle is simply that the truth need not *always* be revealed. There are instances in which a person is entitled or (as will become clear later on) even *obligated* to hide the truth. The second and closely related principle explains that context – especially the *legal* context – sets the terms for when the truth may be hidden. In the particular case of court appeals, Aquinas explains that "it is lawful for a person who is unjustly oppressed to have the recourse of appealing to a higher authority, either before or after the sentence is declared,"[70] but she may not appeal if the reason is simply to subvert justice and avoid punishment. Witnesses, likewise, may or may not be bound to reveal secrets that were told to them by the defendant. If the secret is such that it contributes to the corruption of the community or a grave personal injury, then the witness is not only bound to reveal this information when asked about it but at the moment in which it is brought to her knowledge. If the moral gravity falls short of these criteria, however, then the witness must honor the secret and remain silent. Aquinas writes, "In this case one is not bound to make the matter known even if commanded by an authority, because the service of fidelity [*servare fidem*] belongs to natural right [*de iure naturali*], and no one has the power to command a person to do what is contrary to natural right."[71] There are special cases, however, such as the sacrament of penance. The "seal of confession," to which all priests are solemnly bound, admits of no exceptions. When a priest hears the confession of a penitent, he knows things about the penitent "not as man but as God's minister, and the sacrament binds stronger than any

---

[69] *ST* II-II.69.1: "Et ideo ex debito tenetur accusatus iudici veritatem exponere quam ab eo secundum formam iuris exigit. Et ideo si confiteri noluerit veritatem quam dicere tenetur, vel si eam mendaciter negaverit, mortaliter peccat. Si vero iudex hoc exquirat quod non potest secundum ordinem iuris, non tenetur ei accusatus respondere, sed potest vel per appellationem vel aliter licite subterfugere, mendacium tamen dicere non licet."

[70] *ST* II-II.69.3 ad 1: "Et ideo licitum est ei qui contra iustitiam gravatur, ad directionem superioris potestatis recurrere appellando, vel ante sententiam vel post."

[71] *ST* II-II.70.1 ad 2: "Et tunc nullo modo tenetur ea prodere, etiam ex praecepto superioris, quia servare fidem est de iure naturali; nihil autem potest praecipi homini contra id quod est de iure naturali."

human precept."[72] Even in a court of law, a priest is not allowed to reveal information that was revealed in the confessional. This of course remains a controversial legal question in the present day.[73] But the point is that, for Aquinas, silence is not a neutral moral choice. Sometimes we are morally or legally bound to reveal the truth; at other times we are bound to hide it.

The sin of false testimony in the courtroom remains, for Aquinas, the paradigmatic violation of the eighth commandment. Unlike other kinds of lies, false witness is always a mortal sin. False judicial testimony exhibits a threefold deformity, Aquinas explains. The false testifier (1) commits perjury, (2) violates the order of justice, and (3) utters a falsehood (II-II.70.4). The second point, according to Aquinas, explains why the text of the Decalogue in Exodus 20:16 takes the form, "You shall not bear false witness against your neighbor." Take, for example, the case of a witness who *knows* that the defendant is innocent, yet worries that the evidence is stacked against her. Would it be permissible to provide false testimony in this instance? Would not such a falsehood count as a beneficent (*officiosum*) lie? No, according to Aquinas. He would grant that the lie considered in itself is venial (touching on the third point) and that it does not violate the order of justice (touching on the second). The reason for the mortal sin lies in the fact the falsehood still amounts to perjury (addressing the first point), since the witness testifies under oath (II-II.70.4 ad 2).

---

[72] Ibid.: "Ad secundum dicendum quod de illis quae homini sunt commissa in secreto per confessionem, nullo modo debet testimonium ferre, quia huiusmodi non scit ut homo, sed tanquam Dei minister, et maius est vinculum sacramenti quolibet hominis praecepto." Aquinas further addresses this and related questions on the seal of confession in *Supplementum* 11.

[73] See, for example, the 2016 case, *Mayeux v. Charlet*, decided by the Supreme Court of Louisiana in favor of maintaining the clergy–penitent privilege. For an extensive analysis of this case and the broader legal concerns it touches on, see Caroline Donze, "Breaking the Seal of Confession: Examining the Constitutionality of the Clergy-Penitent Privilege in Mandatory Reporting Law," *Louisiana Law Review* 78:1 (2017): 268–310. Donze argues, "Abrogation of the clergy-penitent privilege in the context of confidential communications is constitutional because the compelling state interest of protecting children outweighs the narrow infringement upon the religious rights of clergy. A change in the law may have only a limited effect on Catholicism as long as priests continue to place canon law ahead of their legal duty to report. Imposing legal accountability on priests would send a strong message to the Catholic Church that perhaps it should reevaluate its absolute stance on the seal of confession" (310). See also Albert R. Jonsen and Stephen Toulmin, *The Abuse of Casuistry: A History of Moral Reasoning* (Berkeley, CA 1988), 199–200. For a comprehensive history of the seal of confession (now somewhat dated, although still unsurpassed), see Bertrand Kurtscheid, *A History of the Seal of Confession*, trans. F. A. Marks (London 1927).

Aquinas's understanding of perjury, like all the scholastics, is thoroughly theological, and we only find echoes of it in contemporary Western conceptions of perjury. For Aquinas, perjury is defined as the act of calling God as a witness to one's false testimony, which is a sin against the virtue of *religio*, since it "implies either that God is oblivious to the truth or that he wills to testify to the falsehood."[74] It is therefore a false *oath*. The falsehood itself, considered in isolation and in the abstract, may by nature only be a venial sin, but it becomes mortal when it is told out of contempt for God (II-II.98.3). The power of an oath is such that even when it is made under coercion it is still binding. Of course, the categories of *oath* and *perjury* still serve important functions in contemporary society, even if they have been stripped of their religious contexts. Italian philosopher Giorgio Agamben, in his provocative theory of language, suggests that the function of oath reveals, first and foremost, the inherent power of speech.[75] It is the possibility of the oath that creates the domains of law and religion, rather than the other way around:

> The testimony is given by language itself and the god names a potentiality implicit in the very act of speech. The testimony that is in question in the oath must therefore be understood in a sense that has little to do with much of what we normally understand by this term. It concerns not the verification of a fact or an event but the very signifying power of language.[76]

Regardless of what we make of Agamben's claims, there is no denying that the act of oath taking displays the power of language. Lying under oath still constitutes perjury under American law, even if we do not believe that God is involved in the judicial process. Aquinas would maintain that an oath – an oath in which the speaker truly believes herself to be calling upon God as her witness – is an act of *religio*, insofar as it acknowledges God's omnipotence and omniscience, and thereby displays reverence to God (II-II.89.4). The courtroom raises the stakes for lying and truthtelling, because the liars either commit perjury or an injustice (or both), while the oath-takers and truth-tellers exhibit the virtue of *religio* and further the ends of justice.

---

[74] *ST* II-II.98.2: "Respondeo dicendum quod, sicut supra dictum est, iurare est Deum testem invocare. Pertinet autem ad Dei irreverentiam quod aliquis eum testem invocet falsitatis, quia per hoc dat intelligere vel quod Deus veritatem non cognoscat, vel quod falsitatem testificari velit. Et ideo periurium manifeste est peccatum religioni contrarium, cuius est Deo reverentiam exhibere."
[75] Giorgio Agamben, *The Sacrament of Language: An Archeology of the Oath*, trans. Adam Kotsko (Stanford, CA 2011), 19.
[76] Ibid., 33.

While Aquinas takes judicial sins of speech as paradigmatic violations of the eighth commandment, this does not mean that extrajudicial falsehoods are all necessarily venial. There is no shortage of harmful lies uttered outside the walls of the courtroom that violate the norms of justice. Citing the frequently glossed Psalm 5:6, "You destroy those who speak lies," Aquinas reminds us that it is *pernicious* lies that violate the law of God and place one under the penalty of mortal sin.[77] Such lies of course can be uttered at any time and in any place, and the harm they invoke can be either spiritual or temporal. But in any event, they are to be distinguished from beneficent lies or jocose lies. Pernicious lies have more in common with other malicious speech acts (i.e., those that do not necessarily involve falsehoods) than they do with venial lies. Thus, pernicious lies, combined with other kinds of harmful words, constitute a special category of sinful speech. What are these sins of speech? Aquinas finds several noteworthy examples in St. Paul's litany of sins in Romans 1:29–31. Some involve falsehood; some do not. They include contention, deceit, spite, gossip, slander, and insult. "And lest these sins be disregarded as trivial due to the fact that they are committed by words alone," Aquinas explains, "[St. Paul] adds that those who commit these deeds are 'hateful to God,' since they primarily attack what God loves in human beings, which is mutual love."[78] As theologian John Webster writes, "Words are signs, and when they function well they signify not only that to which they refer and to which they direct the hearer, but also the speaker's inner life or intention from which they flow. [...] Evil speech expresses and serves the realisation of an evil intention."[79] Even though these various sins of speech differ in their precise aim, as Aquinas explains, they "say something evil about one's neighbor."[80]

The *Summa* takes a more systematic approach to the extrajudicial sins of speech. Questions 72–76 of the *secunda secundae* catalog these

---

[77] Thomas Aquinas, *Sancti Thomae de Aquino in psalmos Davidis expositio*, in *S. Thomae Aquinatis opera omnia ut sunt in indice thomistico*, ed. Roberto Busa, SJ (Stuttgart-Bad Cannstatt 1980), vol. 6, pp. 48–130; cited at 5:6 § 3: "Perniciosum vero semper est mortale: et de isto hic intelligitur."

[78] *In Rom.* 1:30 § 162: "Et ne putentur ista peccata esse levia, quia solo ore committuntur, subdit *Deo odibiles*. Impugnant enim id maxime quod Deus in hominibus amat, scilicet mutuum amorem."

[79] John Webster, "Sins of Speech," *Studies in Christian Ethics* 28:1 (2015), 35–48; cited at 40–41.

[80] *In Rom.* 1:30 § 162 "Sic ergo haec tria vitia in materia conveniunt, quia omnes mala dicunt de proximo. Differunt autem in fine, nam susurro intendit discordiam, detractor infamiam, contumeliosus iniuriam."

"verbal injuries" (*iniuriae verborum*), and Aquinas offers a justification for classifying them as such:

> Words, according to their essence, do not cause injury, unless we mean a person hurts someone's ears by speaking too loudly. But insofar as words are signs that convey things for others to understand, they can cause harm in many ways. For example, harm is done to a person when something is said that is detrimental to his honor, or against the respect that others owe to him. Thus, it is worse to insult someone in the presence of others, but a person may still be guilty of insulting even if it is done privately, insofar as he acts against the respect due to the recipient.[81]

In these Questions, Aquinas reveals the subtlety of the mortal–venial distinction along with the fine layers of moral analysis one must deploy in order to determine culpability. Each of the speech acts listed is mortally sinful *ex genere* (with the exception of *derisione*, or mockery), yet they may only amount to venial sin depending on the circumstances or intention of the speaker. Hurling an insult (*contumelia*) at someone, for example, when done with the intention of dishonoring that person, is a mortal sin no less than theft or robbery (II-II.72.2).[82] Yet, if the intention is simply to correct someone (perhaps even harshly), this only counts as an "insult" accidentally and materially, and thus may only be a venial sin, or perhaps not a sin at all. Then again, someone might not intend to attack another person's honor yet still commit a mortal sin, since he should have thought through the harmful effect of his actions.[83] "Just as if someone were to cause serious injury while incautiously striking another person in fun," Aquinas explains, "he would not be without blame."[84] Aquinas is

---

[81] *ST* II-II.72.1 ad 1: "Ad primum ergo dicendum quod verba secundum suam essentiam, idest inquantum sunt quidam soni audibiles, nullum nocumentum alteri inferunt, nisi forte gravando auditum, puta cum aliquis nimis alte loquitur. Inquantum vero sunt signa repraesentantia aliquid in notitiam aliorum, sic possunt multa damna inferre. Inter quae unum est quod homo damnificatur quantum ad detrimentum honoris sui vel reverentiae sibi ab aliis exhibendae. Et ideo maior est contumelia si aliquis alicui defectum suum dicat coram multis. Et tamen si sibi soli dicat, potest esse contumelia, inquantum ipse qui loquitur contra audientis reverentiam agit."

[82] Aquinas in fact goes as far as to claim that insult and slander are worse than theft *ex genere*, because the former attack a person's spiritual goods, whereas the latter attack physical goods (II-II.73.3 cor. and ad 2).

[83] On slips of the tongue, bursting into speech, and other nondeliberate speech acts, see E. Jennifer Ashworth, "Aquinas on Significant Utterance: Interjection, Blasphemy, Prayer," in *Aquinas's Moral Theory: Essays in Honor of Norman Kretzman*, ed. Scott MacDonald and Eleonore Stump (Ithaca, NY 2008), 207–234 (esp. 229–231).

[84] *ST* II-II.72.2: "Sicut etiam si aliquis, incaute alium ex ludo percutiens, graviter laedat, culpa non caret."

not interested in casuistry or articulating an exhaustive list of all possible forms of insult. Rather, to borrow a phrase from Jean-Pierre Torrell, his approach to moral questions in the Summa can be described as "speculatively practical."[85] In other words, he provides us with the vocabulary necessary to categorize our moral actions, including our speech acts, while still allowing everyday experience to inform the nuances and subtleties of these moral categories.

As Aquinas is well aware, moral injury through speech can take on a multitude of forms. Slander (*detractio*), like insult, is a verbal attack, but it is performed in secret rather than in the open (II-II.73.1). The recipient is unaware (at least initially) that she is being spoken of by her peers. Moreover, slander has a specific end, or purpose, that is distinct from insult, namely, that it injures a person's reputation (*famae*) rather than her honor (Ibid.). The sin of slander is so grave that it is a sin even to listen to slander without rebuking it (II-II.73.4). Similarly, gossip (*susurratione*) involves tale-bearing behind a person's back, but it serves a different, and perhaps more sinister, end: to sow discord among friends (II-II.74.1). Citing Aristotle, Aquinas explains that a friend is better than honor, and to be loved is better than to be honored; thus, gossip, with its destruction of friendship, is the greater sin (II-II.74.2).[86] Mockery (*derisione*) is also a sin, but its end is distinct from the others insofar as it is not necessarily aimed at the spiritual goods of the recipient. The mocker does intend to shame the recipient,[87] but since this is usually done merely for amusement rather than out of contempt, mockery is not a mortal sin *ex genere* (II-II.75.2). A person who mocks out of contempt, however, is guilty of mortal sin, and in this case, the sin is even worse than a generic insult (II-II.75.2 ad 4). Finally, Aquinas considers the act of cursing

---

[85] Jean-Pierre Torrell, *Aquinas's* Summa, 31.

[86] For a qualified defense of gossip, see Linda Radzik, "Gossip and Social Punishment," *Res Philosophica* 93:1 (2016): 185–204. The sort of gossip Radzik wishes to defend can be described as "private, informal, somewhat idle" (190) and non-vengeful. She argues that such gossip can play an important social function. Some of the examples she provides might be defensible on Thomistic grounds; others would be classified as merely venial sins. Radzik's essay is helpful insofar as it helps to distinguish and clarify the point that the *susurratione* Aquinas has in mind is inherently malicious. For a Thomistic defense of gossip and an analysis of the set of conditions under which gossip might be both permissible and obligatory, see Matthew Lee Anderson, "(When) Is there a Christian Responsibility to Gossip?" *Journal of the Society of Christian Ethics* (forthcoming).

[87] *ST* II-II.75.1: "Sicut autem aliquis conviciando intendit conviciati honorem deprimere, et detrahendo diminuere famam, et susurrando tollere amicitiam; ita etiam irridendo aliquis intendit quod ille qui irridetur erubescat."

(*maledictione*). The act of cursing is a complex speech act, and while it is mortally sinful *ex genere* (II-II.76.3), this designation only applies when a person commands or desires another's evil, *as evil* (II-II.76.1). It is possible to command or desire another's evil under the aspect of good, however, as when a judge condemns a person to a just punishment, or when the Church pronounces an anathema. In such cases, we only call this "cursing" accidentally, since the intention of the speaker is directed to good rather than evil (Ibid.).

These extrajudicial sins of speech (II-II.72–76), when taken together with those uttered in a judicial context (II-II.67–71), comprise the *iniuriae verborum* that Aquinas classifies as mortal sins. These are the speech acts that most clearly and obviously violate the norms of justice and the requirements of the eighth commandment. Importantly, not all these sins of speech are concerned with formal falsehood. While many of the judicial speech acts (e.g., unjust accusation) are concerned with the truthfulness of the speaker, the primary concern lies with the harm done to the recipient. Moreover, the extrajudicial sins of speech have little or nothing to do with falsehood. One can insult, gossip, mock, or curse without telling a lie. Thus, in order to address the problem of lying *per se*, Aquinas must construct a new set of questions. These questions will be the focus of Chapter 4.

4

Aquinas on the Virtue of *Veracitas*

As we saw in Chapter 3, Aquinas's strategy to bring Aristotle into the scholastic conversation on lying is an innovation. We find this even in his early commentary on Lombard's *Sentences*, and especially in his commentary on Aristotle's *Nicomachean Ethics*. The import of Aristotle's views on truthfulness, and its contribution to the moral analysis of lying, would not have been immediately obvious to many medieval readers. For one, Aristotle does not display great concern about lying as a moral problem; rather, he praises the truthful man who presents himself accurately and honestly to his peers and within his community. But, as readers of Aquinas have long recognized, his debt to Aristotle often runs deeper than it appears on the surface. To discern the Aristotelian shape of Aquinas's mature thoughts on truthfulness and lying, we must consider what Aquinas has to say about the way human beings use words and the way in which words can be said to be truthful. In the course of my exposition, I also propose a definition of lying that will serve as a reference point for the remainder of the book, namely: A lie is told when there is a lack of correspondence between *what one believes to be the case* and *that which one intends to assert*.

THE NATURE OF TRUTH

In his commentary on Aristotle's *Peri hermeneias*, Aquinas articulates three modes in which words function: (1) intellectual concepts, (2) vocal utterances, and (3) written texts.[1] Aristotle actually says that

---

[1] Thomas Aquinas, *Sententia super Peri hermeneias* I, lt. 2 § 4 (Turin 1955): "Uno quidem modo, in conceptione intellectus; alio modo, in prolatione vocis; tertio modo, in conscriptione litterarum" ("In one mode, by intellectual concept; in another mode, by vocal utterance; in a third mode, by written letters").

words are signs of the "passions of the soul" (ψυχῇ παθημάτων), but, as Aquinas explains:

> He is speaking here of vocal sounds that gain their significance through human institution. "Passions of the soul" must therefore be understood as concepts in the intellect. Names, verbs, and expressions signify these concepts in the intellect immediately, according to the teaching of Aristotle. They cannot signify things in themselves immediately (as is made clear by their mode of signification), just as the term "human" signifies human nature in the abstract, apart from singulars. Thus it is impossible that it should signify immediately a singular human.[2]

This is not the only division of *verbum* ("word") that Aquinas draws upon in his writings, however. In the *Sentences* commentary, he articulates three proper senses of *verbum*: (1) the word of the heart (*verbum cordis*), (2) the interior word (*verbum interius*), and (3) the vocal word (*verbum vocis*).[3] As Daniel De Haan carefully demonstrates, each *verbum* is proper to a different cogitative faculty: The word of the heart is proper to the intellect; the interior word is proper to the imagination; the vocal word is proper to the voice (or vision, in the case of the written word).[4] It is important to note that, "Concerning the hierarchy of words, the 'word of the heart' is the primary instance of *verbum*, which all other senses of *verbum* signify. It is this sense of *verbum* that is intrinsically meaningful in its intentional content and is therefore necessarily required as the principle by which all other *verbum* are able to carry any semantic value."[5] It is this word of the heart that is the exclusive domain of the intellect; all other senses of *verbum* are somehow tied to matter, through signification. Elsewhere, Aquinas explains that the concept, *ratio*, or intention formed by the intellect belongs to this *verbum cordis* (SCG I.53). Lest we are tempted to dismiss this threefold division as an early experiment in the *Sentences* commentary, we find that he repeats a nearly identical division

---

[2] *In PH* I, lt. 2 § 5: "Sed nunc sermo est de vocibus significativis ex institutione humana; et ideo oportet passiones animae hic intelligere intellectus conceptiones, quas nomina et verba et orationes significant immediate, secundum sententiam Aristotelis. Non enim potest esse quod significent immediate ipsas res, ut ex ipso modo significandi apparet: significat enim hoc nomen homo naturam humanam in abstractione a singularibus. Unde non potest esse quod significet immediate hominem singularem."

[3] *In Sent.* I, Dist. 27, q. 2, a. 1.

[4] Daniel D. De Haan, "Linguistic Apprehension as Incidental Sensation in Thomas Aquinas," *Proceedings of the American Catholic Philosophical Association* 84 (2011): 179–196; cited at 183–184. I have lightly adapted the enumeration of these senses from De Haan's version in order to simplify and better capture the overlap between the *In Sent.* and *In PH* divisions.

[5] Ibid., 184.

in *ST* I.34.1. In both texts, he cites John Damascene's *De Fide Orthodoxa* I.17 as his source. It should be noted that this division is perfectly compatible with the threefold division in the *Peri hermeneias* commentary, but it also adds a crucial distinction to Aquinas's theory of signification.

The notion of the *verbum cordis* illuminates some of the otherwise puzzling aspects of Aquinas's intellectualist approach to signification. For Aquinas, a word – a vocal utterance, a written term – can *signify* a concept or a thing, but it does not *mean* either of them.[6] Terms can signify concepts in an immediate sense, but they can only signify external objects in a mediate sense (*In PH* I, lt. 2 § 5). But the important point is that words *signify*, and what they ultimately signify is the *verbum cordis* – the word of the heart, which is the concept, *ratio*, or intention that resides in the speaker's intellect. This is true whether the *verbum* that is doing the signifying is spoken, written, or even articulated privately in one's own mind.[7] The significance of this framework is magnified, as Jennifer Ashworth explains, by contrasting Aquinas's position with another popular theory of signification in the Middle Ages. Drawing upon a passage of *Peri hermeneias*, in which Aristotle explains that to signify is to generate or establish an understanding, Peter of Spain declares, "A significant utterance is one that represents something to the hearer, for instance, 'man,' or the groan of an invalid."[8] This theory shifts the mode of signification from the speaker to the hearer, and it even opens the possibility of irrational or animal noises counting as signifying utterances. In other words, even if the speaker does not intend to signify, the utterance is significant. Since Aquinas interprets Aristotle's claim that words are signs of passions of the soul to mean "signs of concepts," he maintains that the speaker's intellectual capacity and intentions are

---

[6] For a helpful guide to Aquinas's theory of signification (and a defense of the claim that Aristotle intends a direct relationship between words and things, as Aquinas reads him), see Chapter 1, "Aristotle's Semantic Triangle in St. Thomas," in John O'Callaghan's *Thomistic Realism and the Linguistic Turn: Toward a More Perfect Form of Existence* (Notre Dame, IN 2003), 15–39. See also E. J. Ashworth, "Signification and Modes of Signifying in the Thirteenth-Century Logic: A Preface to Aquinas on Analogy," *Medieval Philosophy and Theology* 1 (1991): 39–67.

[7] Of course, one of the problems with this approach is that it suggests, not a *dyad* between "word" and "thing," but rather a *triad* of "word"-"concept"-"thing." Or so it seems. For a convincing refutation of this "third thing thesis," see John O'Callaghan, *Thomist Realism and the Linguistic Turn*, 159–198. As O'Callaghan explains, "'Concept' is a nominalized form of talking about our act of conceiving, not a way of referring to an additional class or category of objects or things in addition to our acts" (169).

[8] Peter of Spain, *Tractatus, Called afterwards Summule logicales*, ed. L. M. de Rijk (Assen 1972), pp. 1–2. Cited in Ashworth, "Aquinas on Significant Utterance," 209.

necessary components of signification. Since words are signs of concepts that reside in the intellect, the speaker *generates* (or at least attempts to generate) an understanding in the mind of the hearer.[9]

What then does it mean for an utterance to be true? First, we must understand the meaning of *truth* as Aquinas uses the term. There are many texts to which we could turn to find a definition of truth, each yielding slightly different results depending on the context, but in the *prima pars* Aquinas states, "[Truth] must be defined as the conformity between the intellect (*intellectus*) and thing (*rei*). To know this conformity is to know the truth."[10] While truth describes the conformity between the thing itself and the intellect's apprehension of the thing, it is more correct to say that truth resides in the intellect.[11] That is to say, truth does not reside in the thing itself, at least not properly speaking. This may strike us rather obvious (or, if you are a contemporary epistemologist, a truism), but Aquinas finds himself having to adjudicate between two inherited traditions on the nature of truth. The first tradition, neoplatonic in origin and evident in the writings of Augustine, emphasizes the truth of being. We find this tradition voiced in the first objection of *ST* I.16.1, which contends that, according to Augustine, if truth were dependent upon the knower, then nothing could be true unless someone could know it. This may be a mere a tautology, but it is problematic on Augustinian terms, since it implies that the things God created are not necessarily true. Aquinas wants to acknowledge this tradition and grant its basic intuitions, but he is also concerned to incorporate the Aristotelian insight that things are the *cause* of truth in our intellects, just as we say that medicine is the cause of health in a person, but we do not say, properly speaking, that health resides in the medicine (*ST* I.16.1 ad 1). In other words, it is not as if truth is transferred from the thing to the intellect, but rather that it causes truth in the intellect through the intellect's conformity to it.[12]

---

[9] To foreshadow a point I argue in Chapter 5, this is one reason why equivocation does not escape the category of lying.

[10] *ST* I.16.2: "Et propter hoc per conformitatem intellectus et rei veritas definitur. Unde conformitatem istam cognoscere, est cognoscere veritatem."

[11] For those concerned about the possibility of knowing a "thing in itself" and the naïve realism of this approach, I commend, in addition to O'Callaghan's monograph cited above, John Deely's *Intentionality and Semiotics: A Story of Mutual Fecundation* (Scranton, PA 2007). See also John Deely, *Realism for the 21st Century: A John Deely Reader*, ed. Paul Cobley (Scranton, PA 2009).

[12] For more on the Aquinas's development of the notion of truth and its various senses, see John F. Wippel, "Truth in Thomas Aquinas," *The Review of Metaphysics* 43:2 (1989): 295–326 and "Truth in Thomas Aquinas, Part II" *The Review of Metaphysics* 43:3 (1990): 543–567.

Despite Aquinas's insistence that truth is understood as conformity between the intellect and thing, he is sensitive to the many ways in which we might (correctly) use this term. He is therefore a pluralist when it comes to defining truth, and we see this displayed throughout Question 16 of the *prima pars*. He explains that there are three ways in which we can understand the notion of truth. The first and most proper sense ascribes truth to the intellect, insofar as its grasp of a thing corresponds to the thing itself. In a secondary sense, truth can be said to reside in things, but only analogically, since they are able to produce truth in the intellect (*ST* I.16.1). There is another sense in which we might say that things are true, by which we mean that each thing that exists is a sign of God's intellect: "Natural things are said to be true insofar as they exemplify the likeness of the species that exist in the divine mind. A stone is called true, for example, when it possesses the nature proper to a stone, according to the preconception in the divine intellect."[13] And this leads us to a third sense in which we can understand truth, namely that God is truth. Indeed, God is truth in the fullest sense of the word, since "his being is not only conformed to his intellect, but it is the very act of his intellect."[14] Thus, if we were to ask the question of whether there is one truth according to which all things are true, we must make a distinction: "If we speak of the truth as it exists in the intellect, according to its proper *ratio*, then there are many truths in many created intellects." However, "If we speak of truth as it is in things, then all things are true by one primary truth, to which each is assimilated according to its own entity."[15] Does this mean that God is necessary to explain how our words and concepts can conform to things in reality? No, at least not in an empirical sense. This is not a "god of the gaps" theory. Thus, John Milbank and Catherine Pickstock oversell Aquinas's claims when they write, "Aquinas's fundamental theory of truth is as theological as it is philosophical, and is only a correspondence

---

[13] *ST* I.16.1: "Et similiter res naturales dicuntur esse verae, secundum quod assequuntur similitudinem specierum quae sunt in mente divina, dicitur enim verus lapis, qui assequitur propriam lapidis naturam, secundum praeconceptionem intellectus divini."

[14] *ST* I.16.5: "Nam esse suum non solum est conforme suo intellectui, sed etiam est ipsum suum intelligere." It should be noted that Question 16 on truth in the *prima pars* is situated amid a series of questions, not on the nature of language or knowledge, but on the nature of God. For more on God's being as the act of his intellect, see *ST* I.14.4.

[15] *ST* I.16.6: "Si ergo loquamur de veritate prout existit in intellectu, secundum propriam rationem, sic in multis intellectibus creatis sunt multae veritates. [...] Si vero loquamur de veritate secundum quod est in rebus, sic omnes sunt verae una prima veritate, cui unumquodque assimilatur secundum suam entitatem." See also *ST* I.21.2 on the claim that the justice of God is truth.

theory in a sense which depends entirely upon the metaphysical notion of participation in the divine Being."[16] Aquinas believes that God created our intellects, but he also believes that our intellects are capable of their own operations without appealing to a metaphysic of participation. His understanding of truth may be classified as a correspondence theory, but it is neither a purely theological model nor a contemporary analytic construction.[17]

THE VIRTUE OF TRUTHFULNESS

Thus far, our concern for the correspondence between word and thing has been in the domain of material truth and falsity. Falsity, like truth, resides in the intellect, and it occurs when there is a lack of correspondence between thing and word (*ST* I.17.3). But falsity is not merely a *lack* of truth, or privation – it is the *contrary* of truth (*ST* I.17.4). If I am simply unable to solve a difficult math problem, my problem is not falsity but ignorance. If, however, I were to utter the statement, "17+18=34" as if it were fact, then my statement would exhibit (material) falsity. If I had uttered this statement *knowing* that the equation was incorrect – say, to play a joke on someone by making him question his mathematical abilities – then my statement would also exhibit *formal* falsehood, which denotes a lack of correspondence between the words I use and the contents of my intellect. Thus, material falsehood occurs when words or concepts do not conform to things in themselves; formal falsehood occurs when words do not correspond to the concepts or thoughts in one's intellect – the *verbum cordis*. Formal falsehood is not limited to statements of fact, either. If I make a promise that I will pay you back tomorrow, yet I have no intention of actually doing so, there is a formal falsehood in my utterance. I do not mean what I say. This is the *contra mentem* principle we find recurring throughout the scholastic debates: *to lie is to speak against one's mind*.

In Aquinas's earlier writings, this notion of formal truth was subsumed under the broader discussion of truth as such. For example, in

---

[16] John Milbank and Catherine Pickstock, *Truth in Aquinas* (New York 2001), 3.
[17] Peter Geach offers a succinct defense of Aquinas's theory of truth, arguing that it is immune to the objections levied against modern correspondence theories, in *Truth and Hope* (Notre Dame, IN 2001), 67–78. For a more recent and more sophisticated interpretation and defense of Aquinas's correspondence theory, see Bruce D. Marshall, "'We Shall Bear the Image of the Man of Heaven': Theology and the Concept of Truth," in *Rethinking Metaphysics*, ed. L. Gregory Jones and Stephen E. Fowl (Oxford 1995), 93–117, and *Trinity and Truth* (New York 2000), 108–140 and 242–281.

De veritate, he articulates something very similar to the three senses of truth outlined above (truth in the intellect, truth in things, God as truth), yet he adds a fourth, namely, that "true or false may be predicated of a person insofar as he chooses to express truth, or insofar as he gives a true or false impression of himself (or others) by what he says or does. This is because truth can be predicated of words in the same way that it can be predicated of the things in the intellect that they convey."[18] By the time he writes the *Summa*, however, this understanding of truth has been set aside, to be discussed later under the auspices of moral virtue. In *ST* I.16.1, Aquinas explains, "Everything is said to be true absolutely insofar as it relates to the intellect on which it depends. [...] And speech [*oratio*] is considered true insofar as it offers signs of truth in the intellect,"[19] but this is an *application* of truth, not its essence. Truthfulness of expression concerns a very different kind of truth from what he has been describing, and thus he passes over it when discussing the nature of truth in the *prima pars*.[20] His purpose here is to clarify the distinction between *truth* and *truthfulness*.

Although it is important to distinguish truth and truthfulness, they are nevertheless intimately related. In the first place, they both describe a kind of conformity between the words we use and the things they signify. Truth describes the conformity between (1) a concept in our intellect or words used to express the concept and (2) the reality to which the concept corresponds. Truthfulness describes the conformity between (1) the words we use and (2) the content of our intellect. Thus, a materially true utterance is one that corresponds in an *outward* direction, from our words to reality;

---

[18] *De veritate* I.3: "Patet ergo ex dictis quod verum per prius dicitur de compositione vel divisione intellectus; secundo dicitur de definitionibus rerum, secundum quod in eis implicatur compositio vera vel falsa; tertio de rebus secundum quod adaequantur intellectui divino, vel aptae natae sunt adaequari intellectui humano; quarto dicitur de homine, *propter hoc quod electivus est verorum vel facit existimationem de se vel de aliis veram vel falsam per ea quae dicit vel facit*. Voces autem eodem modo recipiunt veritatis praedicationem, sicut intellectus quos significant." Emphasis added. See also *ST* I.16.4 ad 3.

[19] *ST* I.16.1: "Unde unaquaeque res dicitur vera absolute, secundum ordinem ad intellectum a quo dependet. [...] et dicitur oratio vera, inquantum est signum intellectus veri."

[20] See also the question on God's justice, which is truth, where Aquinas explains that *truthfulness in expression*, as Aristotle describes it, is a *virtue* in which a person shows herself, in word or deed, to be who she really is. This is to be distinguished from the truth of justice, which consists in a conformity between an effect and its cause or rule: "Ad secundum dicendum quod veritas illa de qua loquitur Philosophus ibi, est quaedam virtus per quam aliquis demonstrat se talem in dictis vel factis, qualis est. Et sic consistit in conformitate signi ad significatum, non autem in conformitate effectus ad causam et regulam, sicut de veritate iustitiae dictum est" (*ST* I.21.2 ad 2). See also *ST* II-II.109.3 ad 3.

a formally true utterance is one that corresponds in an *inward* direction, from our words to our mind. There is a second and very important way in which truth and truthfulness are related. Aquinas explains this relationship when he introduces the virtue of truthfulness in Question 109 of the *secunda secundae*, namely, that truth is the *end* of the virtue of truthfulness (*ST* II-II.109.1). When truth is spoken, there is equality between the sign (word) and the thing signified. Generically, it is good to speak the truth: "To state that which concerns oneself is good generically, insofar as it is a true statement,"[21] and "this truth (*veritas*) or truthfulness (*veracitas*) must be a virtue, because to say what is true is a good act."[22] Since it is good to speak the truth, there must be a virtue that facilitates our truthful speaking. Yet, as Aquinas explains, speaking the truth is only a necessary, not sufficient, condition for the virtue of truthfulness.

The moral virtues, according to Aquinas, are concerned with the operation of our external members insofar as they are commanded by the will. Since truth involves the use of words – uttered by our tongues, written by our hands, or signified in some other way – that express our thoughts and intentions, it, too, must be the subject of a moral virtue (*ST* II-II.109.1 ad 1). As with all the moral virtues, the virtue of truthfulness is context dependent. That is, whether an act of speaking the truth is an act of virtue will depend on a number of factors. Aquinas writes,

> [To state the truth] is not sufficient for an act of virtue, since it is necessary that the act should also be clothed with the due circumstances. Apart from these due circumstances, the act will be sinful. Thus, it is sinful to praise oneself without due cause, even if the praise is true, and it is also sinful to announce one's sin by praising oneself for it or by proclaiming it pointlessly.[23]

The virtue of truthfulness not only discerns due circumstances but also the appropriate mean. Aquinas describes two ways in which it is a mean between excess and deficiency: (1) on the part of the object and (2) on the part of the act. Regarding the object, his analysis closely follows Aristotle.

---

[21] *ST* II-II.109.1 ad 2: "Ad secundum dicendum quod confiteri id quod est circa seipsum, inquantum est confessio veri, est bonum ex genere."

[22] *ST* II-II.109.1: "Et talis veritas, sive veracitas, necesse est quod sit virtus, quia hoc ipsum quod est dicere verum est bonus actus; virtus autem est quae bonum facit habentem, et opus eius bonum reddit."

[23] *ST* II-II.109.2: "Sed hoc non sufficit ad hoc quod sit actus virtutis, sed ad hoc requiritur quod ulterius debitis circumstantiis vestiatur, quae si non observentur, erit actus vitiosus. Et secundum hoc, vitiosum est quod aliquis, sine debita causa, laudet seipsum etiam de vero. Vitiosum etiam est quod aliquis peccatum suum publicet, quasi se de hoc laudando, vel qualitercumque inutiliter manifestando."

Truth denotes a kind of equality, and equality is a mean between more and less. When a person speaks truly about herself, she observes the mean between a person who says more than the truth about herself and a person who says less about herself (*ST* II-II.109.1 ad 3). Regarding the act, the observance of the mean is to tell the truth *when* one ought and *as* one ought, whereas excess is to speak out of turn or to hide one's faults when they ought to be revealed (Ibid.). These distinctions serve to underscore Aquinas's claim that truthfulness is a distinct virtue, worthy of its own classification.

In order to demonstrate that truthfulness is a special virtue, he must distinguish it not only from virtue in the generic sense but also from an overly broad conception of truthfulness. In our own day and in Aquinas's, the multivalence of terms like *truth* and *truthful* lend themselves to a wide variety of applications. Many theologians and Christian ethicists have emphasized the need to "live the truth," which is usually meant to evoke ideals of integrity and sincerity. This is a frequent motif in the writings of Stanley Hauerwas, for example, whose book *Sanctify Them in Truth* argues that Christianity is not about possessing "the truth" but rather learning to live as a faithful community that embodies a (true) narrative.[24] In a similar vein, John Henry Newman, in his sermon "Unreal Words," declares, "That a thing is true, is no reason that it should be said, but that it should be done; that it should be acted upon; that it should be made our own inwardly."[25] Aquinas would gladly affirm the importance of living truthfully, but he would also want to make an important distinction. This more generic sense of truthfulness he calls the "truth of life," which refers to a life that attains its rule and measure. For human beings, this rule and measure is the divine law (*ST* II-II.109.2 ad 3; also II-II.109.3 ad 3). But this "truth" is common to all the virtues; it is not unique to the virtue of *veracitas*. The specific difference of *veracitas* is the feature of simplicity (*simplicitas*) in one's speech, as opposed to the duplicity by which a person "pretends one thing yet intends another" (*ST* II-II.109.2 ad 4).

---

[24] Stanley Hauerwas, *Sanctify Them in Truth: Holiness Exemplified* (Nashville, TN 1999). I should note that Hauerwas does not mean to exclude the more specific notion of truthful speech from his description of truthful living. Elsewhere, for example, he writes, "Regular people are meant to exemplify truthful living and truthful speech. What does it mean for us to be able to sustain people capable of truthful speech in a world where most people don't even know what truthful speech is?" in "Christianity: It's Not a Religion: It's an Adventure," *The Hauerwas Reader*, ed. John Berkman (Durham, NC 2001), 531.

[25] John Henry Newman, "Unreal Words," in *Parochial and Plain Sermons*, Vol. V (San Francisco, CA 1997), 987.

If truthfulness is a specific moral virtue, then where does it fall within the taxonomy of moral virtues? As we saw in the previous chapter, Aquinas annexes *veracitas* to the virtue of justice. I have already articulated the various sins of speech that are directly opposed to justice. But what does it mean to oppose the virtue of truthfulness? Does lying bear any relationship to justice? Aquinas is aware that he must address such questions. While lying *per se* is not directly opposed to justice, it nevertheless violates a debt that is owed to another person. The nature of this debt, however, is not legal, but moral, insofar as, "one person owes another the manifestation of truth" (*ST* II-II.109.3). Besides having the *ratio* of debt, the virtue of truthfulness resembles the virtue of justice in two specific ways. First, it is directed toward another. This may strike us as rather obvious, but it is important for distinguishing from the self-regarding virtues, such as prudence, temperance, and fortitude. Second, *veracitas* sets up a kind of equality between things, "as it makes equal a person's signs and the things concerning himself."[26] Moreover, the manifestation of the truth is an act of the will, which is where the virtue of justice resides (*ST* II-II.109.3 ad 2). Thus, while truthfulness is to be distinguished from justice proper, it nevertheless bears a close family resemblance, which is why it is annexed as a secondary virtue.

Why do we owe each other the truth? Aquinas does not think that our obligation to speak the truth is unqualified or universal. We are not required to reveal our true thoughts whenever we are asked or to whomever asks us. We are permitted to hide the truth when it is prudent to do so.[27] But when we do choose to speak (or to write, or to signify in some way), we owe it to our interlocutors – no matter who they may be – to communicate truthfully. This claim is grounded in the observation that human beings are social animals:

Since humans are social animals, naturally one human owes another that without which human society could not be preserved. It would be impossible for humans to live together, unless they believed one another as declaring the truth. Thus, the virtue of truth regards the *ratio* of due, in a certain way.[28]

---

[26] *ST* II-II.109.3: "Et hoc etiam facit virtus veritatis, adaequat enim signa rebus existentibus circa ipsum."

[27] *ST* II-II.110.3 ad 4: "Licet tamen veritatem occultare prudenter sub aliqua dissimulatione, ut Augustinus dicit, contra mendacium." ("Yet, it is permissible to hide the truth prudently by concealing it somehow, as Augustine says in *Contra mendacium*.")

[28] *ST* II-II.109.3 ad 1: "Ad primum ergo dicendum quod quia homo est animal sociale, naturaliter unus homo debet alteri id sine quo societas humana conservari non posset. Non autem possent homines ad invicem convivere nisi sibi invicem crederent, tanquam sibi invicem veritatem manifestantibus. Et ideo virtus veritatis aliquo modo attendit rationem debiti."

Interestingly, Aquinas does not cite any authorities in support of this argument. He likely has Aristotle's *Politics* I in mind, in which the Philosopher explains that it belongs to human nature to live in communities, like other creatures such as bees and ants. But while Aristotle has much to say about the social nature of human beings, as well as the importance of language for our existence as rational beings, he seldom considers these ideas in conjunction. It is just as likely that Aquinas has Augustine in mind, who frequently reflects upon the social aspects of language. In *De civitatis Dei*, for example, Augustine writes,

[T]he diversity of languages estranges people from each other. If two people meet, neither knowing the other's language, and are compelled by some necessity to stay together rather than moving on, it is easier for dumb animals, even if of different species, to associate together than it is for these people, even though they are both human beings. For, when people cannot communicate their thoughts to each other, because of nothing more than the diversity of their languages, their likeness of nature is of so little use in bringing them together that a man would rather be with his dog than with a foreigner.[29]

The emphasis here is on the fact that language is constitutive of human nature. When communication breaks down at such a fundamental level, we feel less than human. In other words, the point here is less about the accurate transfer of information from one mind to another, and more about the role that language plays in strengthening the communal bonds within human communities. Augustine and Aquinas believe that God designed human language for this purpose. Even the deist Thomas Jefferson, reflecting on this phenomenon centuries later, cannot avoid describing language in teleological terms:

He who receives an idea from me, receives instruction himself without lessening mine; as he who lights his taper at mine, receives light without darkening me. That ideas should freely spread from one another to over the globe, for the moral and mutual instruction of man, and improvement of his condition, seems to have been peculiarly and benevolently designed by nature, when she made them, like fire, expansible over all space, without lessening their destiny in any point.[30]

Aquinas's brief argument in II-II.109.3 ad 1 is drawing upon similar insights. It is not meant to be a stand-alone, airtight argument against lying. Nor is it a slippery slope, making alarmist claims that society will

---

[29] Augustine, *The City of God* XIX.7, trans. William Babcock (Hyde Park, NY 2013).
[30] Letter from Thomas Jefferson to Isaac McPherson (August 13, 1813) in *The Writings of Thomas Jefferson*, vol. 13, ed. Andrew A. Lipscomb and Albert Ellery Bergh (Washington, DC 1903), 333–334.

unravel unless everyone speaks truthfully on every occasion. Rather, he is simply making the point that *veracitas* is a virtue insofar as it is conducive to the communal bonds that make us human.[31] If truthfulness is a virtue, then every act of lying is an act opposed to that virtue.

THE NATURE AND DEFINITION OF LYING

The foregoing analysis can in many ways be read as Aquinas's extended answer to the question left unanswered by Augustine: What property do all lies share that makes them morally bad? In short, all lies are sins against the virtue of *veracitas*, and thus by definition they can never be morally good.[32] While Aquinas's analysis is indebted to Augustine, the latter never gives this exact explanation for his opposition to lying. The closest Augustine comes to offering such an explanation is found in his brief comment in the later *Enchiridion*: "Surely words were not instituted so that people could deceive each other with them, but so that each person could make his or her thoughts known to each other. Thus, using words for the purpose of deceiving, and not for what they were instituted, is a sin."[33] It is unclear whether Augustine means to clarify his earlier arguments against lying by articulating this singular feature of all lies. And while this argument depends on notions about the function of language, it does not depend on the notion of truthfulness as a virtue. Thus, Aquinas steps in to unite the disparate threads of the tradition he inherits in order to make a cohesive argument against lying as such. His unifying principle is the virtue of truthfulness.

Having established *veracitas* as a distinct virtue annexed to the virtue of justice, Aquinas then turns to the sins opposed to truthfulness (*ST* II-II.110–113). The first and most paradigmatic sin against truth, of course, is lying *simpliciter* (*ST* II-II.110). Aquinas defines the lie,

---

[31] For more on the social nature of *veracitas*, see White, "The Virtues of Man the *Animal Sociale*."

[32] According to Aquinas, an act that is evil in its genus (*malum ex genere*) can never be considered good or morally licit. See *ST* II-II.110.3: "Respondeo dicendum quod illud quod est secundum se malum ex genere, nullo modo potest esse bonum et licitum, quia ad hoc quod aliquid sit bonum, requiritur quod omnia recte concurrant; bonum enim est ex integra causa, malum autem est ex singularibus defectibus, ut Dionysius dicit, IV cap. de Div. Nom" ("That which is evil by its very genus can in no way be good or licit, because in order for it to be good, it must have rectitude in every respect. This is so because good is the result of an integrated cause, whereas evil results from a single defect, as Dinoysius says").

[33] *Enchiridion*, 22.

following Augustine, as a falsehood told in order to deceive.[34] To this classical definition, he adds a few important qualifications, some of which were, at best, only implicit within the tradition. The first concerns the matter of deception. Aquinas surprises many readers when he declares that deception is not an essential feature of the lie. Deception, he explains, does not belong to the species of lying but rather to its perfection (ST II-II, Q. 110. A. 1). What does this mean? Simply put, while people typically tell lies for the purposes of deceiving others, it is technically possible to lie without this intention. Aquinas is concerned to isolate the formal features of the lie, and for him this amounts to formal falsehood, or duplicity: "The *ratio* of a lie is taken from formal falsehood, in which a person wills to utter something false. Moreover, the term 'lie' [*mendacium*] is derived from that which is in opposition to one's mind [*contra mentem*]" (ST II-II.110.1).[35] It is important here to distinguish between two different senses of deception. While Aquinas is clear that it is not essential for the liar to intend to deceive her listener *about the state of affairs in the world*, the definition just given necessarily implies that the liar always intends to deceive her listener *about what the speaker believes to be the case*. This is what it means to speak *contra mentem*, against one's mind.

This brings us to another important qualification of the *contra mentem* principle, namely, that lies always involve deception in the second sense. If formal falsehood were enough to constitute a lie – full stop – then this would mean that many speech acts, such as storytelling, acting, and joking would count as lies. But Aquinas mercifully does not think such acts are lies (at least in most cases). He acknowledges that we often speak with a shared understanding among our listeners that what we are speaking is neither true nor believed to be true by the speaker. An actor on the stage, for example, declaring that he is King Henry V, is not understood by his audience to be a king, nor do they think that he

---

[34] ST II-II.110.1 sc: "Sed contra est quod Augustinus dicit, in libro contra mendacium, nemo dubitet mentiri eum qui falsum enuntiat causa fallendi. Quapropter enuntiationem falsi cum voluntate ad fallendum prolatam, manifestum est esse mendacium. Sed hoc opponitur veritati. Ergo mendacium veritati opponitur." ("On the contrary, Augustine says, in his book *Contra mendacium*, 'No one should doubt that a lie is a falsehood that is told with the intention of deceiving. Thus, a false statement uttered with the intention of deceiving is a manifest lie.' But this is opposed to truth. Therefore lying is opposed to truth.")

[35] "Sed tamen ratio mendacii sumitur a formali falsitate, ex hoc scilicet quod aliquis habet voluntatem falsum enuntiandi. Unde et mendacium nominatur ex eo quod contra mentem dicitur."

believes himself to be a king. Thus, the meaning of one's statements – and as a corollary, the criterion of formal falsehood – is determined in part by the shared, understood *context* in which the words are spoken.[36] There is always the possibility of miscommunication, of course, but such errors are not acts of the will and are thus not lies. Aquinas is sensitive to this fact, and he draws upon Augustine as a resource to clarify this point: "As Augustine says, 'it is not a lie to say or do something figuratively. Every utterance must be referred to the thing uttered, and when a thing is done or spoken figuratively, it utters that which it is understood to signify to its audience'" (*ST* II-II.110.3 ad 6).[37] Elsewhere, he explains,

> As Augustine says, "It is not always a lie to pretend. But when the pretense is without signification, it is a lie. When our pretense is signified, however, there is no lie but rather a representation of the truth." He mentions figures of speech as an example, in which a thing is pretended, i.e. we do not mean for it to be taken literally, but as a figure of something else we want to say.[38]

On this account, formal falsehood is a necessary but not sufficient condition for lying. It is possible for an utterance to lack correspondence between one's thoughts and one's words and yet not amount to a lie, so long as this lack of correspondence is *signified* in some way. What this also means is that the presence of an interlocutor (and how the speaker perceives the interlocutor to understand her words) is an integral component of moral analysis when it comes lying. Put more crudely: There must be another person present in order to tell a lie.[39]

---

[36] On the inherent difficulties of using language and the necessity of communal effort in order to understand one another, see Williams, *The Edge of Words*, esp. 86–94.

[37] "Nec est simile de hyperbolicis aut quibuscumque figurativis locutionibus, quae in sacra Scriptura inveniuntur, quia, sicut Augustinus dicit, in libro contra mendacium, *quidquid figurate fit aut dicitur, non est mendacium. Omnis enim enuntiatio ad id quod enuntiat referenda est, omne autem figurate aut factum aut dictum hoc enuntiat quod significat eis quibus intelligendum prolatum est.*"

[38] *ST* II-II.111.1 ad 1: "Ad primum ergo dicendum quod, sicut Augustinus dicit, in libro de quaest. Evang., non omne quod fingimus mendacium est. Sed quando id fingimus quod nihil significat, tunc est mendacium, cum autem fictio nostra refertur ad aliquam significationem, non est mendacium, sed aliqua figura veritatis. Et subiungit exemplum de figurativis locutionibus, in quibus fingitur quaedam res non ut asseratur ita esse, sed eam proponimus ut figuram alterius quod asserere volumus."

[39] Although we might wonder whether this is a moot point if God is always aware of our utterances. Perez Zagorin recalls the saying of Augustine that "it is perjury to swear falsely even on a stone, for although the stone does not hear one speaking, God does and punishes the deceit." Perez Zagorin, *Ways of Lying: Dissimulation, Persecution, and Conformity in Early Modern Europe* (Cambridge, MA 1990), 26.

In order for there to be a lie, the following conditions must be met: (1) an interlocutor must be present who is capable of understanding the speaker's words or other signification, (2) the speaker must utter a formal falsehood (a lack of correspondence between sign and thing signified), and (3) the speaker must intend for the interlocutor to believe that the speaker maintains a correspondence between sign and thing signified. Or, stated in a less loquacious formulation: The speaker must assert a formal falsehood to an interlocutor. This assessment comports with the notion of *assertion* developed by Roderick Chisholm and Thomas Feehan, who in turn are drawing upon insights from C. S. Pierce:

> What distinguishes lying as such from the other types of intended deception is the fact that, in telling the lie, the liar "gives an indication that he is expressing his own opinion." And he does this in a special way – by getting his victim to place his faith in him. The sense of "say," therefore, in which the liar may be said to "intend to say what is false" is that of "to assert."[40]

Actors do not assert. Nor does someone who begins a story with the words, "A priest, a rabbi, and an imam walk into a bar."[41] There are manifold ways in which one may signify that one is not asserting, and by doing so, one avoids lying. In fact, it is quite possible, as Augustine reminds us, to testify to the truth using figurative language.

LYING AS A SIN AGAINST TRUTHFULNESS

Having established the nature and definition of lying – and the important clarification that the act of lying is to be distinguished from other malicious speech acts – we are in a better position to consider the sinfulness of lying. Our analysis thus far has shown an exceptional willingness on Aquinas's part to insist that lying *per se* is only venially sinful and to delineate clear boundaries between lying and other sins of speech. As Dallas Denery notes, "While Thomas is no less vociferous in his assertion that every lie is a sin, his decision to discuss the nature and severity of different kinds of lies, to separate them into mortal and venial sins,

---

[40] Roderick M. Chisholm and Thomas D. Feehan, "The Intent to Deceive," *The Journal of Philosophy* 74:3 (1977): 143–159. Cited at 149.
[41] Of course, the interlocutor's ability to understand that a joke is being told depends on her familiarity with certain social and linguistic cues. It is possible that she will miss these and fail to realize that the speaker isn't telling a true story. Nevertheless, the joke-teller is not guilty of lying, since she at least attempted to signify her pretense (to use Augustine's phrase). For an illuminating and entertaining analysis of the conditional nature of jokes, see Ted Cohen, *Jokes: Philosophical Thoughts on Joking Matters* (Chicago 1999), 12–32.

suggests a lessening of that tension that so tortured Augustine."[42] This does not solve every problem, however. Aquinas must still explain why lies that are seemingly told from a good will are still sinful. Moreover, he feels compelled to justify his position in light of the received tradition on lying, a tradition which (against his own position) frequently suggests that lying *simpliciter* is mortally sinful.

Aquinas does concede that some lies are mortal sins, but only if they meet some additional conditions beyond those outlined above. Every mortal sin is opposed to charity (*ST* II-II.24.12; II-II.35.3), and there are three ways in which a lie can be opposed to charity (*ST* II-II.110.4). First, a lie can be mortally sinful by the nature of its false signification. If the lie concerns divine things, for example, it hides or corrupts the truth of God. In this case, it is not only opposed to charity but also the virtues of faith and *religio*. Similarly, if the lie concerns a certain domain of knowledge that affects a person's good (for example, one's perfection of knowledge [*scientia*] or morals), this amounts to an injury against one's neighbor, in which case it, too, is a mortal sin. Second, any lie, regardless of its formal aspects, is a mortal sin if the ultimate intention, or end, is to harm one's neighbor or to express contempt for God. Finally, a lie may be mortally sinful by accidentally causing scandal or some other injury. Thus, while it remains true that lying *simpliciter* is venially sinful, any of these conditions can elevate a discrete act of lying to the status of mortal sin.[43]

One of Aquinas's challenges – and perhaps the one of most concern in our own day – is to explain why certain kinds of lies are sinful at all. This is especially pressing in the case of the beneficent (*officiosum*) lie, told for the purpose of helping or saving someone. We must remember that, unlike our own cultural milieu, Aquinas's primary interlocutors do not look very favorably on beneficent lies. He introduces a major innovation here, but it is one that easily escapes the contemporary eye. It is found in his treatment of one of the classical biblical texts that frequently appears in medieval debates about lying: the Hebrew midwives who lied to the Egyptians to save the Hebrew children (Exodus 1:15–21). Aquinas addresses this text in two different places in *ST* II-II.110. In the first instance, he gives a seemingly straightforward interpretation of the

[42] Dallas G. Denery, *The Devil Wins: A History of Lying from the Garden of Eden to the Enlightenment* (Princeton, NJ 2015), 121.
[43] For a more thorough analysis of the way in which circumstances can specify sins, see *De malo* II.6.

Hebrew midwives' lie: "The midwives were not rewarded for their lie but for their fear of God and their benevolence, out of which they were led to tell a lie. Thus, it is written in Exodus 1, 'And because the midwives feared God, he built them houses.' But the lie that followed was not meritorious."[44] It is significant that he attributes the lie to the midwives' benevolence. He does not go so far as to say that their act of lying was *good*, but he acknowledges that their action, albeit misguided, originated in a good will. Aquinas's reasoning, only implicit in this text, is made explicit elsewhere: "Not every act proceeding from a will informed by charity is meritorious, otherwise venial sins that are occasionally performed by a person with charity would be counted as meritorious. Yet it is true that every act performed out of charity is meritorious."[45] Aquinas's insight is a subtle one, and it relies on a distinction between acts performed out of charity and acts performed by a person whose will is informed by charity (but not the act itself).[46] The Hebrew midwives exemplified the latter, but not the former.

Aquinas addresses this text again in *ST* II-II.110.4 ad 4, and here his deviation from the received tradition is more obvious. The issue at stake is Gregory the Great's interpretation of the Exodus passage about the Hebrew midwives, which asserts that the midwives' lie resulted in a downgrade of their reward. On Gregory's account, the midwives were given the opportunity to merit an eternal reward, but they squandered it by telling a lie. Instead, they only received "houses," a meager substitute for eternal blessedness (*ST* II-II.110.4 obj. 4). Aquinas offers a rather different interpretation, although he does not signal any disagreement with Gregory. In fact, he informs the reader that "we must understand the words of Gregory in this sense," namely, that the midwives began with a disposition that was worthy of eternal reward (a desire to save

---

[44] *ST* II-II.110.3 ad 2: "Ad secundum dicendum quod obstetrices non sunt remuneratae pro mendacio, sed pro timore Dei et benevolentia, ex qua processit mendacium. Unde signanter dicitur Exod. I, *et quia timuerunt obstetrices Deum, aedificavit illis domos.* Mendacium vero postea sequens non fuit meritorium." Note that virtually every modern English translation of Ex. 1:21 states that God gave the midwives "families," but the Latin text familiar to Augustine and Aquinas reads *aedificavit illis Deus domos* ("God built them houses").

[45] *De malo* II.5 ad 7: "Ad septimum dicendum, quod non omnis actus procedens a voluntate informata caritate est meritorius, si voluntas pro potentia accipiatur; alioquin venialia peccata essent meritoria, quae committunt interdum etiam caritatem habentes. Sed verum est quod omnis actus qui est ex caritate, est meritorius."

[46] For more on charity and its relation to merit, see Joseph P. Wawrykow, *God's Grace and Human Action: "Merit" in the Theology of Thomas Aquinas* (Notre Dame, IN 1995), esp. 177–233.

the Hebrew children), and they still remained worthy of that reward despite telling the lie. The lie they told did not merit anything, nor did it downgrade their reward, but it was nevertheless compatible with the reward they received. This is more of a correction than an interpretation of Gregory, and it indicates a willingness on Aquinas's part to deviate from the received tradition if he finds its resources inadequate. In the earlier *Sentences* commentary, he addresses this same passage, and he gives two possible interpretations of what Gregory means (as well as several opinions of various church doctors), but he does not state which one he prefers.[47] By the time he writes the *Summa*, however, his mind is settled, and he is confident that his interpretation is more faithful to scripture (if not to Gregory).[48]

While Aquinas's differences with Gregory the Great are readily apparent to the attentive reader, his differences with figures like Augustine are more subtle. His analysis of lying is in many ways indebted to Augustine's, but there are a number of important differences between the two. For Augustine, there is a specifically eschatological dimension in his arguments against lying. The rigor of his position is informed in large part by his belief that the loss of goods that might obtain by being truthful in a difficult situation pales in comparison to the eternal goods attainable in the next life. As Boniface Ramsey writes, "Augustine's unwillingness to accept a lie under any circumstances at all – even to protect someone from rape, death or the most loathsome uncleanness – is consistent with his belief in the absolute precedence of eternal with respect to temporal goods."[49] Aquinas does not incorporate this concept into his argument, and the omission allows him to downplay the sinfulness of venial lies. It is not merely the case that some lies are worse than others (as even Augustine is willing to admit); for Aquinas, venial lies are simply not the

---

[47] *In Sent.* III, Dist. 38, a. 4, ad 3.

[48] In an earlier text, Aquinas describes the midwives as those who have not yet achieved the "perfection" (*perfectio*) of virtue but who are active in the "progress of virtue" (*profectus virtutis*), and this is meant to explain how they could still tell a lie even when acting from mercy (*propter misericordiam*). See *Quaestiones de quolibet* VIII.6.4 ad 2, in *S. Thomae Aquinatis opera omnia ut sunt in indice thomistico*, ed. Roberto Busa, vol. 3 (Stuttgart-Bad Cannstatt 1980). He alludes to this notion of perfect virtue again in *ST* II-II.110.3 ad 1. For more on the distinction between *profectus virtutis* and *perfectio*, see *ST* I.43.6 ad 2; and *Reportatio super evangelium Matthaei* 25:16 § 2045, in *S. Thomae Aquinatis opera omnia ut sunt in indice thomistico*, ed. Roberto Busa, vol. 6 (Stuttgart-Bad Cannstatt 1980).

[49] Boniface Ramsey, "Two Traditions on Lying and Deception in the Ancient Church," *Thomist* 49 (1985): 504–533, cited at 513.

sort of action that jeopardizes one's eternal status. They belong to a different species of moral action compared to their mortal counterparts. Or, to use Thomistic terminology, venial lies and mortal lies have different *objects* of moral action.

This is not to say that Aquinas's arguments against lying are atheological or that they are not eschatologically inflected. Paul Griffiths believes that Aquinas shows himself to be "insufficiently serious as a Christian thinker" for failing to incorporate the "Augustinian Trinitarian analysis of the act of speech" in his discussion of lying.[50] While it is undeniably true that Aquinas differs in many respects from (Griffiths's interpretation of) Augustine, this is not because one thinker is theological and the other is not. To the contrary, Aquinas is quite sensitive to the spiritually harmful effects of lying and to the ways in which it can damage one's relationship with God. He writes, for example, "Since God is truth, and every lie is against the truth, whoever uses lying to display the greatness of God acts against God in that very act" (*In Iob* 13:7). Moreover, Aquinas's categorization of lying as venially sinful *ex genere* serves to underscore the eschatological nature of venial sin. The fact that venial sin exists as a moral category is itself a result of the Fall, according to Aquinas (*ST* I-II.89.3). As Lawrence Dewan writes, "[V]enial sin is part of the doctrine of human nature as fallen nature."[51] Venial sins are committed due to the disorder of the lower powers of the soul, the passions, or they are the result of disordered reasoning about ends in the exercise of practical reason. But such disorder did not exist in Adam's original state, and thus, venial sins are only a result of the Fall. In fact, Aquinas argues that it was not possible for Adam to commit a venial sin in his original state (*De malo* VII.7),[52] and for the same reason, he argues that angels are incapable of committing venial sins (*De malo* VII.9). When a person commits a mortal sin, however, she acts against (*contra*) the law by choosing a transitory good over her eternal good, which is God.[53] When a person

---

[50] Paul J. Griffiths, *Lying: An Augustinian Account of Duplicity* (Grand Rapids, MI 2004), 183.
[51] Lawrence Dewan, "St. Thomas, Lying, and Venial Sin," in *Wisdom, Law, and Virtue: Essays in Thomistic Ethics* (New York 2008), 382.
[52] See also *De malo* VII.1 *ad* 17.
[53] William Mattison offers an exceptionally insightful analysis of venial sin within the broader Thomistic vision of the moral life in "A New Look at the Last End: Noun and Verb, Determinate Yet Capable of Growth," *Journal of Moral Theology* 8:2, Special Issue (2019): 95–113. For an accessible and pastorally sensitive description of venial sin, see the sermon "Ash Wednesday" by Herbert McCabe, OP in *God Matters* (New York 2005), 243–245.

commits a venial sin, she acts outside (*praeter*) the law, but not against it.⁵⁴ Mortal sin severs the bond of charity and merits eternal punishment; venial sin is forgivable (*De malo* VII.1).

In short, Aquinas's classification of lying *simpliciter* as venially sinful is meant to accommodate the harsh realities of a fallen world. While he never condones lying – nor does he modify the original Augustinian definition, for that matter – he seeks to minimize as much as possible the sinfulness of beneficent lies. In an unfallen world, there would be no fear of someone knocking on your door and asking if you have refugees hiding in your basement. The temptation to lie would not even arise. In a fallen world, however, even those with the grace of charity will sometimes feel compelled to lie, especially in moments of duress. Those who do so are not acting *against* the law.⁵⁵ Lest any uncertainty remain, Aquinas makes clear in Questions 109 and 110 that lying *simpliciter* is neither directly opposed to justice nor directly opposed to the eighth commandment (*ST* II-II.109.3 ad 3; II-II.110.4 ad 2).⁵⁶ While he affirms, with Augustine, that lying is never without sin, his analysis is marked by a sensitivity to humanity's fallen condition.⁵⁷ Aquinas is often labeled a rigorist for his

---

⁵⁴ *De malo* VII.1 ad 1: "Unde praedicta definitio peccati perfecte quidem convenit peccato mortali, imperfecte autem et secundum quid peccato veniali; unde convenienter dicitur, quod peccatum veniale non est contra legem, sed praeter legem: quia si in aliquo recedit ab ordine legis, non tamen ipsam corrumpit, quia non corrumpit dilectionem, quae est plenitudo legis, ut dicitur Rom. XIII, 10" ("So the definition of sin referenced here ['sin is a word or deed or desire contrary to the eternal law'] is perfectly fitting in regard to mortal sin, yet imperfectly (and only in a certain sense) in regard to venial sin. Thus, it is fittingly said of venial sin that it is not contrary to the law, but outside the law; that is, it in some way departs from the order of law. This is not to say that it destroys law's order. Venial sin does not destroy love, which is the fulness of the law (as Rom. 13:10 says).") See also *ST* I-II.74.9; I-II.88.1 ad 1; II-II.105.1 ad 1.

⁵⁵ For a helpful commentary on this distinction found in *ST* I-II.74.9 and elsewhere in Aquinas's works, see Dewan, "St. Thomas, Lying, and Venial Sin," 374–381.

⁵⁶ I am grateful to an anonymous reviewer for pointing out that, on Aquinas's terms, lying *simpliciter* is unjust in a certain sense. It is opposed to justice, even if it is not opposed to the perfection of justice (our public relationships). Nonetheless, I am relying on Aquinas's own remarks that "the truth of which we are now speaking" is not concerned with public manifestations of truth in which there is a legal due (*debitum legale*), such as those in a court of law, in which case a lie is directly opposed to justice (*ST* II-II.109.3 ad 3). Lying *simpliciter* always violates a moral debt (*debitum morale*), however, and it is appropriate to characterize all lies as unjust in a qualified sense (II-II 109.3).

⁵⁷ One of Janet Smith's criticisms of Aquinas's position on lying is precisely that it does *not* adequately account for humanity's fallen condition. I disagree with Smith's assessment, for reasons I articulated in Chapter 1. See Smith, "Fig Leaves and Falsehoods," *First Things* 214 (June/July 2011), 45–49.

position on lying, but when read in light of these qualifications and distinctions, his position comes across as rather lenient.[58]

Given this leniency, we might wonder why we should be concerned at all about venial lies if they do not sever the bond of charity and are so easily forgivable. Aquinas would likely remind us that a virtuous person would never feel compelled to ask this sort of question. The person whose actions are guided by virtue always aims at the good (*ST* I-II.5.3). Furthermore, the soul informed by charity loves God above all else and avoids actions that are not conducive to this love – even if such actions are not explicitly proscribed by the law (*ST* II-II.23.7). Aquinas offers two basic answers to this question, one conceptual and one psychological. From a conceptual standpoint, he reminds us that lying is generically evil (*secundum se malum ex genere*) and can thus never be considered good (*bonum*) or lawful (*licitum*). He continues, "It is an action bearing on undue matter. Since spoken words are by nature signs of one's thoughts, it is unnatural and undue that anyone should signify with words that which is not in one's mind."[59] We should interpret the term *undue* in light of the virtue of truthfulness and not as an indicator of crude naturalism.[60] But the important point is that lying is intrinsically disordered by nature of its incompatibility with the virtue of *veracitas*.[61]

Still less should we claim that there are instances in which one *should* tell a lie. There is a disorder in the action of lying, and since a disordered action can never be a good action, we can never say that a lie *should* or *ought to* be told. It is one thing to claim that venial sins are *outside* of the law, as Aquinas does; it is another thing entirely to claim that

---

[58] The role of the mortal–venial distinction in Aquinas's analysis of lying becomes all the more important when one notices its absence in contemporary interpretations of Aquinas's thought. Joseph Boyle, for example, never even mentions, aside from a fleeting reference to jocose lies as venial sins on p. 54, this distinction in his explanation of Aquinas's position in his essay "The Absolute Prohibition of Lying and the Origins of the Casuistry of Mental Reservation: Augustinian Arguments and Thomistic Developments," *American Journal of Jurisprudence* 44:1 (1999): 43–65.

[59] *ST* II-II.110.3: "Est enim actus cadens super indebitam materiam, cum enim *voces sint signa naturaliter intellectuum*, innaturale est et indebitum quod aliquis voce significet id quod non habet in mente."

[60] The point being that we should not think about words merely as naturally occurring artifacts but rather as acts of the will. The proper object of an assertion (*manifestationis*) or a statement (*enuntiationis*) is the true or the false (*ST* II-II.110.1).

[61] *ST* II-II.110.1: "Sic ergo patet quod mendacium directe et formaliter opponitur virtuti veritatis" ("Thus it is evident that lying is directly and formally opposed to the virtue of truth").

one *ought* to commit a venial sin. Aquinas writes, "It is not permissible (*licet*) to use something that is inordinate (*illicita inordinatione*) for the purpose of preventing harm or defect caused by someone else," and "therefore it is not permissible (*licet*) to lie for the purpose of saving someone from any kind of danger."[62] For Aquinas, to claim that a person *should* commit a venial sin (even in very limited circumstances) is simply a contradiction in terms.[63]

The second answer to the question of why we should refrain from committing venial sins, from the perspective of Aquinas's moral psychology, is simply that venial sins predispose us to commit mortal sin. He writes,

> A venial sin can dispose one to a sin that is mortal on the part of the agent, as a consequence. The disposition or habit may be strengthened by acts of venial sin, and the desire of sin increases to the extent that the sinner fixes his end on that venial sin: since the end for one who has a habit is to work in accordance with that habit. As a result, he becomes disposed to a mortal sin by sinning venially on a frequent basis.[64]

When it comes to lying, however, Aquinas is not interested in providing a psychological profile of the liar. As Gérard Courtois reminds us, he is describing the lie as an *act* in Q. 110. This is a theory of lying (*mendacium*), not of the liar (*mentiens*).[65] Experience bears out just how easy it is to lie, however. As Ludwig Wittgenstein confesses, "It is often only

---

[62] *ST* II-II.110.3 ad 4: "Ad quartum dicendum quod mendacium non solum habet rationem peccati ex damno quod infert proximo, sed ex sua inordinatione, ut dictum est. Non licet autem aliqua illicita inordinatione uti ad impediendum nocumenta et defectus aliorum [...]. Et ideo non est licitum mendacium dicere ad hoc quod aliquis alium a quocumque periculo liberet." Dewan explains that *illicitus* in this context "means not 'against the law' but rather 'not a thing that should be done' in a more general way; '*licet*' is not cognate with '*lex*,' but appears closer to the '*lib-*' in '*liber*.' One is not altogether free to do what is illicit," "St. Thomas, Lying, and Venial Sin," 610, fn. 20.

[63] See, for example, *ST* II-II.43.7 ad 5: "Ad quintum dicendum quod quidam dixerunt quod peccatum veniale est committendum propter vitandum scandalum. Sed hoc implicat contraria, si enim faciendum est, iam non est malum neque peccatum; nam peccatum non potest esse eligibile."

[64] *ST* I-II.88.3: "Sed per hunc modum peccatum veniale potest disponere, per quandam consequentiam, ad peccatum quod est mortale ex parte agentis. Augmentata enim dispositione vel habitu per actus peccatorum venialium, intantum potest libido peccandi crescere, quod ille qui peccat, finem suum constituet in peccato veniali, nam unicuique habenti habitum, inquantum huiusmodi, finis est operatio secundum habitum. Et sic, multoties peccando venialiter, disponetur ad peccatum mortale." See also *ST* III.87.1 ad 1.

[65] Gérard Courtois, "Mensonge et parjure selon saint Thomas d'Aquin," *Rue Descartes* 8/9 (1993): 85–97, cited at 87.

very slightly more disagreeable to tell the truth than a lie; only about as much as is drinking bitter rather than sweet coffee; & yet even then I have a strong inclination to tell the lie."[66] Moreover, most of us have encountered habitual liars, and what we typically find is that the habitual liar has eroded her sensitivity to lying through the repeated act of telling lies. As a general principle, the more we lie, the easier it becomes. We do not need formal studies to confirm this principle, but such studies have been conducted. One set of brain imaging studies concludes that "lying involves intentional suppression of the predominant truth response," and the results showed that "frequent truth telling made lying more difficult, and that frequent lying made lying easier."[67] The relevant concern for our present purposes, however, is not merely that lying disposes one to tell *more* lies; the concern is that frequent lying disposes one to tell lies of a certain kind, namely, those that are opposed to justice and charity.

The analysis in this and the preceding section reveals that the mortal-venial distinction is crucial for understanding Aquinas's position on lying, and it is a distinction that has unfortunately been lost on many contemporary Thomists. Without this distinction, lying becomes a monolithic category, and now the most important feature of *all* lies is their intrinsic disorder. While a harmful lie may be morally worse than a beneficent lie, the feature that these lies have in common (their intrinsic disorder) becomes more important than what distinguishes them, namely, whether or not they intend harm. On this account, if there is an exceptionless moral norm against lying, then the intent of the lie is not morally relevant. Such an account can only lead to absurd conclusions, exemplified by John Skalko's comparison of a beneficent lie to murder:

If lying may be done for the sake of the common good when lives are in danger, then cannot the same rationale apply to other actions as well? Could not adultery, murder, or homosexual actions be justified in similar situations? Imagine a blackmail situation: a gang breaks into a bank and recognizes you as their old lost enemy. They insist that they will murder everyone else in the bank and leave the gun in your cold dead hands unless you kill one of the innocent bank tellers. If you can lie for the sake of the common good, then why can you not murder?[68]

---

[66] Ludwig Wittgenstein, *Culture and Value: A Selection from Posthumous Remains*, trans. Peter Winch (New York 1998), 45.
[67] Bruno Verscheure, et al., "The Ease of Lying," *Consciousness and Cognition* 20 (2011): 908–911.
[68] John Skalko, Disordered Actions: A Moral Analysis of Lying and Homosexual Activity (Neunkirchen-Seelscheid 2019), 301.

This analogy is not only morally tone deaf – it is not Thomistic, either. Skalko writes, "Aquinas never backs down on his statement that every lie is a sin. If Aquinas really had held that the officious lie is not a lie in some cases, then he would have said so."[69] But one does not have to affirm that officious lies are not sins at all in order to acknowledge that they are a fundamentally different kind of act than malicious lies. Skalko misses this important principle because he fails to acknowledge the mortal–venial distinction in Aquinas's thought on lying. Aquinas is no consequentialist, but he is at least willing to concede that the Hebrew midwives' lie was compatible with charity and did not diminish their reward. He would never say the same about a person who commits murder for the sake of the common good.[70]

OTHER VICES OPPOSED TO TRUTHFULNESS

The division between lies that are mortally sinful and those that are merely venial maps onto an older division of lies into those that are beneficent (*officiosum*), jocose *(iocosum)*, and pernicious *(perniciosum)* (*ST* II-II.110.2). This threefold division originates in antiquity, and Aquinas must account for it somehow. The problem is that, while beneficent and pernicious lies are clearly delineated, there has never been a clear consensus as to what constitutes a jocose lie. Aquinas's interpreters do not agree on the criteria for jocose lies, nor on the question of whether he considers jocose lies to be sinful. Marcia Colish, for example, interprets Aquinas as

---

[69] Ibid., 235, fn. 1.
[70] Here I must also address (all too briefly) the concerns of an anonymous reviewer who identifies a potential inconsistency in Aquinas's thought. Why does Aquinas acknowledge that in the cases of murder and theft there is a distinction to be made between the act in its natural species (killing another person, taking what another person has) and the act in its moral species (murder, theft) yet fail to make a similar distinction in the case of lying? What is special about lying that causes such asymmetry in Aquinas's thought? If we proceed from the premise that Aquinas does not make such a distinction in regard to lying, then I agree with the reviewer that any reason we might come up with to justify this asymmetry will be unsatisfying. We might wonder, then, whether the first edition of the Catechism of the Catholic Church was right to distinguish "just lying" from unjust lying (in which case, the former is not really lying at all). My response is to suggest that Aquinas does, in fact, make this distinction. The natural species we are looking for is "uttering a formal falsehood." One can utter a formal falsehood without lying – for example, one might be telling a joke or a fairytale, or playing the part of a fictional character. The moral species of lying is constituted by an additional feature, namely, *intentionally asserting* a formal falsehood. On the distinction between pretense and lying, see *ST* II-II.111.1 *ad* 1. Thus, Aquinas *does* make a distinction that is comparable to the distinction between killing and murder.

holding the position that "The jocose lie is no lie at all,"[71] even though Aquinas states plainly that it is.[72] The twentieth-century manualists, John McHugh and Charles Callan, insist that jokes clearly signaled as such should not be considered jocose lies:

> Jocose lies include all kinds of humorous and interesting narrations and descriptions meant only to afford pleasure, but given out as facts by one who does not believe them to be facts. Untruths told in such a way (e.g., with a laugh or in a playful tone, especially if the auditors have a sense of humor) that it is clear they are not meant to be taken seriously, are not jocose lies or lies of any kind.[73]

Aquinas does not appear to grant this exception, however. He explicitly acknowledges that jocose lies are *not* told with the intention to deceive, nor do they have the effect of deceiving (*ST* II-II.110.3 ad 6), yet they are still lies and thus sinful. This admittedly appears to be at odds with Aquinas's more humane qualification that figures of speech are exempt from the charge of lying (Ibid.). What, then, is a jocose lie? And why is it sinful?

First, we must consider the context in which the jocose lie appears in Aquinas's schema. In the *sed contra* of *ST* II-II.110.2, he cites a gloss on Psalm 5:7 that lists the threefold division of lies. This division is originally found in Augustine's commentary on the same text, but Augustine also provides a different, eightfold division of lies in *De mendacio*.[74] Aquinas wants to account for both of these lists (as well as Aristotle's twofold distinction between boasting and mock-modesty), and he mentions all of them in the body of the article. He complicates things, however, when he begins to articulate Augustine's eightfold division. In Augustine's original composition, the fifth kind of lie is described as a lie that is told with the aim of pleasing someone through "smooth talking."[75] But Aquinas adds his own gloss, which changes the meaning. He writes, "The fifth kind is the jocose lie, which is told with a desire to please."[76] While Augustine mentions jocose lies in his threefold division in *De mendacio*, it does not actually appear in the eightfold division of the Psalms commentary,

---

[71] Colish, "Rethinking Lying in the Twelfth Century," 170.
[72] See *ST* II-II.119.2 and 110.3 ad 6
[73] John A. McHugh and Charles J. Callan, *Moral Theology: A Complete Course Based on St. Thomas Aquinas and the Best Modern Authorities*, Vol. 2 (London 1929), § 2392 (a).
[74] See Table 2.1.
[75] *De mendacio*, 25: "Quintum, quod fit placendi cupiditate de suaviloquio."
[76] *ST* II-II.110.2: "Nam quintum est mendacium iocosum, quod fit placendi cupiditate."

as Aquinas seems to suggest. This is Aquinas's own interpretation – or perhaps more accurately, interpolation. Aquinas is likely attempting to synthesize these two lists,[77] and since the jocose lie needs to fit somewhere within the eightfold division, he assumes that the "smooth talking" lie and the jocose lie are synonymous.

What is the significance of this arcane detail? For one, it has been a source of confusion for Aquinas's interpreters, as I have already noted. Second, it created a real conundrum for Catholic moral theologians in the manualist tradition, who were unsure of whether they should classify jokes as sinful. The problem lies in the observation that Aquinas seems inconsistent on this matter. Why does he make provisions for forms of communication such as hyperbole and figurative language, but not jokes? If shared context determines the meaning of an utterance and thus figurative language does not meet the criteria for lying, then it seems that jocose "lies" should also be exempt. Aquinas acknowledges that jocose lies are not told with the intention of deceiving anyone, although he curiously adds that they have the *ratio* of deception from their genus of action.[78] We might be tempted to say that jocose lies are sinful because they are only told for the sake of pleasure. But Aquinas explains elsewhere that speaking solely for the purpose of amusement or pleasure is not necessarily sinful.[79] Thus, pleasure and amusement as such are insufficient criteria for a jocose lie.

We might, then, be led to think that mocking someone with explicitly harmful intentions (or at least a disregard for the harm inflicted by one's words) is what Aquinas has in mind with the jocose lie. This recalls the well-known (probably apocryphal) anecdote about Aquinas among his fellow Dominicans:

---

[77] Aquinas's first attempt at this synthesis can be found in *In Sent.* III, Dist. 38, a. 2, ad 4.
[78] *ST* II-II.110.3 ad 6: "Mendacium igitur iocosum ex ipso genere operis habet rationem fallendi."
[79] See, for example, *ST* II-II.72.2 ad 1: "Ad primum ergo dicendum quod ad eutrapelum pertinet dicere aliquod leve convicium, non ad dehonorationem vel ad contristationem eius in quem dicitur, sed magis causa delectationis et ioci. Et hoc potest esse sine peccato, si debitae circumstantiae observantur. Si vero aliquis non reformidet contristare eum in quem profertur huiusmodi iocosum convicium, dummodo aliis risum excitet, hoc est vitiosum, ut ibidem dicitur" ("It belongs to *eutrapelia* ['wittiness'] to taunt lightly, not with intent to dishonor or inflict pain on the person who is the object of the reproof, but rather for the sake of fun and entertainment. This can be done without sin so long as due circumstances are observed. On the other hand, if someone does not hold back and inflicts pain while taunting, just for the sake of making others laugh, this is sinful, as stated in the passage above [Aristotle, *Ethics* IV]").

Once when he was busy, quietly withdrawn in his cell, the voice of a companion called to him from the adjoining garden: "Brother Thomas, come quickly! See! There is a flying ox!" The one summoned, whose imagination was immersed in a more profound world of wonders, likely believed that a rare and marvelous bird, a griffin or a phoenix, was soaring through the air and he actually hurried into the garden, to the immense amusement of his companions. When they teased him on his credulous simplicity he responded in his peaceful, measured way: "I have never believed that an ox could fly; until now I believed even less that a religious could lie."[80]

This would seem like a good candidate for the jocose lie. Indeed, Edward Synan writes, "The 'Come quickly! See! There is a flying ox!' would be classified as a jocose lie since it would have been contrived only to amuse and to please all who heard it except, of course, the simple-minded butt of the story who was on other grounds 'the dumb ox from Sicily.'"[81] The problem with this interpretation is that Aquinas has another classification for this kind of speech. He would indeed regard such actions as sinful, but *mockery* is a distinct genus of moral action. Mockery is distinct from other sins of speech insofar as "the scoffer intends to shame the person he ridicules."[82] The jocose lie, if it is truly a distinct genus, must be something other than mockery.

I contend that Aquinas has, in fact, told us what constitutes the jocose lie. It has simply been overlooked. For Aquinas, the jocose lie amounts to *boasting*. To my knowledge, no recent interpreters of Aquinas have made this connection, but there is clear textual evidence for it. Failure to notice this connection has led interpreters to misread him.[83] The real

---

[80] Karl Werner, *Der heilige Thomas von Aquino* (Regensburg 1858) 1: 96. Cited in Edward A. Synan, "Thomas Aquinas: Propositions and Parables," in *The Gilson Lectures on Thomas Aquinas*, ed. James P. Reilly (Toronto 2008), 107–124; cited at 109.

[81] Synan, "Thomas Aquinas: Propositions and Parables," 110.

[82] ST II-II.75.1: "Sicut autem aliquis conviciando intendit conviciati honorem deprimere, et detrahendo diminuere famam, et susurrando tollere amicitiam; ita etiam irridendo aliquis intendit quod ille qui irridetur erubescat. Et quia hic finis est distinctus ab aliis, ideo etiam peccatum derisionis distinguitur a praemissis peccatis" ("Just as the person taunting aims to injure the honor of the person he taunts, the backbiter to deprecate one's reputation, and the tale-bearer to destroy friendship, so too the mocker aims to shame the person he mocks. Since this aim is distinct from the others, it follows that the sin of mockery is distinct from the previously mentioned sins.")

[83] Alexander Pruss, for example, does not realize that the jocose lie means "boasting" for Aquinas, and he criticizes Aquinas for failing to account for the basic features of language: "To call jokes that are not intended to deceive and that do not deceive 'lies' is as much a misunderstanding of language as to say that the Psalmist's quoting the fool's 'There is no God' (Ps 10:4; 14:1) is a lie or to say that Dostoevskii was a liar when he penned *The Brothers Karamazov* because there never was such a person as Ivan Karamazov. Saint Thomas's mistake here is not so much a philosophical one as one of linguistic theory," in "Lying and Speaking Your Interlocutor's Language," *Thomist* 63 (1999): 439–453; cited at 443 fn. 4.

problem with the jocose lie, which gives it the nature of sin, is not merely that it belongs to the genus of lying or to the genus of "statements whose nature is to deceive." Nor is it concerned with the harm inflicted. Rather, the sinfulness of jocose boasting is that it is performed for the sake of pleasure – a particular *kind* of pleasure. Once again, Aquinas draws upon Aristotle to reinforce an Augustinian argument: "It is a vain, meaningless thing to boast for mere pleasure of boasting, as the Philosopher remarks. Thus it amounts to a jocose lie."[84] Of course, Aristotle does not use the term *jocose lie* or its equivalent; it is Aquinas's own gloss, and he deploys it to give definition to a term in the tradition that has thus far been indeterminate. The text he has in mind here is Aristotle's *Ethics* IV.7, and Aquinas's commentary on this passage sheds further light on the problematic nature of pointless boasting:

> [Aristotle] first states that sometimes a person speaks boastfully about things that are untrue or exaggerated regarding himself, for no other purpose than the enjoyment he finds in it. Such a person is said to have a semblance of evil, otherwise he would not find pleasure in lying, which arises from a disordered soul. He should not be considered wicked, however, since he does not intend any malice; he is only vain for taking pleasure in something that is neither truly good nor useful.[85]

To be clear, this is not the boasting a person does so that she can get ahead or distinguish herself above her colleagues. That would amount to a beneficent (or, more accurately in this case, "useful," *officiosum*) lie. The boaster who boasts for the mere pleasure of it is what Aquinas has in mind. It simply has no moral value. It is not quite as bad as lying out of a lust for lying' (which holds the fourth place in Augustine's and Aquinas's taxonomy; see *ST* II-II.110.2), in which case *lying* itself is the end of the action. With jocose lies, the lie is accidental, since it is not necessarily the source of the boaster's pleasure. What we typically refer to in English as *jokes* would not fall under the rubric of jocose lies; rather they would fall under the category of hyperbole or figurative speech. We recall that Aquinas is drawing on Aristotle's understanding of truthfulness, which in its original context is the mean between boasting and mock-modesty.

---

[84] *ST* II-II.112.2 ad 3: "Quod autem aliquis se iactet quasi hoc ipso delectatus, est quiddam vanum, ut philosophus dicit. Unde reducitur ad mendacium iocosum."
[85] *In Eth.* IV.7 § 842: "Dicit ergo primo, quod quandoque aliquis iactat de se quae non sunt, vel maiora quam sint, non propter aliquem alium finem, sed quia in hoc delectatur, et talem dicit habere quamdam mali similitudinem, alioquin non gauderet de mendacio. Hoc enim ex inordinatione animi provenit. Non tamen talis est omnino malus, quia non intendit aliquam malitiam. Sed est vanus, inquantum delectatur in re, quae secundum se, nec est bona nec utilis."

Aquinas dedicates two Questions to these vices (112 and 113, respectively), which are opposed to truth. Yet here we also find him drawing upon the vice of boasting and incorporating it into his analysis of lying proper. By inserting it into Augustine's classic eightfold division of lies, as a synonym for the jocose lie, he once again attempts to clarify what was unclear in the Augustinian tradition on lying.

Another clarification Aquinas brings to the discourse on lying concerns the broader category of *dissimulation*. There can be no doubt that Aquinas does not limit the vice of lying to signification with words:

> It belongs to the virtue of truth to show oneself outwardly as one actually is, by the use of outward signs. Now outward signs are not limited to words but also include deeds. Thus, just as it is contrary to truth to signify something with words differently than what one has in mind, it is also contrary to truth to use signs of *deeds* or *things* to signify the opposite of what is in oneself, and this is what is properly called dissimulation. Thus, dissimulation is properly a lie told through the signification of outward deeds.[86]

We can think of dissimulation as a species of the genus *lying* (*ST* II-II.111.3 sc). It is possible to assert something, as well as violate the *contra mentem* principle, by using signs other than words. A citizen who wears a police officer's uniform for the purpose of making others believe he is a police officer is guilty of dissimulation; someone who wears the uniform as a Halloween costume is not. As with lying proper, the problem of dissimulation raises thorny questions. They rarely, however, add complicating factors that are not already present in instances of lying. Aquinas does occasionally consider some peculiar examples, for instance: a priest giving an unconsecrated host to someone while pretending that it is consecrated (*ST* III.80.6 ad 2). For the most part, however, his analysis of dissimulation mirrors his analysis of lying.[87] Some moral theologians and ethicists have attempted to articulate a morally significant distinction between lying and dissimulation,[88] but Aquinas does not share this intuition.

---

[86] *ST* II-II.111.1: "Respondeo dicendum quod, sicut dictum est, ad virtutem veritatis pertinet ut aliquis talem se exhibeat exterius per signa exteriora qualis est. Signa autem exteriora non solum sunt verba, sed etiam facta. Sicut ergo veritati opponitur quod aliquis per verba exteriora aliud significet quam quod habet apud se, quod ad mendacium pertinet; ita etiam veritati opponitur quod aliquis per aliqua signa factorum vel rerum aliquid de se significet contrarium eius quod in eo est, quod proprie simulatio dicitur. Unde simulatio proprie est mendacium quoddam in exteriorum signis factorum consistens."

[87] See, for example, Aquinas's description of Jehu's actions (2 Kings 10:18–27) in *ST* II-II.111.1 ad 2.

[88] For example, Elizabeth Anscombe considers the classic "Nazis at the door" scenario and suggests that "feigning a faint or a fit of madness" might be a preferable alternative to

The difficult cases include the use of dissimulation in situations such as warfare – or, in our contemporary context, state-sponsored intelligence agencies. Aquinas only offers a few remarks on this subject, but they are worth quoting in full:

> Ambushes are executed for the purpose of deceiving the enemy. Now a person may be deceived by another's word or deed in two ways: First, by being told a falsehood, or by a broken promise. And this is always illicit. No one should deceive the enemy in this way, since there are certain rights of war and covenants, which should be observed even among enemies, as Ambrose states in *De officiis*.[89]

Thus, Aquinas does not make exceptions to prohibition against lying in times of war. But there are other means of hiding the truth that do not include lying, and sometimes they are permissible:

> Second, a person may be deceived by what we say or do because we do not reveal our purpose or meaning to him. We are not always bound to do this, since even in sacred doctrine many things must be concealed, especially from unbelievers, because they might ridicule it. As it is written in Matthew 7: "Do not give that which is holy to the dogs." More still, war campaigns should be hidden from the enemy. The soldier should hide his purpose from the enemy so that it does not become known, as stated in Frontinus's *Stratagemata*. This concealment is what is meant by "ambush," which is licit in a just war.[90]

The description of licit ambushes during wartime is thus limited to the use of concealment. For Aquinas, the conceptually wider category of dissimulation does not open the door for deceptive practices, even in times of war. Needless to say, it is impossible to imagine such standards being applied in contemporary warfare, and these standards were likely no

---

lying. See G. E. M. Anscombe, "Two Moral Theologians," in *Faith in a Hard Ground: Essays on Religion, Philosophy and Ethics by G.E.M. Anscombe*, ed. Mary Geach and Luke Gormally (Charlottesville, VA 2008), 157–169; cited at 163.

[89] *ST* II-II.40.3: "Respondeo dicendum quod insidiae ordinantur ad fallendum hostes. Dupliciter autem aliquis potest falli ex facto vel dicto alterius uno modo, ex eo quod ei dicitur falsum, vel non servatur promissum. Et istud semper est illicitum. Et hoc modo nullus debet hostes fallere, sunt enim quaedam iura bellorum et foedera etiam inter ipsos hostes servanda, ut Ambrosius dicit, in libro de officiis."

[90] Ibid.: "Alio modo potest aliquis falli ex dicto vel facto nostro, quia ei propositum aut intellectum non aperimus. Hoc autem semper facere non tenemur, quia etiam in doctrina sacra multa sunt occultanda, maxime infidelibus, ne irrideant, secundum illud Matth. VII, *nolite sanctum dare canibus*. Unde multo magis ea quae ad impugnandum inimicos paramus sunt eis occultanda. Unde inter cetera documenta rei militaris hoc praecipue ponitur de occultandis consiliis ne ad hostes perveniant; ut patet in libro stratagematum Frontini. Et talis occultatio pertinet ad rationem insidiarum quibus licitum est uti in bellis iustis."

more realistic in Aquinas's own day. But these are the only "deceptive" practices that he considers licit in war. As he goes on to write, "Nor can these ambushes be properly called deceptions. They are neither contrary to justice nor to a rightly ordered will. Rather, a person would have an inordinate will if he did not allow others to hide anything from him."[91] Whatever we might think about the practicability of Aquinas's position, he can at least be credited with consistency.

Finally, Aquinas considers a sin against truth that can be described as a species of dissimulation, namely, hypocrisy. More precisely, hypocrisy describes the kind of action in which "one person simulates another, for example when a sinner simulates the *persona* of a just person."[92] Like boasting, it involves claiming something for oneself that is not actually the case; as a species of dissimulation, hypocrisy exercises a broader form of representation of oneself, which may not even involve the use of words. He explains, "An outward deed is a natural sign of one's intention. When a person performs works to the service of God (which are good by their genus), yet in performing them intends to please humans rather than God, he simulates a rectitude of intention that he does not actually possess."[93] He gives the example elsewhere of a person in mortal sin who presents himself to receive the Eucharist: "He commits a falsehood by signifying that he has charity when he does not."[94] These are all significations that can be performed without words, and they are performed with the intention of making others think that one is a person other than who she really is. We may, of course, conceal our sins without being guilty of dissimulation (II-II.111.1 ad 4), but we may not actively indicate through use of signs

---

[91] Ibid.: "Nec proprie huiusmodi insidiae vocantur fraudes; nec iustitiae repugnant; nec ordinatae voluntati, esset enim inordinata voluntas si aliquis vellet nihil sibi ab aliis occultari."

[92] *ST* II-II.111.2: "Sic dicendum est quod hypocrisis simulatio est, non autem omnis simulatio, sed solum illa qua quis simulat personam alterius; sicut cum peccator simulat personam iusti."

[93] *ST* II-II.111.2 ad 1: "Ad primum ergo dicendum quod opus exterius naturaliter significat intentionem. Quando ergo aliquis per bona opera quae facit, ex suo genere ad Dei servitium pertinentia, non quaerit Deo placere, sed hominibus, simulat rectam intentionem, quam non habet."

[94] *In I Cor.* 11:27 § 691: "Cum igitur peccator careat caritate, et sit separatus merito ab Ecclesiae unitate, si accedat ad hoc sacramentum, falsitatem committit, dum significat se habere caritatem, quam non habet," in *Super primam Epistolam ad Corinthios lectura*, in *Super epistolas S. Pauli lectura*, 8th rev. edn, vol. 1, ed. Raphael Cai (Turin 1953).

that we are blameless. The exercise of the virtue of *veracitas* requires a unity of sign and thing signified, and this holds true whether our signs are spoken, written, gestured, worn, or suggested in any way. If we assert something other than what we believe to be true, we have told a lie. In Chapter 5, we will consider the question of whether it is possible to evade the truth in our assertions and whether this could ever be morally good.

5

Lying, Asserting, and Evading

A Linguistic and Moral Analysis

Many of the thorny questions surrounding the morality of lying hinge on the definition of a lie. For example, as we saw in Chapter 1, Alexander Pruss offers a novel take on the age-old question of how we should account for the way an utterance is *heard* by one's interlocutor. The arguments may be novel, but the basic proposal is not new. As we saw in Chapter 2, some thinkers in the early Christian tradition approve of equivocation and other forms of evading the truth that appear to fall short of outright lying. To address the moral significance of equivocation, we must move beyond the realm of signification and into the realm of *meaning*.

The foregoing analysis has shown that the definition of lying as "a lack of correspondence between one's thoughts and one's words" – to equate lying with duplicity, in other words – is insufficient. Words *signify*, as Augustine and Aquinas frequently remind us. But words in isolation cannot *mean* anything; the meaning of one's utterance is determined by its context.[1] And context is established through the shared norms and practices of a community of language users. An utterance has no meaning in a vacuum. Ludwig Wittgenstein famously makes this point in his arguments against the notion of "private language." He writes, "'So you are saying that human agreement decides what is true and what is false?' – It is what human beings *say* that is true and false; and they agree in the *language* they use. That is not agreement in opinions but in

---

[1] For a helpful analysis of the concept of meaning, as well some helpful pre-modern concepts that illuminate our understanding of meaning, see John A. Oesterle, "Another Approach to the Problem of Meaning," *The Thomist* 7:2 (1944): 233–263.

form of life (*Lebensform*)."[2] He describes imaginary human beings who only speak in monologue, who accompany their activities by talking to themselves. While an explorer who watches and listens to them might be able to translate their "language" into ours, this would not amount to an authentic *language* but rather an ability on the part of the explorer to predict those people's actions correctly by hearing them make resolutions and decisions.[3] Our purpose here, then, is to consider the role of language and the nature of meaning – and more precisely, what it means for one person to assert something to another person – as they relate to the morality of lying. Since Aquinas does not give us a detailed account of assertion in his analysis of lying (although he does have much to say elsewhere about the relationship between thought and language[4]), the best we can do is to develop an account that is broadly Thomistic. If that seems too modest, I should add that I not only think that the account I develop here is consistent with Aquinas's thought but that his analysis logically demands such an account (or something very close to it). I do, of course, draw upon Aquinas's writings where relevant, but I recognize that my analysis takes me beyond what Aquinas says himself, at least explicitly. The first section of this chapter is concerned with the formal features of assertion and its relationship to lying. In the second section, I extend my analysis to the "Nazi at the door" dilemma and consider the moral relevance of assertion.

EQUIVOCATION AND LYING

In order to understand the relationship between the problem of private language and the problem of equivocation, we must reflect on what it means for words to express meaning. We recall Aristotle's claim that words are signs of the "passions of the soul"[5] and Aquinas's claim that words are "signs of one's thoughts" (*ST* II-II.110.3). But neither of these

---

[2] Wittgenstein, *Philosophical Investigations*, I.241. See also I.269.
[3] Ibid., I.243.
[4] *ST* I.85 serves as a helpful starting point for understanding Aquinas's views on this relationship. For an illuminating discussion on the contemporary relevance of these views, see the exchange between Nicanor Pier Giorgio Austriaco, OP and Marie George in *American Catholic Philosophical Quarterly* 95:1 (2021) 117–152. See also John O'Callaghan, *Thomist Realism and the Linguistic Turn: Toward a More Perfect Form of Existence* (Notre Dame 2003). For a sophisticated constructive account of the moral dimensions of speech, see Terence Cuneo, *Speech & Morality: On the Metaethical Implications of Speaking* (New York 2014).
[5] Aristotle, *Peri Hermeneias* I.1.

thinkers is claiming that human vocal utterances are natural, one-to-one expressions of mental sensations. As Aquinas explains, "Brute animals manifest things, yet they do not intend to manifest anything; they do something by natural instinct, and a manifestation is the result."[6] The act of human manifestation, however, is a communal enterprise; we cannot avoid thinking about the meaning of our utterances as they are received by our interlocutors. This is the very essence of language. Wittgenstein offers a helpful illustration:

> Look at the blue of the sky and say to yourself "How blue the sky is!" – When you do it spontaneously – without philosophical intentions – the idea never crosses your mind that this impression of colour belongs only to *you*. And you have no hesitation in exclaiming that to someone else. And if you point at anything as you say the words you point at the sky. I am saying: you have not the feeling of pointing-into-yourself, which often accompanies "naming the sensation" when one is thinking about "private language." Nor do you think that really you ought not to point to the colour with your hand, but with your attention. (Consider what it means to "point to something with the attention.")[7]

In other words, we have a default assumption of *shared context* when we think about the meaning of our words. Just as shared knowledge of a spoken language (English, Dutch, Japanese, etc.) is requisite for verbal communication,[8] so is the shared assumption that our words and utterances mean the same thing in the minds of both interlocutors. Wittgenstein continues, "But how is it even possible for us to be tempted to think that we use a word to *mean* at one time the colour known to everyone – and at another the 'visual impression' which *I* am getting *now*?"[9] It is only when one self-consciously reflects on *my sensation* or *my thought* or *my meaning* that one moves from the domain of human language into the realm of "private language."

This is precisely what happens in the act of equivocation. When we equivocate, we ignore – or pretend to be unaware of – the fact that "what *I* mean by *x*" may in fact contradict what *x* will mean when uttered in a given context. In the words of C. L. Hamblin, "Equivocation, if we

---

[6] ST II-II.110.1: "[U]nde etsi bruta animalia aliquid manifestent, non tamen manifestationem intendunt, sed naturali instinctu aliquid agunt ad quod manifestatio sequitur."
[7] Wittgenstein, *Philosophical Investigations*, I.275.
[8] Recall Augustine's remark, "For, when people cannot communicate their thoughts to each other, because of nothing more than the diversity of their languages, their likeness of nature is of so little use in bringing them together that a man would rather be with his dog than with a foreigner," in *The City of God* XIX.7.
[9] Wittgenstein, Philosophical Investigations, I. 277.

think of the *meanings* of sentences or terms as extralinguistic entities, becomes in essence the association of a single sentence or term with two or more such entities instead of one."[10] While the material truth or falsity of an utterance often depends on context (e.g., "It is 4:00 pm" is true when it is 4:00, but false at any other time), we cannot neglect the fact that the *formal* truth and falsity of an utterance also depends on context. The fatigued worker who greets his colleague on Monday morning by saying, "Gotta love Mondays! It's my favorite day of the week," is not asserting a falsehood. He does not expect his colleague to believe that he genuinely loves Mondays. If she *does* misunderstand her colleague's sarcasm, then she is likely not a native English speaker, or for whatever reason she has not been initiated into the cultural and linguistic habits of the American workplace. If the colleague recognizes that there has been a failure in communication, he may seek to correct it by explaining what he means, but he has not told a lie. Similarly, a person who begins a story with the words, "Once upon a time," is not asserting that the events described are historical, but a listener who is unfamiliar with the conventions of fairy tales might mistake the story as an assertion of historical fact. But the speaker is not lying. Aquinas learns this principle from Augustine: "As Augustine says, 'it is not a lie to say or do something figuratively. Every utterance must be referred to the thing uttered, and when a thing is done or spoken figuratively, it utters that which it is understood to signify to its audience.'"[11] And elsewhere,

As Augustine says, "It is not always a lie to pretend. But when the pretense is without signification, it is a lie. When our pretense is signified, however, there is no lie but rather a representation of the truth." He mentions figures of speech as an example, in which a thing is pretended, i.e., we do not mean for it to be taken literally, but as a figure of something else we want to say.[12]

---

[10] C. L. Hamblin, *Fallacies* (London 1970), 286.
[11] *ST* II-II.110.3 ad 6: "Nec est simile de hyperbolicis aut quibuscumque figurativis locutionibus, quae in sacra Scriptura inveniuntur, quia, sicut Augustinus dicit, in libro contra mendacium, *quidquid figurate fit aut dicitur, non est mendacium. Omnis enim enuntiatio ad id quod enuntiat referenda est, omne autem figurate aut factum aut dictum hoc enuntiat quod significat eis quibus intelligendum prolatum est.*"
[12] *ST* II-II.111.1 ad 1: "Ad primum ergo dicendum quod, sicut Augustinus dicit, in libro de quaest. Evang., non omne quod fingimus mendacium est. Sed quando id fingimus quod nihil significat, tunc est mendacium, cum autem fictio nostra refertur ad aliquam significationem, non est mendacium, sed aliqua figura veritatis. Et subiungit exemplum de figurativis locutionibus, in quibus fingitur quaedam res non ut asseratur ita esse, sed eam proponimus ut figuram alterius quod asserere volumus."

The point is that when my pretense is signified – when I indicate by some shared locutionary convention that my words are meant to be understood in a certain way or possess an additional layer of meaning – I am not lying.

We can think of these of these speech acts as containing *implicit premises*, which, when taken together with their corresponding explicit utterances, constitute the *meaning* of the utterance. This meaning is what the person *asserts* with her words. Here I am drawing upon Paul Grice's concept of conversational implicature:

> [W]hen somebody asks me where he can get some petrol and I say that there is a garage around the corner; here I might be said to imply, not just that there is a garage around the corner, but that it is open, and that it has stocks of petrol, etc. Or, if in response for a request to a testimonial for somebody who is a candidate for a philosophical job and whom I have taught, I write back and say that his manners are excellent and that his handwriting is extremely legible, I could be said to be implying that he was not all that good at philosophy.[13]

An utterance that begins with the words, "A priest, a rabbi, and an imam walked into a bar," contains the implicit premise: ["I am speaking in the genre of a joke. The events I'm describing did not actually occur in history"].[14] Or, when a non-Jewish actor on the stage declares, "I am a Jew,"[15] his words contain the implicit premise: ["I am not asserting that I am a Jew; I am speaking in the voice of my character, Shylock"]. Implicit premises are not limited to special circumstances; they belong to even the most mundane utterances. Take for example, the utterance, "No, thanks, I'm not hungry." If a person says these words in response to an offer for lunch, there is an implicit premise: ["but I will be later"]. The speaker is not asserting that she has definitively lost her appetite and that she will never be hungry again. Since lying is concerned with formal falsehood, we are ultimately concerned with the meaning of a person's utterance, and meaning must take into account the explicit utterance understood in light of the utterance's implicit premises.

Thus, it will not suffice to define a lie as a lack of correspondence between one's thoughts and one's words – as if "words" could have any

---

[13] Paul Grice, "Presupposition and Conversational Implicature," in *Radical Pragmatics*, ed. Peter Cole (New York 1981), 183–198; cited at 184.
[14] See Cohen, "Jokes are Conditional," in *Jokes*, 12–32.
[15] William Shakespeare, *The Merchant of Venice* (New York: Oxford University Press, 2008), Act 3, Scene 1, Line 1292.

meaning independent of a specific utterance.[16] This is why we have been using the following definition of lying: A lie is told when there is a lack of correspondence between *what one believes to be the case* and *that which one intends to assert*. Without this additional refinement, it would be unclear why speech acts such as jokes, sarcasm, playacting, and storytelling should not count as lies. In the most formal, technical sense, such speech acts *do* exhibit a lack of conformity between a person's thoughts and the words she utters. The reason they are not lies, however, is because the person does not intend to *assert* something opposed to what is in her mind, and she uses linguistic cues and recognized social conventions to "signify her pretense," as Aquinas would say. While Aquinas never discusses equivocation as a discrete topic,[17] his comments on hyperbolic expression and figurative language provide resources for thinking about the role that context plays in shaping the meaning of our utterances.[18] When placed under closer scrutiny, these resources lead us to the conclusion that our shared context is always normative when determining the meaning of one's words. We cannot ignore this reality in some cases while affirming it in others.

[16] Kevin Flannery suggested in personal correspondence that perhaps the original definition would work so long as we take "one's words" to mean "one's words as generally understood." My concern is that the clause "generally understood," while it ostensibly takes context into account, verges on the kind of "pure Platonism" Hamblin describes, below (fn. 22). This can be seen in cases of equivocation, in which the speaker relies on the way a word or phrase may be "generally understood," yet, in his own mind, adapts the meaning to suit his own purposes. The actual meaning of an utterance depends not only on the meaning of the words as they are "generally understood" but also on more complex and context-specific features of the utterance.

[17] I must disagree with John Skalko when he writes, "Aquinas in numerous cases allows for equivocation or various types of mental reservation," in "Why Did Aquinas Hold That Killing is Sometimes Just, But Never Lying?" 238 fn. 36. Skalko cites *ST* II-II.110.3 ad 3 and ad 6 in support of this claim, but 110.3 ad 3 is concerned with figurative and prophetic speech, whereas 110.3 ad 6 is concerned with jokes, hyperbole, and figurative expression. Neither explicitly addresses (let alone affirms) equivocation or mental reservation. See the footnote below for further considerations.

[18] Aquinas states, "It is lawful to hide the truth by concealing it somehow" (*Licet tamen vertitatem occultare prudenter sub aliqua dissimulatione*) in *ST* II-II.110.3 ad 4. Unfortunately, he does not provide any examples of such *dissimulatione*, but we can safely assume that they would not include instances of "dissimulation" (*simulatio*), or false signification that does not involve words (see II-II.111.1). Elsewhere, he approvingly cites Augustine's defense of Abraham's claim that Sarah is his "sister" (II-II.110.3 ad 3). Augustine explains that Abraham wished to "hide" the truth rather than tell a lie (*veritatem voluit celari, non mendacium dici*), but clearly, he is doing more than merely withholding information. He *asserts* something, namely, that Sarah is his sister (I discuss this in the present chapter, below). If Aquinas wishes to avoid classifying

Now we are in a position to understand why equivocation, as I have been describing it, must be a species of lying. We must either accept the claim that *implicit premises are constitutive of an utterance's meaning*, or we must reject it. We cannot have it both ways. If we accept this claim, then we must acknowledge that equivocation is a form of lying (according to the above definition of lying). If we reject this claim, however, then we are forced to embrace the view that jokes, sarcasm, playacting, and storytelling are lies – a view that I suspect very few will find appealing. To illustrate, we need only to distill the implicit premises from utterances that equivocate their meaning. Take, for example, the case of Athanasius we encountered in Chapter 2. When encountered by his pursuers, he declares, "Athanasius is not far." His pursuers carry on in their search, leaving Athanasius unharmed. Clearly, this is the intended effect of Athanasius's words, with the upshot that he avoids telling a lie – or so it seems. Had he declared, "I saw him run that way!" there would be no question that a lie had been told. But some might defend Athanasius on the grounds that his words appear to be both materially true (Athanasius is, in fact, "not far") and formally true (Athanasius believes the statement "he [i.e., himself] is not far" to be true). The problem arises once we ask: What does Athanasius *assert*? His explicit utterance is, "He is not far," but in the context in which it is uttered, it contains the implicit premise: ["and I am not Athanasius"]. Thus, Athanasius asserts a formal falsehood. There is a lack of correspondence between *the thoughts in his mind* and *that which he intends to assert*. Athanasius has told a lie.

Or take, for example, the case of Abraham telling the Egyptians that Sarah is his sister in Genesis 20. He makes this declaration out of fear that if the Egyptians realize that he is married to Sarah, they will kill him so that the Pharaoh can take Sarah for himself. He later offers the following justification for his words: "Besides she is indeed my sister, the daughter of my father but not the daughter of my mother; and she became my wife" (Gen. 20:12). As with the case of Athanasius, the context of his words necessitates an implicit premise. If we are inclined to think that it

---

Abraham's assertion as an equivocation, it is unclear why it should not be considered as such. If, on the other hand, Aquinas would acknowledge that the assertion is an equivocation and, furthermore, that this is not an instance of lying, then he would need to explain why such equivocations are not lies. Perhaps Aquinas is simply inconsistent on this point. On the other hand, since he never provides his own examples of "hiding the truth prudently by concealing it," his own view on the matter of equivocation remains somewhat of a mystery.

is the listener, and not the speaker, who adds the additional premise, we only need to recall that Abraham (as with Athanasius) *intends* to assert the implicit premise; in fact, the equivocation fails if the listener does not "hear" this premise. In Abraham's case, the explicit utterance is, "She is my sister," and the implicit premise is: ["and she is not my wife"]. This is in fact what he intends to assert, as the Genesis text makes clear. Abraham explains, "I did it because I thought, 'There is no fear of God at all in this place, and they will kill me because of my wife'" (Gen. 20:11). Athanasius and Abraham *want* their words to be taken in a different sense than that which they hold in their own minds, and this is precisely why they word their statements so carefully. But we cannot determine whether their "words" fail to correspond to their thoughts – such a task would be incomprehensible. We must ask whether their *assertions* fail to correspond to their thoughts. Of course, thoughts themselves are subjective, and therefore only the liar can ever know with absolute certainty whether a lie has been told. But in many cases of equivocation (such as the case of Abraham), the equivocator implicates himself by providing the reasons for his choice of words.

One of the more notorious contemporary examples of equivocation was uttered by former US President Bill Clinton during his Senate trial, in which he was being charged with perjury and obstruction of justice. In a prior deposition, Clinton's attorney had asserted that there "is absolutely no sex of any kind in any manner, shape, or form" between Clinton and Monica Lewinsky, a former intern and Department of Defense employee.[19] The truth is that there had been a sexual relationship between Clinton and Lewinsky. During the grand jury testimony in the Senate trial, independent counsel Solomon Wisenberg confronted Clinton: "[That] was an utterly false statement. Is that correct?" Clinton responded, "It depends on what the meaning of the word *is* is. If the – if he – if *is* means is and never has been, that is not – that is one thing. If it means there is none, that was a completely true statement."[20] In other words, Clinton acknowledged that the claim "there is no sex" between him and Lewinsky can be taken to signify two different (and incompatible) assertions. In his own mind – according to his own private language – Clinton's statement meant that there was not *at present* a sexual relationship. In everyone else's mind, the statement meant

---

[19] Peter Baker, *Breach: Inside the Impeachment and Trial of William Jefferson Clinton* (New York 2012), 29.
[20] Ibid.

that there had never been such a relationship (which is, arguably, what Clinton intended to assert). He had every reason to know that this is how his statement would be understood, given the fact that one of the purposes of the trial was to ascertain whether or not there had been such a relationship. Even Clinton's lawyers conceded that his words *implied* a falsehood. In a legal brief filed to a committee of the Arkansas Supreme Court, his attorneys wrote, "Many categories of responses which are misleading, evasive, nonresponsive or frustrating are nevertheless not legally 'false' [including] literally truthful answers that imply facts that are not true."[21] Clinton's explicit utterance was: "There is no sex." The implicit utterance was: ["and there never has been"]. If he knew that this is how his statement would be understood and in fact *wanted* it to be understood this way, then that is what he intended to assert. If he intended to assert something that did not correspond to his own thoughts, then he told a lie.

To be clear, my argument that equivocation is a species of lying has nothing to do with the effect or outcome of one's words. Thus, it will not do to object that we cannot determine the *effect* of our words as they are heard by our interlocutors. This objection, as stated, can mean two different things – but both are irrelevant. In the first sense, we might want to say that we cannot directly control how our interlocutors will *respond* to our words. But this is only trivially true. When Athanasius told his pursuers that he is not far, he could not know whether they would carry on or whether they would see through his ruse. But that is not the point. In the second sense, we might want to say that, since we can *never* be certain how our words will be understood by someone else, then the only criterion relevant to the moral analysis of lying is whether my words are true *as I understand them*. But this is a false dilemma. It also presupposes the possibility of private language. It pretends that we can evaluate the meaning of an utterance exclusively within the context of the speaker's mind, as if it has a "pure meaning" apart from the way in which language functions and apart from what it intends to communicate to her interlocutors.[22] While it is true that we can never know

---

[21] Charles Babington, "Clinton Reply in License Case: Testimony 'Not Legally False,'" *The Washington Post*, May 9, 2000.

[22] On this point it is worth quoting Hamblin at length: "The meaning of a term is, it is true, not just a matter of what a speaker or writer intends it to mean but also a matter of what a hearer or reader understands by it, what an average speaker or an average hearer would mean by it in normal circumstances, and so on; but we can determine what a hearer takes a word to mean by asking him, and we can determine what an average

how our words will be heard or interpreted, this has no bearing on the one question that is really relevant to the present analysis, namely: *What do I intend to assert?* We must ask this question because it is the only way to assess the status of equivocation while recognizing that: (1) language is an inherently social and communal enterprise, and correlatively, (2) we cannot resort to the notion of private language to explain the meaning of our utterances.

Many have tried to defend equivocation on the grounds that we cannot control others' perception of our words. Perez Zagorin describes one such argument, from the early Jesuit theologians, which follows this strategy:

> The argument also treated the use of "pious equivocation" as different from lying. It justified responding to questions by means of equivocation, contending that responsibility for the resulting deceit would not rest with the respondent but with the questioner, who by taking the answer in his own sense deceived himself. The opinion concluded generally that one could keep silent about the truth or hide it as long as one did not directly deny it.[23]

This view reflects a long struggle within Catholicism to determine whether (and what kind of) "mental reservation" is a species of lying.[24] The answer to this question has never been definitively settled in canon law or official Church teaching, although certain views have been condemned by the magisterium. For example, some Jesuit casuists in the seventeenth century (most prominently Thomas Sánchez) argued in favor of strict mental reservation, that is, the view that it is licit to speak duplicitously so long as one mentally directs the "true" meaning of one's words to God. The boundaries of strict mental reservation are virtually

---

speaker, hearer, reader, or writer means by conducting a poll. We can, perhaps, determine what a fictional speaker or hearer means by devising an imaginary explanation-request and answer in accordance with the canons of fiction. Thus 'hearer's meaning', and the others, can be defined analogously to 'speaker's meaning'. But a second answer is appropriate to those who remain unsatisfied with this extension of the criterion and insist on asking for a definition of '*the* meaning'. It is to ask: What other kind of meaning can there be? Besides the various possible explanations of meaning that could be elicited by asking users, it is difficult to see that any other source of explanations is possible. This pure Platonism must be rejected," *Fallacies*, 288–289.

[23] Perez Zagorin, *Ways of Lying*, 187.
[24] This is a question that has been confronted by many other faith traditions, as well. For a representative exposition of equivocation in the Islamic tradition, see Abu Al-Ghazali, "An Exposition of the Reality of Truthfulness, Its Meaning and Levels," in *Al-Ghazali on Intention, Sincerity and Truthfulness: Kitab al-niyya wa'l-ikhlas wa'l-sidq*, trans. Anthony Shaker (Cambridge 2013), 85–98. Al-Ghazali argues that equivocation is better than lying but nevertheless ought to be avoided.

limitless. A person may say, "I did not steal the bag of gold," yet in his mind, he speaks directly to God: "by this statement I mean that I did steal the bag of gold." He may be guilty of robbery, but on this view, he is not guilty of lying. In 1647, however, Pope Innocent XI condemned strict mental reservation,[25] which effectively ended all Catholic arguments in its favor. But it remained an open question as to whether other sorts of mental reservation might be permissible.

EQUIVOCATION AND THOMISTIC MORAL THEOLOGY

The eighteenth-century scholastic bishop-theologian Alphonsus Liguori is one of the most famous defenders of equivocation or "wide mental reservation." On Alphonsus's view, "Equivocation, the use of words so as to create an impression in the mind of the hearer which is different from the real sense of the words in the mind of the speaker, is lawful in a number of cases, when there is a 'just cause.'"[26] Importantly, however, wide mental reservation must rely on an ambiguity in the utterance itself; the speaker can simply insist that she meant something other than what she said. On this account, Athanasius's utterance ("He is not far") as well as Abraham's ("She is my sister") are examples of licit equivocation and thus fall under the category of wide mental reservation. This view was not without its critics,[27] but it also had staunch defenders. Some of these defenders appealed to Aquinas in making their case, if not for direct support, then at least to show that their view does not contradict his. For example, in 1854 the editors of *The Dublin Review* write,

Thus we are told "whenever there is an attempt to deceive, whether by a material truth or by a material false hood, there is moral falsehood." We were not likely to forget this fact, since it is conceded to the full by all our theologians, although some of them maintain with St. Thomas that the special malice of a lie, *as such* is to be sought from *the intention of saying that which is false*. But equivocations and mental reservations as held permissible by Catholic Divines

---

[25] Propositions 26–27 in Pope Innocent XI, "Sixty-Five Propositions Condemned in the Decree of the Holy Office, March 2, 1679," in *Enchiridion symbolorum, definitionum et declarationum de rebus fidei et morum*, ed. Heinrich Denzinger (San Francisco, CA 2012), Latin-English, 43rd Edition; 2101–2167.

[26] Josef L. Altholz, "Truth and Equivocation: Liguori's Moral Theology and Newman's Apologia," *Church History* 44:1 (1975): 73–84; cited at 74.

[27] See, for example, J. and C. Mozley, "St. Alfonso de Liguori's Theory of Truthfulness," in *Moral Theology of the Church of Rome*, No. 1 (London 1855).

cannot be objects forbidden by the negative precept in virtue of the intention to deceive which accompanies their use, for they are only allowable under the hypothesis that such intention be absent.[28]

Since wide mental reservation was not explicitly condemned by the Church, and since Aquinas's writings did not address this question in any detail, moral theologians continued to debate both the licitness of the practice and its conformity to Thomism.

Interpreters and defenders of Aquinas continued to disagree on the permissibility of equivocation well into the twentieth century. A debate between two manualists illuminates the difficulty of squaring the idea of licit equivocation with Aquinas's position on lying. Arthurus Vermeersch, writing in Latin in the quarterly journal of the Gregorian University, constructs a long and detailed argument that the malice of lying, according to Aquinas, is found in its opposition to social utility.[29] His argument hinges on a subtle shift regarding the act of *locutio*, the end of which he claims is human communication rather than the accurate expression of ideas. J. Brodie-Brosnan offers a rebuttal to Vermeersch's interpretation of Aquinas, and in the process, he elegantly summarizes the real problem of equivocation:

> Even though his words are really ambiguous, and there be a reasonable outward ground that he is not expressing his present conviction, what is there herein to prevent the speaker himself from wishing personally to use his words in the very meaning that contradicts his mind? Whenever he does so, he undoubtedly lies. Father Vermeersch's theory embraces not this contingency and therefore is inadequate. [...] The judgment that the language is truly ambiguous or reasonably non-expressive of his mind (where he wishes to use it as such) must be made by the speaker himself, previous to its use rather than consequently by his hearers.[30]

Some twentieth-century manualists share Brodie-Brosnan's rejection of equivocation while also proposing a more sophisticated understanding of mental reservation. For example, in his commentary on *ST* II-II.110,

---

[28] In *The Dublin Review* 37:74 (1854) Art. III: 326–403. This article, written by the editors without attribution, is simultaneously a review of *The Works of St. Alphonsus Maria de Liguori* and a response to another review of the Liguori volume, which was published in the journal *The Christian Remembrancer*.

[29] Arthurus Vermeersch, *De mendacio et necessitatibus commercii humani*, Parts 1 and 2, Gregorianum 1:1 (1920): 11–40, and *De mendacio et necessitatibus commercii humani*, Part 3: *Necessitatibus commercii humani quo pacto providendum sit*, Gregorianum 1:3 (1920): 425–474.

[30] J. Brodie-Brosnan, "Father Vermeersch on Mental Restrictions," *The Irish Ecclesiastical Record* 18 (1921): 602–609; cited at 605. See also J. Brodie-Brosnan, "Father Vermeersch on the Malice of Lying," *The Irish Ecclesiastical Record* 18 (1921): 266–274.

Michel Labourdette argues that there are limited cases in which the ambiguity of language can licitly be exploited to avoid asserting something one does not wish to assert.[31] Yet, in these cases, the ambiguity is a result of objective circumstances and not a result of the speaker secretly concealing one's true meaning to oneself.[32] Labourdette rightly contends that such acts should not even be classified as mental reservation, precisely because the reservation is not "mental."[33] What he is describing is similar to what I call vagueness in Chapter 6.[34]

While there is no consensus among Thomists, historical or contemporary, on the relationship between lying and equivocation, the framework proposed in this book necessitates that equivocation is a species of lying. The major flaw in the efforts to condone equivocation is that they assume that uttering an equivocal statement falls within the same genus of locutionary acts as "keeping silent." While, on the one hand, keeping silent may very well count as an assertion in some contexts (a question I consider in the next section of this chapter), it is patently false that equivocation merely "hides" the truth. As my foregoing analysis shows, our utterances contain implicit premises, and it is entirely possible to assert something without explicitly stating it. To defend equivocation is to imagine that we can ignore our own implicit premises, which is to say that we can ignore our own explicit intentions. Elizabeth Anscombe offers a succinct refutation of this line of thinking:

This is an idea infected by the notion of an act of meaning, the notion that you have to be *thinking* about meaning something in order to be meaning it and not the other thing. Whereas I would suppose that you only had to think, if at all, "well, it's true in *that* sense, anyway," and the question at issue is whether the fact that you hope and intend that the hearer will take it in the sense in which it is false means that you are telling a lie.[35]

When the only way to justify one's utterance as "technically truthful" is by mentally articulating unspoken features that endow a *different meaning* upon one's utterance than the meaning given by the immediate, linguistic context (and, importantly, the meaning the speaker intends to

---

[31] Michel Labourdette, OP, *Grand cours de théologie morale, 13: La religion* (IIa–IIae, qu. 80–122) (Paris: Parole et Silence, 2018), 263ff.
[32] Ibid., 267–268.
[33] Ibid., 264.
[34] See Chapter 6, Thesis 5.
[35] G. E. M. Anscombe, "Two Moral Theologians," in *Faith in a Hard Ground: Essays on Religion, Philosophy and Ethics by G. E. M. Anscombe*, eds. Mary Geach and Luke Gormally (Charlottesville, VA 2008), 159.

convey to her interlocutor), then the utterance is rightly classified as a lie.[36] The greatest Anglican moral theologian of the twentieth century, Kenneth Kirk, describes the effort to defend equivocation as lending itself "to that debased form of casuistry which, while maintaining the letter of the law, eviscerates its spirit." He deftly observes that Vermeersch's defense of equivocation inevitably ends up exonerating many lies that "sound common sense" would recognize as mendacious.[37]

The foregoing analysis is concerned exclusively with the question of whether equivocation is a species of lying. Considered in isolation, it is a purely formal question. Thus far, I have only argued that equivocation meets the formal criteria for lying, given the definition of lying in the present Thomistic framework. I do not mean to suggest that the examples I have cited share the same moral status. We recall Aquinas's principle that "the greater the good intended, the more the culpability of lying is diminished" (*ST* II-II.110.2). Even if no lie is without sin, this does not preclude us from recognizing that some lies are much worse than others. Aquinas continues,

> Thus, if we carefully consider the enumeration of these lies, we will order them according to the gravity of their culpability: the useful good is to be preferred over the pleasurable, the life of the body is to be preferred over money, and virtue is to be preferred over the life of the body.[38]

---

[36] Griffiths offers a helpful explication of such mental gymnastics: "When you specify the meaning of your utterance to yourself in a creative way in order to avoid duplicity, you're typically doing something extra, something you don't do when you're speaking figuratively in the ordinary sense. You're making a second-order judgment about the meaning of your utterance, a judgment that cancels or places under erasure the first-order act of uttering it by offering (to yourself) a radical reconstrual of its meaning," *Lying*, 36. He provides an example: "When I'm asked to write a check for a good cause and I say, 'My checkbook's at home,' while knowing that it's in my pocket, I may specify to myself that what I mean by 'at home' is 'in my pocket.' But such a specification requires a conscious and fairly elaborate specification of meaning," Ibid., 36–37. Griffiths is inconsistent in his application of this principle, however. He acquits Abraham's deception in telling the king that Sarah is his "sister" by explaining that "the woman is in fact his (half-) sister, and he thinks so," Ibid., 34. While this statement may be "technically" true, it nevertheless requires a "conscious and fairly elaborate specification of meaning" (i.e., a meaning of "sister" that specifies, "well, not my full sister, and also my wife, even though the category of 'sister' would typically preclude this possibility, according to the way most people use the word") in order for Abraham to believe his own statement to be true.

[37] Kenneth Kirk, *Conscience and Its Problems: An Introduction to Casuistry* (Louisville, KY 1999), 395.

[38] *ST* II-II.110.2: "Patet autem quod quanto bonum intentum est melius, tanto magis minuitur culpa mendacii. Et ideo, si quis diligenter consideret, secundum ordinem praedictae enumerationis est ordo gravitatis culpae in istis mendaciis, nam bonum utile praefertur delectabili; et vita corporalis praefertur pecuniae; honestas autem etiam ipsi corporali vitae."

With this in mind, it is not difficult to arrive at the conclusion that Clinton's equivocation is morally far worse than the equivocal statements of Athanasius and Abraham. While all three would broadly fall under the category of "useful" or *officiosum* lie, they are told for different ends. Abraham and Athanasius were protecting the good of the body – their very lives – while Clinton was lying in order to hide his previous sins. To compound the matter, Clinton's lie was told under oath, which amounts to perjury. Here, we see the extent to which circumstances and intention can alter the moral status of an equivocation (or any kind of lie): In one case, it amounts to a mortal sin; in the others, it amounts to a minor, venial sin that is immediately forgivable and still compatible with charity.

The formal analysis of equivocation is, however, an important prerequisite for discerning its moral status. If equivocation meets the definition of lying, and lying cannot be considered a morally good action, then equivocation bears the culpability of lying. As I have shown, to argue that equivocation somehow evades the formal criteria of lying is to rely on the possibility of private language. Such a notion is not only problematic from the perspective of the philosophy of language; it also reflects an inadequate understanding of what it means to be a human being. Throughout this book, I have defended the notion of truthfulness as a virtue, and it is a virtue that pertains to our social nature as human beings. Just as truthfulness is constitutive of human society, and human language cannot function without a presumption of truthfulness (*ST* II-II.109.3 ad 1), so it is that the presumption of "meaning-constancy" (to borrow a phrase from Hamblin) is necessary condition for meaningful discourse.[39] It is in this sense that equivocation is opposed to truthfulness and cannot be considered a moral good, insofar as it subverts the virtue that is constitutive of human communication.

None of these observations undermine the important subjective and individual aspects of language and communication. Consider the way Marilynne Robinson beautifully captures the mystery of our individuality in her novel *Gilead*, through the voice of her protagonist, the Reverend John Ames:

---

[39] Hamblin, *Fallacies*, 295. For an excellent contemporary analysis and application of Hamblin's notion of meaning-constancy, see Fabrizio Macagno, "The Presumptions of Meaning: Hamblin and Equivocation," *Informal Logic*, 31:4 (2011): 367–393.

In every important way we are such secrets from one another, and I do believe that there is a separate language in each of us, also a separate aesthetics and a separate jurisprudence. Every single one of us is a little civilization built on the ruins of any number of preceding civilizations, but with our own variant notions of what is beautiful and what is acceptable – which, I hasten to add, we generally do not satisfy and by which we struggle to live.[40]

But just as our own "separate jurisprudence" does not negate the necessity and importance of an objective jurisprudence in human society, neither does one's subjective understanding of language negate the normative aspects of human communication. The affirmation of human individuality should not require a denial of the fact that human beings are also social animals. As Augustine explains, God instituted human language as a communal enterprise, as a means of fulfilling the uniquely social aspects of human nature. Without an objective language, he writes, "[T]here would be no way for love, which ties people together in the bonds of unity, to make souls overflow and as it were intermingle with each other, if human beings learned nothing from other humans."[41] In the history of Christian literature, there is a tradition that associates private language with a private hell. In the *Inferno*, when Dante encounters Nimrod (traditionally ascribed as the builder of the Tower of Babel in Genesis 11), Virgil explains,

> He incriminates himself.
> He's Nimrod; owing to his evil plan
> there's no one language used in all the world.
> Let's leave him and not toss our words away,
> for no one's ever heard the tongue he speaks,
> and every tongue is gibberish to him.[42]

Nimrod is responsible for thwarting human communication, and as punishment he is confined to his own private language.

THE NAZI AT THE DOOR

The topic of equivocation frequently arises when theologians and moral philosophers consider the ethics of lying in the context of moral dilemmas.[43] If a fugitive is hiding in one's basement, what are we supposed to tell the

---

[40] Marilynne Robinson, *Gilead* (New York 2006), 197.
[41] Augustine, *On Christian Teaching*, Preface 13–14.
[42] Dante Alighieri, *The Divine Comedy: Inferno*, Canto 31, lines 76–81; trans. Anthony Esolen (New York 2003), 321.
[43] The material in this section also appears in adapted form in my essay, "Lying to the Nazi at the Door: A Thomistic Reframing of the Classic Moral Dilemma," *Journal of Religious Ethics* 49:1 (2021): 6–32.

pursuer at the door who asks if we know the fugitive's whereabouts?[44] What are we to do when faced with a situation in which it seems that we have no other option than to tell a lie? If a fugitive is hiding in the basement, what are we supposed to tell the pursuer at the door who asks if we know the fugitive's whereabouts? If it would be wrong to lie to the pursuer, then perhaps there is some other acceptable locutionary device that we could deploy. Would such an evasion of the truth be morally blameless, or at least *better* than telling an outright lie?

In his essay, "Truth, Truthfulness, and Trust," Peter Geach suggests that equivocation is preferable to outright lying. "Equivocal utterances may produce the very same false impressions as direct lies," he writes, "but they do not, like lies, debase the currency of language."[45] In defense of this position, he cites the example of Jesus Christ in the Gospels, who declares, "Destroy this temple and I will raise it up in three days" (John 2:19), meaning his own body by "this temple" (Ibid.). While the meaning of Jesus's statement would likely have been unclear to his audience, it is not obvious to me that this is an example of equivocation. Jesus's intention was not to make his hearers believe (that is, he did not *assert*) that he would physically rebuild the Temple in Jerusalem in the span of three days; he intended to teach them that *he* is in fact the true Temple. Aquinas would classify this locution under the rubric of *prophetic speech*. When exemplars in sacred Scripture utter statements that appear to be untruthful, he explains, "such statements must be understood to be figurative and prophetic."[46] Aquinas believes that God is the primary agent in acts of prophetic speech, and God, knowing that these words would be recorded in Scripture, is speaking to an audience throughout the ages.[47] Thus, to the original audience, the meaning of the utterance may be

---

[44] For some contemporary philosophical analyses of this moral dilemma (which are concerned neither with moral theology nor with the exegesis of historical figures such as Aquinas or Kant), see Seana Valentine Shiffin, *On Lying, Morality, and the Law* (Princeton, NJ 2014), Chapter 1, "Lies and the Murderer at the Door," pp. 5–46; Kate Greasley, "The Morality of Lying and the Murderer at the Door," *Law and Philosophy* 38:5–6 (2019): 439–452.

[45] Peter Geach, "Truth, Truthfulness, and Trust," in *Truth and Hope* (Notre Dame, IN 2001), 58.

[46] ST II-II.110.3 ad 3 "Si qua tamen in eorum dictis appareant quae mendacia videantur, intelligendum est ea figuraliter et prophetice dicta esse" ("If in their words it appears that they lied, such statements must be understood to be figurative and prophetic").

[47] See, for example, ST II-II.173.4 and II-II.174.3. In ST II-II.111.1 ad 1, Aquinas writes, "Thus Ambrose says that Abraham prophesied about that which he knew not. He planned to return alone after sacrificing his son, but by his mouth the Lord expressed what he was going to do."

unclear – not because the speaker is exploiting a specific bivalent sense of the utterance, but rather because it is simply too vague or obscure to be comprehended. Whatever we make of such instances in the Bible, they are insufficient warrant for the claim that garden-variety equivocation wholly escapes the charge of lying.

Geach maintains that lying *per se* devalues human language. He writes, "[E]pistemically no man is an island. The language a man speaks is an institution, just as money is; and it is a *per se* effect of lying that it damages the institution, just as in accordance with the law of Copernicus or Gresham, bad money drives out good."[48] I concur with this judgment, but I would extend it to cover equivocal statements as well. Geach argues that, even in cases in which the culpability for the lie would be very minor, "it is better to mislead the enquirer without lying."[49] He tells the story of a Dutch woman whom the Nazis suspected of hiding Jews in her home. When confronted, the woman tells the Nazis that there are Jews under the table. In a technical sense, there *are* Jews under the table – under the floorboards. But the Nazis interpret her utterance as senile or sarcastic, and they go along their way with no further inquiry. Geach explains, "doubtless she feared God and had an ingrained habit of avoiding lies; so when an emergency arose she saw a way of escape without lying."[50] Of course, this assessment assumes that equivocation is not lying – an assumption that is questionable, at best.[51] Most equivocation still meets the criteria of the lie that I articulated in the first section. It exploits the social nature of language and pretends that I can mislead my interlocutor about the meaning of my words while telling myself that *I* understood their meaning perfectly well. But if equivocation is no better than lying,[52] then the Gestapo Question is still in need of an answer.

---

[48] Geach, "Truth, Truthfulness, and Trust," 53.
[49] Ibid.
[50] Ibid., 57.
[51] Since equivocation is lying and lying can never be morally good, according to the account I am proposing here, then it simply follows that equivocation can never be morally good, either. I recognize that this does not quite get at the question of whether forms of misleading that fall short of outright lying are in some way morally *better* or preferable to outright lying. Jennifer Saul offers a compelling argument that in most cases misleading is not morally better than lying, in Jennifer Saul, *Lying, Misleading, and What Is Said* (New York 2012), 69–100.
[52] I mean, of course, that equivocation is generically no different from lying, whereas Geach is offering a specific assessment of the Dutch woman's character. It may very well be the case that she thought she avoided telling a lie, in which case Geach is correct that

If prevarication with words does not provide an adequate solution to the Gestapo Question, then perhaps some form of nonverbal communication can provide an acceptable way forward. Elizabeth Anscombe suggests that perhaps "feigning a faint or a fit of madness, making a distracting joke or producing some other red herring" might be a preferable alternative to lying.[53] There is no question for Aquinas that nonverbal signification such as "feigning a faint" would still count as lying. More precisely, these actions would be classified as dissimulation (*simulatio*), which is merely "a lie told by signs of outward deeds."[54] There does not appear to be any reason to prefer nonverbal false signification over verbal false signification. Of course, there is another course of action that is nonverbal: to remain silent. A person who remains silent is not trying to create a false belief in the mind of someone else. She is simply not disclosing the truth, or at least she is making it more difficult to obtain the truth. As Augustine writes, "It is not then a lie if something is kept back by silence, but rather when something false is posited through speech" (*Contra mendacium*, 23).[55] The exercise of the virtue of truthfulness requires prudence to determine when and how the truth ought to be manifested. We have a general "moral debt" to one another to share the truth, but this does not amount to an unqualified right (ST II-II.109.3). "If a person were unwilling for others to hide anything at all from him," Aquinas writes, "he would have an inordinate will."[56] Remaining silent in the face of an intruder is not a violation of truthfulness, nor it is it a lie. Silence is in fact what Paul Griffiths commends to those faced with

---

her actions were guided by her fear of God and her ingrained habit of avoiding lies. This assessment parallels Aquinas's assessment of the Hebrew midwives. Even if the Dutch woman is misguided, her intentions are praiseworthy. This has no bearing, however, on the analytical question of whether equivocation is a species of lying.

[53] G. E. M. Anscombe, "Two Moral Theologians," 163. I should note that in this context Anscombe is not expressly advocating such actions as morally preferable to lying; rather, she is criticizing Bruno Schüller's account of lying for its failure to consider such alternatives. It is unclear whether Anscombe herself thinks that nonverbal deception is better than lying.

[54] ST II-II.111.1: "Unde simulatio proprie est mendacium quoddam in exteriorum signis factorum consistens. Non refert autem utrum aliquis mentiatur verbo, vel quocumque alio facto, ut supra dictum est" ("Thus, properly speaking, dissimulation is a lie consisting of outward signification. But it does not make a difference whether a person lies in word or in some other deed, as stated above"). See also II-II.110.1 ad 2 and II-II.111.3.

[55] "Non est ergo mendacium cum silendo absconditur verum, sed cum loquendo promitur falsum." My translation.

[56] ST II-II.40.3: "[N]ec ordinatae voluntati, esset enim inordinata voluntas si aliquis vellet nihil sibi ab aliis occultari."

such a dilemma. He writes, "The community of truth will [...] be one for which silence will become increasingly attractive. If the lie is as ready to the tongue as Augustine says, silence will often be the tongue's only proper use. This is the intuition behind the tradition of encouraging *linguae castitas*, the tongue's chastity."[57] According to Griffiths, silence may be the only option that neither betrays the fugitive nor results in a lie being told.[58]

The problem with remaining silent in the face of the intruder is that in nearly all cases, it *does* betray the fugitive and, as such, is a violation of justice. Let us assume for the moment the more obvious fact that revealing the truth, with words, to the intruder would constitute a betrayal of the fugitive and would thus be a violation of justice. Yet, if the Nazi at the door asks, "Are there Jews hiding in this house?" and I respond with silence, have I not betrayed them? If we are inclined to say that such a response amounts to betrayal (as I believe we ought), this is not merely because one's silence will have the *effect* of leading the Nazi to the Jews. It very well may have this effect, but it may not. The Jews may be so well hidden that the Nazis are unable to find them, try as they may. That is not the point. Rather, the question is whether my silence *asserts* something to the Nazi. Aquinas never addresses this theoretical question explicitly,[59] but there are good reasons for thinking that silence can be a kind of speech act. When a chairperson declares, "All in favor say 'aye,'" those who remain silent are signifying their disapproval. In Rowan Williams's apt description, "We can mean something by not doing or saying; withdrawing from speech allows something to be communicated."[60] As Geach writes, "Describing the circumstances in which someone asserts something by remaining silent would be quite difficult. In a huge number of cases, remaining silent does not amount to any assertion at all."[61] Yet, as he explains, "'Lying by silence' is not an empty or ill-formed concept,

---

[57] Griffiths, *Lying*, 229.
[58] Griffiths maintains that one never lies by remaining silent (ibid., 208, 33). It follows from this that silence cannot *assert*, since, if it could, then it would at least be possible to lie through silence. Initially, Griffiths appears only to be exegeting Augustine, who sets aside the question of whether silence can be a lie, for methodological purposes. Yet, it becomes clear that this is in fact Griffiths's own view when he describes the "community of truth," as seen in the quotation above.
[59] Aquinas explains that we are permitted to "hold the truth back" in some instances, but he never considers whether, in some circumstances, silence can positively *assert* information (*ST* II-II.110.3 ad 4).
[60] Williams, *The Edge of Words*, 156.
[61] Geach, "Truth, Truthfulness, and Trust," 59.

but great care is needed in applying it. There are indeed cases where a failure to speak up may have the purport of an actual statement, and thus of a true or false statement."[62] By my estimation, if any case were a candidate for silence-as-assertion, this would be it. If the Nazi at the door asks me if there are Jews in the basement and I respond with cold silence, then I have effectively given an affirmative answer. As Kevin Flannery puts it, "If, upon the enquiry, you remain resolutely stone-faced, looking off into the distance, it is likely you mean to betray [the fugitive]. You might as well say, 'He's in the attic'."[63] The problem is not that a lie has been told – in fact, it is quite the opposite. The problem is that the *truth* that should have remained hidden has been revealed.

RESOLVING THE DILEMMA: THREE (FAILED) PROPOSALS

If my preceding analysis is correct, then it seems we face a genuine moral dilemma: either tell a lie (commit a sin) or betray the Jews to their murderer (commit a sin). There does not appear to be a sinless option. Here, I will briefly consider three approaches to this dilemma, and all of these approaches share three laudable features: (1) They do not resort to equivocation or wordplay as a way to evade the act of lying, (2) they recognize that the circumstances of the Gestapo Question do not change the utterance of a falsehood to something other than a lie, and (3), they do not allow that the Gestapo Question creates an exception to an otherwise exceptionless moral norm.

First, there is what I call the *confrontation* approach. Christopher Tollefsen, in his analysis of the Gestapo Question, suggests that there *is* an alternative course of action, namely, to confront the Nazi:

> So one should refuse to answer, by keeping silent or by evading in some way the question. Still, the Nazi is a human being, and a child of God, and one cannot assume that his soul is beyond saving. One's obligation, I hold, is to refuse to answer his question regarding the whereabouts of Jews (for he is owed no answer); but I would suggest that it would be responsive to the obligation to love, and the good of sociality, to tell him further that he is engaged in a wicked activity and to encourage his repentance.[64]

---

[62] Ibid.
[63] Flannery, "Being Truthful with (or Lying to) Others about Oneself," 206. Flannery makes an important distinction between the person in this example and the example of a person who freezes up and remains silent out of fear. The latter does not seem to be morally culpable, whereas the former seems to be an act of betrayal.
[64] Christopher O. Tollefsen, *Lying and Christian Ethics* (Cambridge, UK 2014), 177.

This position is admirable insofar as it seeks to confront the dilemma in the most direct way possible. Tollefsen does not attempt to redefine lying or resort to circumlocution. Nor is his position naïve. He recognizes that this response may simply anger the Nazi, which could endanger oneself as well as the Jews. He offers a sobering exhortation:

> I do not think one could in good conscience allow the Nazis to depart alone with the Jews. [...] One could offer to go with the Nazis in place of the Jews, and if that failed, one could insist that one be brought with Jews (it is very likely this decision would already have been made by the Nazis). And one should be willing to accept that a possibly significant degree of physical harm, perhaps even death, would be visited upon one's person while one continued to proclaim the truth to the Nazis about the wickedness of their mission.[65]

Like Griffiths,[66] Tollefsen's commitment to truthfulness mirrors the pacifist's commitment to nonviolence. He is willing to embrace the unattractive consequences of his position. My objection to his position is not simply that it is too extreme or that it is repugnant to modern sensibilities. Rather, my difficulty with this approach is that it does not, in fact, resolve the problem of silence-as-assertion. To be precise, Tollefsen's position amounts to something like *silence plus* – that is, it assumes that responding to the Nazi with silence does not assert anything about the Jews' whereabouts, and then he simply adds an exhortation to tell the Nazi that what he is doing is wrong. He cannot explain how this approach does not amount to a betrayal of the Jews. Elsewhere, Tollefsen implausibly suggests that one could establish a prior habit of denying information to Nazis: "a firm policy never to answer [...] makes it difficult for the Nazi to infer anything accurate from what he hears about the whereabouts of Jews *on any occasion*."[67] This strikes me as special pleading. The classic Gestapo Question assumes a scenario in which one is put on the spot; our moral analysis of this scenario is not enhanced by presupposing that one has had prior encounters with the Nazi that might incline him to walk away when there are Jews hiding in the basement.

Second, there is what I call the *prioritization of goods* approach, exemplified by Alasdair MacIntyre's solution to this dilemma. Like Tollefsen,

---

[65] Ibid., 179.
[66] Griffiths writes, "The consistent Augustinian cannot lie to save innocent life, whether one or a million; he cannot lie to comfort the sad, preserve the public order, prevent physical suffering, or even to prevent apostasy or blasphemy," *Lying*, 230.
[67] Tollefsen, *Lying and Christian Ethics*, 177.

Resolving the Dilemma: Three (Failed) Proposals 145

MacIntyre believes in exceptionless moral norms, and his approach is non-consequentialist.[68] Like Aquinas, he also considers questions about the morality of lying within the broader context of the virtue of truthfulness. MacIntyre differs from many of his intellectual comrades, however, in that he believes the solution to the Gestapo Question is to tell a lie. His argument is nuanced, and I will not attempt to replicate it here in full. In short, MacIntyre's view is one that attempts to articulate an exceptionless moral norm yet allows – indeed, *requires* – one to lie to the Nazi at the door. The norm is not against *lying*, however. Otherwise, he would have to grant an exception to the norm in cases like this one, and MacIntyre does not believe in exceptions to moral norms. He instead proposes the following norm:

Uphold truthfulness in all your actions by being unqualifiedly truthful in all your relationships and by lying to aggressors only in order to protect those truthful relationships against aggressors, and even then only when lying is the last harm that can afford effective defense against aggression.[69]

MacIntyre denies that this formulation grants an exception to the norm against lying – precisely because there is no norm against lying *per se*. As he explains,

It would be misleading to state it as though its form was "Never tell a lie, except when ..." For this would suggest that we were first formulating a rule and only later, as a second thought, introducing an exception. But this is a mistake. The

---

[68] MacIntyre's earlier remarks on exceptionless moral norms illuminate the present discussion: "People who adopt a norm about marriage, about suicide, about truthtelling, which allows for exceptions are not only adopting a different norm. They are also adopting a different attitude to the norm and to norms as such. They are saying, 'I am going to be bound by this most of the time, but I leave open the possibility that I may abandon my commitment at certain points.' And it is rarely possible for such persons to specify with adequate precision in advance just where this will take defection to be justified. [...] Somebody who is thinking about marriage, and who considers marriage dissoluble, is not thinking about marriage in the same sense as someone who holds it to be indissoluble. Each of these envisages a different kind of possibility, one in which there is and one in which there is not an unconditional commitment. So different attitudes to norms involve further difference about the way in which one relates to the institutions in whose life one participates and about the way in which on defines one's relationships to other people. All these issues arise just as much about the moral issue of truthtelling and lying which is one very little discussed in our public life as they do over abortion or over marriage," in Alasdair MacIntyre and John Finnis, "Pastoral Concerns: Faith, Natural Law and Virtue," in *The Twenty-Fifth Anniversary of Vatican II: A Look Back and a Look Ahead*, ed. Russell E. Smith (Dallas 1990), 257–258.

[69] Alasdair MacIntyre, "Truthfulness, Lies, and Moral Philosophers," in *The Tanner Lectures on Human Values*, vol. 17, ed. Grethe B. Peterson (Salt Lake City 1994), 357.

rule that we need is one designed to protect truthfulness in relationships, and the justified lies told to frustrate aggressors serve one and the same purpose and are justified in one and the same way as that part of the rule that enjoins truthfulness in relationships.[70]

While I am deeply sympathetic to the spirit of this formulation, I believe it fails as an analytical principle. When MacIntyre's rule is deconstructed, what we find is an incommensurable set of claims about the goods of truthfulness, the immorality of lying, and the importance of protecting truthful relationships. *Protecting*, for example, is ill-defined in this formulation. What constitutes protecting truthful relationships? May we protect them at any cost? May we use violence? We are given no guiding principles. Moreover, the fact that he adds the qualification that lies are justified "only when lying is the last harm that can afford effective defense against aggression,"[71] suggests that there is something inherently bad – even if by bad we only mean less than ideal – about lying. Otherwise, why add this qualification at all? Why not permit lying unreservedly to those with whom we are not in a truthful relationship? It may be the case that truthful relationships are among the goods achieved by being truthful, but MacIntyre's formulation belies the fact that there is something problematic about lying in itself, such that it should only be used as a last resort.

More importantly, perhaps, is the imprecision of the term *relationships*. If we are to be "unqualifiedly truthful" in all our relationships, then why must we not also be truthful to the Nazi? Are we not in a relationship with Nazi? If the answer is that we are not in a *truthful* relationship with the Nazi, then this merely begs the question of what constitutes a truthful relationship. Thus, MacIntyre's rule falls prey to two errors. First, it is circular. It assumes that, since the Nazi is the kind of person to whom we must lie, our relationship with him is not a truthful relationship, and therefore, we are entitled to lie to him in order to protect our truthful relationships. Second, when this rule is deconstructed, we find that it is nearly indistinguishable from the more commonplace strategy of annexing a clause about those who have *a right to the truth* to the norm against lying. Despite MacIntyre's insistence, it appears that his formulation is, in fact, an exception added to a norm against lying.

Finally, there is what I call the *sympathy for the liar* approach. This approach better captures the spirit of Aquinas than the previous two

[70] Ibid.
[71] Ibid.

approaches, although it remains unsatisfactory. Under this heading, I will consider proposals by two Thomistic philosophers: Lawrence Dewan and Kevin Flannery. Neither Dewan nor Flannery condone lying, but they emphasize the fact that lying to the Nazi is a very small matter from a moral standpoint. In his essay, "St. Thomas, Lying, and Venial Sin," Dewan speculates about Aquinas's answer to the Gestapo Question: "His answer is quite simply that one ought not to lie, no matter what the consequences. He indicates that evasiveness should be exploited, but lying is not a thing to do."[72] On the surface, this looks very much like the rigorism we find in Tollefsen or Griffiths. Yet, one crucial component of Dewan's analysis that sets him apart is his acknowledgment that the lie to the Nazi is only a very minor venial sin. He softens the edges of this answer as he explains,

[Lying to save the Jews] would be a venial sin, and one should never commit a venial sin, no matter what good might come of it. *However, given the human condition, most good people, most saints (we might even say), will tell the lie,* that is, will commit the venial sin. For their charity, which consists in their good-will toward their neighbors, God will reward them with eternal life. It is even possible that for the venial sin God might reward them with some terrestrial goods, though that is hardly of interest to such people.[73]

While I find it odd to suggest that God might reward someone for an action that ought never be done,[74] Dewan is right to downplay the sinfulness of such lies, and in doing so he echoes Aquinas.

Of course, it is one thing to acknowledge that most good people *will* lie to the Nazi; it is quite another to suggest that one *should* lie to him. Dewan asks rhetorically, "Might it not be a terrible moral fault not to tell the lie?" He suggests, further, "it is the answer to this challenge that seems to me to show the importance of the entire question of venial sin."[75] The distinction between mortal and venial sin is a theological one, and as such, it presupposes commitments that will not necessarily be shared by, or even acceptable to, the moral philosopher. Dewan concedes that perhaps the claim "even beneficial, life-saving lies ought not be told"

---

[72] Dewan, "St. Thomas, Lying, and Venial Sin," 378. It should be noted that Dewan does not include equivocation as an acceptable form of evasion.
[73] Ibid., 381. Emphasis mine.
[74] Recall Aquinas's analysis of the Hebrew midwives and the reward they received despite telling a lie (*ST* II-II 110.4 ad 4). The reward was for their "fear of God," not for the lie itself.
[75] Dewan, "St. Thomas, Lying, and Venial Sin," 381.

is only intelligible in light of theology,[76] but he believes the Christian response is clear: one still should not tell the lie. In sum, his position is that one should not lie to the Nazi at the door, but most people will, and it is only a very minor venial sin. The problem with Dewan's position is that it implies that there is some other, sinless option – some morally *preferable* option – yet he never reveals what that option might be.

Kevin Flannery does better on this front. His position resembles Dewan's very closely, as he explains that the person at the door might have "decided to lie, in effect trusting himself to the mercy of God. If he knows his Thomas Aquinas, he will have done so with some confidence, knowing that such a sin is 'beside [*praeter*] the order of charity' but not repugnant to it."[77] Unlike Dewan, however, Flannery is forthright in proposing an alternative course of action. Acknowledging that to remain silent or to reveal the fugitive's whereabouts are not acceptable options, Flannery writes,

> But it is always possible at least to *attempt* some dodge, even while knowing that it is quite likely to fail. The attempt might manifest itself in nothing other than the person's simply stuttering and then freezing up – or freezing up without stuttering – so that the fugitive is discovered. In any such scenario, the person answering the door can be said to have betrayed the fugitive, in the sense that the pursuers do discover the fugitive (presuming that they do). The person, however, is certainly not guilty of *betrayal*.[78]

He goes on to add, "The person who tries to come up with something but fails does nothing wrong."[79] The person does nothing wrong, according to Flannery, because she does not intend to betray the fugitive. But this raises a difficult question: If one knows (or is at least nearly certain) that her evasion tactics will fail to save the fugitive, then in what sense can the attempted evasion be considered a *good* action? If one responds that it is the intention behind the action that makes it good, this will not suffice. The person who lies to the Nazi also has a good intention. In both instances, the *ends* of these actions – to lie or to attempt evasion – are the same, namely, to save the Jews hiding in the basement. In the case of the liar, the *object* of the action is flawed, insofar as it bears upon "undue matter" (*ST* II-II 110.3). But in the case of the evader, the circumstances (specifically, one's knowledge that the evasion attempt will fail)

---

[76] Ibid., 381–383, 385–386.
[77] Flannery, "Being Truthful with (or Lying to) Others about Oneself," 211.
[78] Ibid., 207–208.
[79] Ibid., 208.

are constitutive of the object of the act and render it morally flawed.[80] This is so precisely because an evasion that is knowingly going to fail will have the effect of communicating to the Nazi that one has Jews hiding in her house, in just the same way that silence communicates this same information. To know this and yet still attempt the evasion cannot be a moral action with a good object.

To make this point clear, let us imagine two scenarios: In the first scenario, a man who is slight of frame spots someone who is much larger drowning in a pond. He pauses for a moment, thinking to himself, "There is no way I will be able to save this person from drowning." Yet he tries, anyway. The object, end, and circumstances of his action are good. He has performed a morally good action, even if he is unsuccessful in saving the drowning person. In the second scenario, involving the Nazi at the door, a person thinks to himself, "I know that I am incapable of evading the Nazi; any attempt will surely fail. And my failure will have the effect of revealing to him that the Jews are hiding in my house." In this case, the person should not attempt the evasion. In the first scenario, the person does not *cause* someone to drown; in the second scenario, the failed evasion (which the person *knew* would fail) *causes* the Jews to be discovered. Flannery claims that this action betrays the Jews yet does not amount to an act of betrayal, but this distinction cannot hold. In choosing to act in a way that will inevitably result in betrayal, one has effectively committed an act of betrayal.

REFRAMING THE DILEMMA

We have finally arrived at the heart of the matter. Even if we wish to say that refraining from action appears to be the only sinless option in the Nazi-at-the-door scenario, in reality it is not possible to refrain from action. A deliberate choice not to respond when confronted by the Nazi who asks for the Jews' whereabouts is perhaps an act of omission, but this does not change the fact that it is also a moral act. As I have argued, in these circumstances, silence asserts something. Choosing to remain silent in response to the Nazi's question is analyzable as a moral action; it cannot be classified as morally neutral non-action. Flannery accepts this

---

[80] *ST* I-II.18 is the *locus classicus* for Aquinas's understanding of good and evil actions, particularly with regard to object, circumstances, and end. He explains that it is possible in some cases for a circumstance to be taken as the essential difference of the moral object, thereby specifying the act as good or evil. See *ST* I-II.18.5 ad 4 and 18.10 ad 2.

logic, as he ought. But if he is to be consistent, then he must also accept that a knowingly-going-to-fail evasion tactic is as morally culpable as cold silence. Both actions assert something, whether we want them to or not.

The fact that one knows that his silence will assert something is enough to preclude it as an acceptable course of action. If Flannery maintains that the evader is blameless because he does not *intend* to betray the Jews, then he should apply the same logic to the response of silence. But he knows that he cannot. The only way out of this dilemma, it seems, is to find a course of action that is morally blameless. All the authors I have engaged in the previous two sections are keenly aware of this problem, but none of them answers it successfully, in my judgment.[81] It appears that the only morally blameless response in this scenario is the response of *stunned* silence – that is, silence that comes as a result of being genuinely tongue-tied when approached by the Nazi. But authentic stunned silence is not an *intentional* action. It cannot be chosen; therefore, it is not a moral action, and as such, it cannot help us resolve this dilemma.

What I suggest, instead, is that any course of moral action – that is to say, any intentional action – in the Nazi-at-the-door scenario will involve at least some small measure of venial sin. Whereas Dewan maintains that the principle "even beneficial, life-saving lies ought not be told" is only intelligible in light of theology, I am taking this theological analysis one step further. I am suggesting that the theological category of venial sin helps us understand why there may be some (perhaps very limited) instances in which one has no choice but to perform some morally defective action. To lie to the Nazi is a regrettable action, but it is also forgivable.[82] This does not mean that it is a *permissible* or *good* action. It is important to clarify our vocabulary here, lest the argument be mistaken

---

[81] To recapitulate: None of these authors is a consequentialist, and none of them attempts to redefine lying to suit his purposes. Geach thinks that one should equivocate (but not lie) in order to mislead the Nazi. Tollefsen thinks that one can choose to remain silent, but, ideally, one should rebuke the Nazi and call him to repentance. MacIntyre thinks that the norm against lying should be replaced with a norm that requires us to protect truthful relationships; as such, one should lie to the Nazi. Dewan does not think one should lie, but if one does, he is of little moral significance; he does not propose any alternative course of action. Flannery's position concurs with Dewan's, but he suggests that if one wishes to avoid sin entirely, one should attempt to evade the Nazi somehow, even if one knows this effort will not succeed and will likely lead to the Jews' discovery. I believe all of these proposals fail.

[82] Dewan's description of regret over venial sin is apropos: "This is important, to place venial sin within a wholesome spiritual life. One should not be satisfied to have done such a thing. One ought to have the purpose of preparing oneself for reducing venial

as a consequentialist solution to the problem.⁸³ Rosalind Hursthouse's description of tragic dilemmas illuminates this point:

> The actions a virtuous agent is forced to in tragic dilemmas fail to be good actions because the doing of them, no matter how unwillingly or involuntarily, mars or ruins a good life. So to say that there are some dilemmas from which even a virtuous agent cannot emerge having acted well is just to say that there are some from which even a virtuous agent cannot emerge with her life unmarred – not in virtue of wrongdoing (for *ex hypothesi*, in making a forced choice, the agent is blameless), and not in virtue of having done what is right or justifiable or permissible (which would sound very odd), but simply in virtue of the fact that her life presented her with this choice, and was thereby marred, or perhaps even ruined.⁸⁴

Of course, moral philosophers like Hursthouse do not attempt to frame tragic dilemmas theologically. On the account I am proposing here, we must understand the possibility of such dilemmas as a result of the Fall. A virtuous agent living in an unfallen world would never find herself in such a situation; she would never encounter Nazis knocking on her door. When we apply this insight to the Gestapo Question, we can now understand the sense in which the lie to the Nazi is not a good action. While the lie told to save the Jews is not, in and of itself, *good*, it is nevertheless compatible with charity and a profound, healthy fear of God – a claim with which Flannery and Dewan both concur. The point of departure is my claim that one has no choice but to lie to the Nazi. If the Nazi at the door asks, "Are there Jews in this house?" one should not reveal the truth. Nor should one simply remain silent, which would assert an affirmative answer. If evasion tactics are unlikely to work (the success of which would rely on intellectual virtues, not moral virtues), then this is not the time for experimentation.⁸⁵ It may be that one has no choice but lie to the Nazi.

---

sin; otherwise, there would be danger of failing, since the appetite for improving, or the appetite for removing the impediments to spiritual progress, would desert one both of which are venial sins," Dewan, "St. Thomas, Lying, and Venial Sin, 610, n. 22.

⁸³ The fact that the consequences of lying to the Nazi would be good is not enough to make it a morally good action. As Flannery correctly explains, "Within a Thomistic theory, one certainly can – and often must – make choices with a view to consequences; consequences, however, never become the basis of the theory: if there is a possible conflict, reason always trumps consequences," Flannery, "Being Truthful with (or Lying to) Others about Oneself," 209. See also Alasdair MacIntyre, *After Virtue: A Study in Moral Theory*, 3rd ed. (Notre Dame, IN 2007), 150–151, on the relationship between virtue, consequences, and rules.

⁸⁴ Rosalind Hursthouse, *On Virtue Ethics* (New York 1999), 74.

⁸⁵ Again, this is where my position is at odds with Flannery's. He thinks that one would not be morally culpable so long as one at least *tries* to evade the Nazi, even if it is almost certain that such evasion will not be successful. While I admit that the morally salient facts in this example are rather murky, it strikes me that the self-aware, unsuccessful evader bears some culpability if she knows that her tactics will fail.

Readers may notice that I have studiously avoided saying that one *should* or *ought to* lie to the Nazi.[86] I prefer to say that there may be situations in which one cannot avoid committing a venial sin, rather than to say that there are situations in which one should commit a venial sin. Some may object that this is a distinction without a difference, but the wording bears moral significance. There is, at least ostensibly, a logical incoherence to the claim that one has a moral obligation to commit a venial sin – an incoherence that is avoided when we say, instead, that because we live in a fallen world, we may find ourselves in a situation in which there are no sinless options.[87] Some may object that this still amounts to the proposition *one ought to lie to the Nazi*. If by this we simply mean that it is better (or at least less sinful) to lie to the Nazi than it is to take any other available course of action, then I have no objection. But if we mean by this that lying to the Nazi is virtuous, or good, or morally licit,[88] then we are mistaken. What we are describing is a moral dilemma in which it is impossible to avoid venial sin but still possible to avoid mortal sin.[89] Moreover, it will invariably hold true in any such dilemma

---

[86] Anscombe is willing to say that one "should" lie to the Nazi if one cannot think of any other course of action, and to support this claim she draws upon the concept of *counsel*: "If it is absolutely clear that someone can't be persuaded to avoid wrongdoing altogether in some matter, it is good to persuade him to commit some lesser sin than what he is minded to do. If *you* cannot see any alternative to committing one sin of another, you act better if you choose the lesser sin," in "Two Moral Theologians," 164. I do not find this move convincing, for reasons that Flannery artfully articulates in "Anscombe on Two Jesuits and Lying," 206–211. Interestingly, Paul Griffiths, although he disagrees with Aquinas's position on lying, finds it to be an obvious implication of Aquinas's position that one *should* tell the lie when facing such a dilemma: "The answer seems obvious: the lie should be told. Aquinas would say so: it would be a venial sin," *Lying*, 230.

[87] My appeal to postlapsarian reality may strike some readers as bearing similarity to Janet Smith's position, which I engaged in Chapter 1. It does not. Smith appeals to postlapsarian reality for the purpose of redefining what it means to lie, a strategy to which I object. I do not believe that humanity's fallen condition forces us or entitles us to redefine speech acts. I am suggesting, rather, that there may be very limited occasions in which we cannot avoid committing a venial sin. The one instance I have described in this chapter – the Nazi-at-the-door – is one that Smith would consider perfectly sinless, but only because she has redefined what it means to lie. Moreover, the scope of the instances I have in mind in which one might have no choice but to lie is far, far narrower than the scope of instances in which Smith would find it acceptable to utter intentional falsehoods. See Smith, "Fig Leaves and Falsehoods."

[88] Recall that, for Aquinas, venial sins are not "against" the law of God, but rather "outside" (*praeter*) the law. See *De malo* VII.1 *ad* 17. Properly speaking, venial sins are neither licit nor illicit.

[89] I maintain, however, with Aquinas, that there will never be a scenario in which we must choose between two *mortal* sins. At least, the only situations in which one finds oneself forced to choose between two mortal sins are those in which the agent bears

that there is prior sin involved, but it will not necessarily be the *agent's* sin. The dilemma only arises as the result of another agent's sinful actions and intentions. The Nazi at the door already has sinful intentions, which is what has led the Jews into hiding in the first place. It is *his* sin that has created this dilemma. We must remember that, according to Aquinas, venial sins can only occur in a fallen world,⁹⁰ and there are no Nazis at the door in the state of paradise. This is the tragic dimension of the Thomistic framework I have been constructing throughout this book, but it comes as a result of the fact that Aquinas's account of sin is irreducibly theological. To claim that life in a fallen world could be otherwise would require us to deny the virtue of *veracitas*. Aquinas leads us not to redefine what it means to tell a lie but rather to conform our moral reasoning to the reality of sin. In Chapter 6, we will consider the ways in which the reality of sin can affect the status of truthfulness in society at large.

---

responsibility for finding herself in the situation. This latter scenario is what Aquinas would consider a *secundum quid* dilemma. See, for example, *De veritate* 17.4 ad 8; *In Sent.* 39.3.3 ad 5; *In Rom.* 14:14 § 1120. Aquinas rejects the notion of the dilemma *simpliciter* (or what he refers to as *perplexus simpliciter*), in which a person, through no fault of her own, has no choice but to violate the law of God. Importantly, he only discusses *mortal* sin in the context of *perplexi* (e.g., *In Rom.* 14:14 § 1120), which shows that he is concerned here with actions that are explicitly against (*contra*) the law rather than those that are "outside" (*praeter*) the law, such as venial lies. For more on Aquinas and moral dilemmas, see M. V. Dougherty, *Moral Dilemmas in Medieval Thought: From Gratian to Aquinas* (New York 2011), 112–167. See also Alan Donagan, "Consistency in Rationalist Moral Systems," *The Journal of Philosophy* 81 (1984): 291–309; Alasdair MacIntyre, "Moral Dilemmas," *Philosophy and Phenomenological Research* 50, Supplement (1990): 367–382, esp. 379–381. For more general, but still illuminating, philosophical reflections on moral dilemmas, see Philippa Foot, "Moral Dilemmas Revisited," in *Moral Dilemmas and Other Topics in Moral Philosophy* (New York 2003), 175–188; Lisa Tessman, *Moral Failure: On the Impossible Demands of Morality* (New York 2014) and *When Doing the Right Thing Is Impossible* (New York 2017).

⁹⁰ See Aquinas, *De malo* VII.7–9. This very important feature of venial sin leads Aquinas to make some major conceptual distinctions between mortal and venial sin. For the human in the original state of grace, it was possible to avoid each and every sin. But in the state of corrupt nature, this is not possible. For those in the present world who are infused with charity, it is only possible to abstain from all *mortal* sin. It is possible to avoid any *individual* venial sin, considered in isolation, by turning one's attention to some other course of action (*ST* I-II.109.8). Yet, while turning one's attention away from the individual venial sin, "it is possible for another inordinate movement to arise, also" (*ST* I-II.74.3 ad 2). "Thus," writes Aquinas, "penance for mortal sin requires one to intend to abstain from all and each mortal sin. But penance for venial sins requires one to intend to abstain from each venial sin, but not *all* venial sin, since the weakness of this life does not allow for this possibility" (*ST* III.87.1 ad 1).

6

A Thomistic Framework for the Ethics of Lying and Truthfulness

This chapter summons the implicit premises that have been developed thus far in this book and makes them explicit. In the first section, I articulate the basic tenets of this Thomistic framework for the ethics of lying and truthfulness in the form of eight theses. In the second section, as a means of illustrating the practical implications of this Thomistic framework, I sketch fifteen vignettes of human communication, each followed by a brief analysis that draws on relevant features of the framework.

EIGHT THOMISTIC THESES ON LYING

In Chapter 5, I articulated some of the more contentious features of my proposed framework for the ethics of lying and truthtelling. In doing so, I have indulged in speculations that reach far beyond Aquinas's own scope of analysis. This is unavoidable if we wish to construct a comprehensive framework that can account for the full range of complexities that pertain to lying and related sins of speech. Aquinas is not a casuist, and he does not bother to apply his moral arguments to every imaginable scenario. I am no casuist myself, but I do believe that there are theoretical lacunae in Aquinas's position on lying that must be addressed. This is why I call the project a "Thomistic framework," insofar as it interprets and defends what is explicit in Aquinas's account while articulating what is missing (or at least only implicit). While I believe that the framework proposed in this book is thoroughly Thomistic, I am less concerned with its fidelity to Aquinas than I am with arriving at the sober truth. In what follows, I bring together the core tenets of this framework in the form of eight theses. The reasoning behind each thesis has been articulated at various points throughout this book, but my hope is that the following summary will better capture the framework as a whole.

Thesis 1: *Lying* is determined by the *contra mentem* principle: to "speak against one's mind," or, to utter a formal falsehood with an intention to deceive. *Deception* in this context refers to *formal* deception, not material deception. To lie requires the *assertion* of a falsehood. A lie is told when there is a lack of correspondence between *one's thoughts* and *that which one intends to assert*.

This thesis accepts Aquinas's definition of the lie (which he inherits from Augustine; *ST* II-II.110.1) yet refines it to address some difficult cases. "The *ratio* of a lie," he explains, "comes from its formal falsehood, that is to say, from the fact that someone intends to say what is false. Thus, the word "lie" (*mendacium*) derives from that which is opposed to the mind (*contra mentem*)."[1] The distinction between formal and material deception comes directly from Aquinas, in the same article: "The intention to deceive someone by causing him to have a false opinion does not belong to the species of lying but rather to its perfection."[2] While it is true that deception regarding the state of affairs in the external world is not an essential feature of lying (a very minor point that has received an inordinate amount of attention from Aquinas's interpreters), it will always be the case the liar intends to deceive his interlocutor about the liar's own thoughts. The additional stipulation about *assertion* is meant to clarify another point that is implicit in Aquinas's position: If a speaker utters something that does not correspond with her own thoughts, it must be clear that she means to *assert* her statement if we are going to call it a lie.[3] In other words, it is not a joke, sarcasm, or stage performance. The speaker's context, as well as the various genres and modes of speech, determines whether an assertion is being made (*ST* II-II.110.3.6; II-II.111.1 ad 1). These considerations lead to the final stipulation, namely that in truthful speech there must be a correspondence between *one's thoughts* and *that which one intends to assert*. This stipulation is meant to implicate speech acts such as equivocation and mental reservation. One's words do not possess any inherent, "pure" meaning; the speaker must take into consideration the established social conventions of language when making an assertion.

---

[1] *ST* II-II.110.1: "Sed tamen ratio mendacii sumitur a formali falsitate, ex hoc scilicet quod aliquis habet voluntatem falsum enuntiandi. Unde et mendacium nominatur ex eo quod contra mentem dicitur."
[2] Ibid.: "Quod autem aliquis intendat falsitatem in opinione alterius constituere fallendo ipsum, non pertinet ad speciem mendacii, sed ad quandam perfectionem ipsius."
[3] See Chisholm and Feehan, "The Intent to Deceive."

Thesis 2: Lying properly refers to verbal and written communication, but more broadly it refers to all human signification.

Lying is a sin against truth that pertains to speech acts. But telling a lie is not the only way to sin against the virtue of truthfulness. Aquinas writes, "It belongs to the virtue of truth to show oneself outwardly with external signs as one is. Now external signs are not only words, but also deeds."[4] Intentional false signification through a nonverbal act is dissimulation (*simulatio*). In Genesis 27, Jacob uses *simulatio* to deceive his father, Isaac, by wearing goat's hair to mimic his brother's hairy arms (although he lies with his words, also). Aquinas describes a more specific form of dissimulation, hypocrisy (*hypocrisis*), which is "when one person imitates another, for example when a sinner pretends to be a righteous person."[5] It is acceptable at times to deceive others, either by word or by deed, insofar as we do not disclose our plans or intentions. This is how Aquinas justifies ambushes in war, for example (*ST* II-II.40.3). One may *hide* one's purposes, but one may not use any kind of signification to *assert* something that contradicts one's own thoughts.

Thesis 3: Lying is a morally bad action because it is opposed to the virtue of truthfulness (*veracitas*). The person who possesses this virtuous habit and acts from it will not willingly violate the *contra mentem* principle.

The act of lying in-and-of-itself – that is, to utter a formally false assertion – is not a direct violation of justice. In life, many lies *are* in fact violations of justice, because they are uttered with the intention of harming someone else. But the speech act "lying" is opposed to the virtue of truthfulness, not justice proper. It is never good to lie, but some lies are very minor indeed. There is a clear hierarchy of lies, and those that are told to save someone else are the most forgivable of all (*ST* II-II.110.2).[6] Venial lies are not good, but neither would it be correct to say that they are "bad" unqualifiedly. Aquinas explains that venial sins are not bad simply (*mala simpliciter*) but only in a relative sense (*secundum quid*).[7] Venial

---

[4] *ST* II-II.111.1: "Respondeo dicendum quod, sicut dictum est, ad virtutem veritatis pertinet ut aliquis talem se exhibeat exterius per signa exteriora qualis est. Signa autem exteriora non solum sunt verba, sed etiam facta."

[5] *ST* II-II.111.2: "Sic dicendum est quod hypocrisis simulatio est, non autem omnis simulatio, sed solum illa qua quis simulat personam alterius; sicut cum peccator simulat personam iusti."

[6] On the stratification of sin within a single species of action, see *De malo* II.7.

[7] *ST* I-II.78.2 ad 1: "Ad primum ergo dicendum quod peccata venialia non excludunt bonum spirituale, quod est gratia Dei vel caritas. Unde non dicuntur mala simpliciter, sed secundum quid. Et propter hoc nec habitus ipsorum possunt dici simpliciter mali, sed

sin is only "sin" in an analogous sense, because the proper notion of sin is opposed to the eternal law of God (*ST* I-II.88.1 ad 1). Venial sin "is not against the law, since the person who sins venially neither does what the law forbids nor omits what the law prescribes; but he acts beside the law, by not observing the mode of reason intended by the law."[8] Venial sin is "infinitely distant" from charity and does not diminish the reward of eternal life (*De malo* VII.2 sc 1 and 2). Still, one should not be indifferent about venial sin, since the repetition of venial sins predisposes one to commit mortal sin (*ST* I-II.88.3). As Geach writes, "Even a habit of telling little lies about contingent matters is very harmful; a soul that should be a mirror of Truth is covered with hundreds of tiny scratches. And one fine day the habitual teller of little lies will in a sudden emergency come out with a big, whopping, utterly inexcusable lie, because he sees no other way out of his predicament."[9] The person whose soul is infused by charity will seek to avoid venial lies, recognizing that they are "out of step" with the eternal law, even if the law does not prohibit them.

Thesis 4: Human language is multifaceted and does not serve a singular function. Not all utterances are assertions. Jokes, acting, imaginative play, etc. involve formal duplicity, but they do not violate the *contra mentem* principle, therefore they are not lies.

Even Augustine recognizes that there are many speech acts that depend on formal duplicity yet should not be counted as lies. Hyperbole and figurative language, while not "true" in a literal sense, do not violate the *contra mentem* principle because they do not *assert* something that is false. Aquinas endorses these qualifications (*ST* II-II.110.3.6; II-II.111.1 ad 1), but he offers a new insight into the Augustinian tradition. Whereas Augustine and those who followed him – all the way through Peter

---

solum secundum quid" ("To the first: Venial sins do not exclude the spiritual good, which is the grace of God or charity. Thus, they are not spoken of as evil simply, but only in a certain sense. For the same reason, their habits cannot be said to be evil simply, but only in a certain sense").

[8] *ST* I-II.88.1 ad 1: "Ad primum ergo dicendum quod divisio peccati venialis et mortalis non est divisio generis in species, quae aequaliter participent rationem generis, sed analogi in ea de quibus praedicatur secundum prius et posterius. Et ideo perfecta ratio peccati, quam Augustinus ponit, convenit peccato mortali. Peccatum autem veniale dicitur peccatum secundum rationem imperfectam, et in ordine ad peccatum mortale, sicut accidens dicitur ens in ordine ad substantiam, secundum imperfectam rationem entis. Non enim est contra legem, quia venialiter peccans non facit quod lex prohibet, nec praetermittit id ad quod lex per praeceptum obligat; sed facit praeter legem, quia non observat modum rationis quem lex intendit."

[9] Geach, "Truth, Truthfulness, and Trust," 57.

Lombard in the Middle Ages – refer to the category of the "jocose lie," meaning a falsehood told for amusement, Aquinas rightly recognizes that jokes of this sort cannot rightly be considered lies. As I demonstrated in Chapter 4, Aquinas reinterprets the jocose lie as the act of *boasting*. Jokes in the traditional sense are not lies at all, and neither are playful exaggerations, tall tales, sarcasm, or related speech acts.

Thesis 5: Equivocation, mental reservation, and other linguistic evasions of the truth – insofar as they intend to mislead about the speaker's actual beliefs – are still lies. This necessary follows from the definition of lying given in Thesis 1. However, many euphemisms and social niceties are intentionally vague and, in their relevant contexts, are not taken to have a singular, fixed meaning. They are not *contra mentem* acts and are not lies. Obscuring one's meaning through vagueness is not the same as equivocation.

I argued in Chapter 5 that equivocation is a species of lying. Here I will only add that many other forms of linguistic evasion are exempt from this classification. Whereas equivocation depends on two distinct meanings being attached to a single utterance with the intention of asserting one and not the other, there are other means of prevarication that are simply too vague to affix a specific meaning to the utterance. In other cases, the ostensible meaning of an utterance differs from its meaning in particular context. When the clerk at the checkout counter asks, "Did you find everything you needed today?" and you reply "Yes, thank you," you most likely have not told a lie, even if there was an item you had hoped to find. Upon hearing the question, you respond with a "yes" because the item was not all that important to you, and you understand the clerk's question to mean, "Please let me know if there is something you would like me to help you find in the store." This social convention is understood between the two of you, and because of this shared context, your speech act is not *contra mentem*.

Thesis 6: While certain factors (external circumstances, the intention of the speaker, etc.) may mitigate the sinfulness of a lie, there are no circumstances that can change the species of a *contra mentem* utterance into something other than a lie. Questions concerning the interlocutor's right to the truth, for example, are irrelevant to the moral description of a lie as a genus of action.

Given the definition of lying proposed by this framework (Thesis 1), there are no good grounds for calling intentional, formally false assertions anything but lies. While we may harbor certain moral intuitions that tempt us to modify our understanding of what counts as a lie in special circumstances, there are no good grounds for doing so: a lie is a lie. I am following Aquinas's lead by maintaining a strict definition of the lie while at the same time downplaying the moral significance of certain kinds of lies – in some cases to a miniscule degree. This model not only enjoys a higher degree of consistency and coherence – it also protects the virtue of truthfulness as something not to be shirked for our own convenience.

Thesis 7: Lying as such is only venially sinful.[10] Nevertheless, there is no situation in which a lie ought to be told (in the moral sense of "ought") or in which it is morally good to tell a lie. In the postlapsarian world in which we find ourselves, however, there are instances when certain lies are especially forgivable and may occur within a broader context of morally praiseworthy actions.

To say that an action "should" or "ought" to be performed means that it is a good action (insofar as it promotes virtue) or that it is prescribed by the law. A venial lie meets none of these conditions. Since venial sin is only possible in a fallen world, the sinfulness of certain venial lies is mitigated by the end for which they are told. As Aquinas observes, the Hebrew midwives were rewarded for saving the Hebrew children from the murderous Pharaoh, even though they told a lie to accomplish this goal (*ST* II-II.110.3 ad 2; II-II.110.4 ad 4). We must remember that in any situation in which it appears that a lie might save someone from danger or death (and the lie would be a venial sin), there is always a corresponding *mortal* sin on the part of the perpetrator, that is, the one who is threatening the life of someone else. As I argued in Chapter 5, there may be limited instances in which we are unable to avoid committing a venial sin – such as lying to the Nazi at the door – and that such actions are still regrettable.[11] As I have shown, this theological distinction has significant implications for moral analysis.

Thesis 8: Sins of speech that include an intention to harm one's neighbor – while they may involve a *contra mentem* assertion – are most accurately categorized not as *lies* but as more specific speech acts (slander, gossip, false accusation, etc.). These actions are violations of justice and sins against charity. They are not only morally impermissible – there is no circumstance in which they can be considered "forgivable" (venial). Methodologically, it is preferable to set aside this class of speech acts when assessing the morality of lying.

---

[10] Lawrence Dewan, whose position in many ways reflects my own, appears to undermine his own argument when he writes, "We see then, that it would be wrong to say that 'lying is only a venial sin.' There are types of lies that are mortal sins, and there is a type of lie that is a venial sin," in "St. Thomas, Lying, and Venial Sin," 379. As I have argued throughout this book, lying *per se* is venially sinful. It is only when some additional feature is added to the lie that it becomes a different species of action that is mortally sinful.

[11] For a fascinating, non-Thomistic analysis of moral responsibility in light of the doctrine of original sin, see Jesse Couenhoven, *Stricken by Sin, Cured by Christ: Agency, Necessity, and Culpability in Augustinian Theology* (New York 2013).

Aquinas describes three ways in which a lie may contradict charity (*ST* II-II.110.4). In the first place, if the subject matter concerns something that pertains to another person's good, whether in matters of knowledge, moral conduct, or things divine, then the lie harms one's neighbor. This is the case because the knowledge in question has consequences for one's life. Second, if the lie is told with the explicit end of injuring one's neighbor (or injuring God), it is a mortal sin, regardless of subject matter or circumstances. "One commits a mortal sin," Aquinas writes, "if one merely *intends* to commit a mortal sin."[12] Third, an otherwise venial lie is a sin against charity if it is told in such a way to cause public scandal. These are the ways in which the act of lying – a sin against truth – can become a mortal sin. In each case, there is some additional, sinful feature of the act that goes far beyond the mere inordinate use of language. Moreover, there are many other sins of speech that involve falsehood yet warrant their own classification: perjury, slander, gossip, and the like. As we saw in Chapter 3, Aquinas has much to say about these as well, but the *ratio* of such speech acts differs in kind from the *ratio* of lying *simpliciter*.

For ease of reference, I list all eight theses, in abbreviated form, in the following table:

TABLE 6.1 *Eight Thomistic theses on lying*

---

1. A lie is told when there is a lack of correspondence between one's thoughts and that which one intends to assert. Such acts are *contra mentem*.
2. Lying properly refers to verbal and written communication, but more broadly it refers to all human signification.
3. An act that is *contra mentem* is opposed to (and cannot originate from) the virtue of truthfulness.
4. Many utterances that involve formal duplicity are not *contra mentem*.
5. Equivocation, insofar as it is intended to deceive one's interlocutor about one's thoughts, is *contra mentem*. Many euphemisms, vague expressions, and social conventions are not *contra mentem*.
6. Circumstances cannot change a *contra mentem* utterance into something other than a lie.
7. Lying as such – a *contra mentem* utterance with no additional moral description – is only venially sinful.
8. Utterances that are *contra mentem* and are also opposed to justice or charity are best described by their proper names; they are not mere lies.

---

[12] *ST* II-II.110.4: "[E]x sola autem intentione peccati mortalis, aliquis mortaliter peccati." Emphasis added.

THOMISTIC VIGNETTES: BRIEF CASE STUDIES IN LYING

In this section, I offer fifteen miniature case studies in lying. The purpose here is not to provide anything approaching a manualist guide to the ethics of lying. Nor am I attempting casuistry – my analysis of these cases is far from exhaustive. Rather, my aim is simply to demonstrate the principles of my Thomistic framework by way of illustration. Sometimes the finer points of one's moral theology can only be seen when they are applied to specific cases. This is what the framework, articulated in the previous section, looks like in action.

Case 1: Jon's children ask him for a bedtime story. He agrees, and he begins with the words, "Once upon a time, there were three bears: a mama, a papa, and a wee bear."

Jon is not uttering a lie. While almost no one would dispute this claim, its significance should not be overlooked. Without the requisite qualifications added to the basic Thomistic definition of lying ("to speak contrary to one's mind"), Jon's story might appear to meet the conditions for lying: It is not true, Jon does not believe it to be true, and yet he states it as if it were true. Why is it not a lie? Because Jon is not *asserting* that his story is true. How not? For one, he is using a linguistic convention – easily recognized by his children – that signifies that his words are not to be taken as literally true. It is not a *false signification*, and thus not a lie. We can imagine a similar scenario in which Jon makes up a story, but he does not add the linguistic cues that indicate it is a make-believe story. If his children are unsure, they might ask, "Dad, is this a *true* story?" If he answers "yes," then he has lied. But if Jon simply tells a fictional story, even without the signifiers of a fairytale, he is not lying.

Case 2: Sophia, age eight, answers a knock at her door, only to find a solicitor. The solicitor asks, "Is your father home?" He is upstairs, but, knowing that he would not want to be disturbed, Sophia answers, "He's not here right now." Hoping that the solicitor will take this to mean that her father is away from the house, she thinks to herself, "Well, at least he's not *here* in our presence right now."

Sophia's statement is a lie. She equivocates by exploiting the valence of *here*, asserting one meaning of the word while affirming another in her mind. There is nothing gravely wrong with her statement, but a truthful response would have indicated clearly that the family does not wish to be bothered. Sophia's response avoids the discomfort of having to speak so bluntly, and we would likely be inclined to say that it is more polite. But it cannot rightly be considered a *truthful* statement.

Case 3: Lucia has just learned that her employer is downsizing and that she will no longer have a job in 3 months. While running errands on her way home from work, she runs into an acquaintance. The acquaintance asks, "How are you?" and Lucia answers, "I'm fine, thanks."

Lucia's response is not a lie. She is not equivocating, either. Rather, she is using a standard convention of American English – a response that is intentionally vague and is meant to convey that one does not necessarily wish to indulge any more information about one's psychological state. The acquaintance is not misled, nor is Lucia asserting that she is, in fact, "fine" in any generic sense. She is recognizing a convention, a sort of script one follows in social settings that is widely recognized and shared by the language users in her community. If she had responded instead by saying, "I'm doing great! Couldn't be better, actually," this most likely would have been a lie.

Case 4: Ben and Amanda, like many parents, tell their children that Santa Claus is real. They explain that if the children are good throughout the year, Santa will bring them presents. He will go down the chimney and place their gifts under the Christmas tree. He drives a sleigh with flying reindeer, they explain, and he does this for all the good children across the world. The children begin to question the physics of the Santa Claus myth, but their parents devise elaborate explanations to assuage the children's doubts. When the children are older, Ben and Amanda reveal to them that the story was only pretend, but it was fun to play along.

While Ben and Amanda's intentions may be harmless, they have lied to their children. They have asserted something that is not true and that they do not believe to be true. They have even defended these false assertions over an extended period of time. We may be reluctant to find them morally blameworthy, but it is not possible, within the proposed framework, to interpret their actions as anything other than lies. There is a case to be made, I believe, that parents should not perpetuate the Santa Claus myth to their children, but I will not attempt to settle that debate here. I draw the reader's attention to the following remarks by Peter Geach: "People often have an odd attitude about lying to children, as if such lies really did not count. Since a child's very learning of language is possible only if, and insofar as, its parents give it true rather than false information, it is hard to see the rationale of this."[13] Parents often justify the practice of telling their children about Santa Claus on the grounds that it gives them "something to believe in." But when that "something" is a falsehood, which the child is bound to realize at some point later in life, it is difficult to see how such a practice is compatible with the virtue of truthfulness.

Case 5: A doctor speaks in an overly optimistic manner to his patient about her prospects for recovery. The doctor is confident that giving the patient false information will increase her overall well being and decrease her degree of suffering. The psychological effects of these falsehoods may even contribute to an increase in the patient's likelihood of recovery.

While the pertinent facts and probabilities of this case are subject to empirical analysis, there is no question that the doctor has lied. This is a frequently discussed subject in the field of medical ethics, and theorists typically frame the problem as a tension between the conflicting principles of *autonomy* and *beneficence*.[14] Some medical ethicists argue that there are cases in which the perceived benefit to the patient justifies telling a lie.[15] On the present framework, however, even these beneficent lies are not without sin. While they are not gravely wrong, they are not good actions and cannot be commended as a course of action.

Case 6: Lydia, aged ten, misses Mass on Sunday through her own fault. The nun at the parochial school asks her before the entire class if she had missed Mass. Lydia answers that she did not.[16]

The statement is a lie. Dorszynski (from whom this example is taken), claims that the statement is not a lie, because his proposed definition of lying contains a clause regarding one's right to the truth. I have also acknowledged the importance of articulating one's right to the truth, but the existence of this right does not (or at least should not) determine whether a lie has been told. Dorszynski is right that Lydia has a "lawful secret" and that the nun has no right to demand this information.

---

[13] Geach, "Truth, Truthfulness, and Trust," 58.
[14] See Theda Rehbock, "Don't Lie! .... Why Not?: How to Argue for Truthfulness in Medical Practice," *Cambridge Quarterly of Healthcare Ethics* 21:2 (2012): 177–187. For an insightful Thomistic analysis of truthfulness in medicine, see John Butler, "Truthfulness and Thomism in Medical Practice," *National Catholic Bioethics Quarterly* 12:4 (2012): 633–651.
[15] See, for example, Claude Richard, Yvette Lajeunesse and Marie-Thérèse Lussier, "Therapeutic Privilege: Between the Ethics of Lying and the Practice of Truth," *Journal of Medical Ethics* 36:6 (2010): 353–357.
[16] Adapted from Dorszynski, *Catholic Teaching about the Morality of Falsehood*, 95 (Case 2).

Aquinas would agree that she "has a right to safeguard [her] reputation,"[17] but this does not justify the lie or make it good. There are other means of safeguarding one's reputation that are consistent with the virtue of truthfulness.

Case 7: In a monastery, Brother Peter entrusts a secret, pertaining to his past private life, to Brother James. The secret involves no danger to the community or to the spiritual or material welfare of Peter, James, or a third party. The Superior asks "in the name of Holy Obedience" if James knows of Peter's secret. Brother James says he does not.[18]

As with the previous case, the person asking the question is not entitled to the information he seeks. There is a relevant question regarding authority in this case. Since Brother Peter has taken a vow of obedience, does he not owe an answer to his superior? If it could be established that the vow covers instances such as these, then the answer would be "yes." But this is unlikely to be the case. Dorszynski appeals to Raus's *De sacrae obedientiae virtute et voto* to make the case that a religious, under the vow of obedience, is never obligated to confess his own crime. The problem with this hypothetical scenario is that the wrongdoing should be ascribed to Brother Peter, not to Brother James. More importantly, the fact that one is not obligated to reveal one's own sin does not allow us to classify Brother James's statement as anything other than a lie. He may refuse to answer and remind his superior that he is seeking privileged information, but he cannot deny that he has any knowledge of Peter's secret.

Case 8: Kate, unmarried, becomes pregnant. She is sent away to the country in order to avoid talk. A neighbor asks Kate's mother about her whereabouts, and her mother tells the neighbor about the splendid new job Kate found in the big city.[19]

This antiquated example is another instance of Dorszynski's effort to redefine lying. Kate has obviously *not* taken a new job, and her mother's statement is a lie. Dorszynski finds a morally and linguistically salient distinction between the mother being *asked* about Kate's whereabouts and the mother *volunteering* this false information. This is because (if the reader has not already surmised) Dorszynski is concerned first and foremost with the question of whether one's interlocutor has a right to

---

[17] Ibid.
[18] Adapted from Dorszynski, *Catholic Teaching about the Morality of Falsehood*, 95 (Case 3).
[19] Adapted from Dorszynski, *Catholic Teaching about the Morality of Falsehood*, 97 (Cases 7 and 8).

the truth. He claims that in the latter scenario, Kate's mother tells a lie, but in the former scenario, she does not. But this question is irrelevant in determining what kind of speech act Kate's mother has performed: it is a lie.

Case 9: David has been struggling with severe depression, and he decides to relocate to another city with a reputable mental health center. He knows that he must find a new source of income in order to make ends meet, so he applies for a part-time job in the new city. David's father, when asked, tells his friends that "David found a new job, and he just needed to make some changes in his life."

David's father has not told a lie. He has neither equivocated nor asserted a falsehood in any way. What he has done is refrain from revealing the *entire* truth. There are times when hiding the truth, or part of the truth, is morally unacceptable, but not in cases in which one's interlocutor is not entitled to the truth. David's father is doing what Aquinas would call "prudently concealing the truth" (*ST* II-II.110.3 ad 4). It is true that David found a new job, and it also true that he needed to make some changes in his life. Both of these statements are true – in the plain sense of the words and in the sense in which his interlocutors took them to mean. There is no equivocation here. His father did not specify that among these changes was David's seeking help at a mental health center, but this information did not need to be revealed.

Case 10: A pro-life group performs a series of undercover "stings" in several Planned Parenthood clinics around the country. In these stings, a man or a woman (or sometimes both) enters a Planned Parenthood clinic posing as persons engaged in the sex industry who were interested in securing care for illegal underage immigrants they had hired for prostitution. During these visits, employees of the targeted Planned Parenthood clinics invariably intimate or explicitly suggest ways to avoid reporting the child sexual abuse to the proper authorities.

This is not a hypothetical scenario. These events, as described by Thomas Petri and Michael Wahl, took place in 2011.[20] The group, Live Action, wanted to portray Planned Parenthood in a negative light, and in this task they succeeded. Regardless of one's views on abortion, few would argue that the procedures carried out by Planned Parenthood (all captured on video, thanks to Live Action's sting operations) were ethically defensible. But the fact that Live Action exposed these practices does not make their sting operations *good*. I concur with Petri and Wahl in their assessment,

---

[20] Thomas Petri, OP and Michael A. Wahl, in their article, "Live Action and Planned Parenthood: A New Test Case for Lying," *Nova et Vetera* 10:2 (2012): 437–462.

"Though it is likely that the sins committed by the Live Action operatives were venial, they remain sins nonetheless."[21] Their actions would fall under Aquinas's category of an *officiosum* lie, since their ultimate aim was to expose corruption and save human babies, not to harm anyone. However, not all sins are equal (not even venial sins), and I suggest that their lies are much worse than the person who lies to the Nazis at the door. In the Gestapo situation, the person at the door is under duress, and in such situations, it is difficult to think of alternative courses of action. A beneficent lie told under duress is far more venial ("forgivable") than Live Action's sting operations. Not all Christian ethicists agree with my assessment. Conservative Catholic philosopher Peter Kreeft argues not only that Live Action's stings were morally right but that "they were very *clearly* right."[22] Kreeft's defense of the organization incorporates a curious blend of intuitionism, pragmatism, and emotivism. He writes:

An undercover policeman saves children from becoming drug addicts by pretending to be a drug customer to expose the drug dealer. Is this pretending "lying" or not? I don't much care, except as a professional philosopher and logician. I do much care that the "sting" works and my kids are protected. Do you care more about protecting your own moral correctness than protecting your kids' lives?[23]

I will allow Aquinas to have the last word on the matter: "One should carefully consider that the person who uses a lie to show the justice and goodness of God not only does something that God does not need – he also offends God in this very thing."[24]

Case 11: A man tells his wife they are going to a restaurant in order to get her to a different location where, in fact, a surprise birthday party has been organized.[25]

Apart from lies that are told to save someone from harm, the lie in this scenario is likely to be considered the most innocent of all. What could be wrong with planning a surprise party for a loved one? Hardly anything, so it seems. It is difficult to image formulating a moral norm against surprise parties. Does the man who plans a surprise party for his wife

---

[21] Ibid., 461.
[22] Peter Kreeft, "Why Live Action Did Right and Why We All Should Know That," *CatholicVote.org* (February 18, 2011), www.catholiceducation.org/en/religion-and-philosophy/apologetics/why-live-action-did-right-and-why-we-all-should-know-that.html. Emphasis original.
[23] Ibid.
[24] Aquinas, *In Iob* 13:7, C. 13 L. 1.
[25] Adapted from Gerald Dworkin, "Are These 10 Lies Justified?" https://opinionator.blogs.nytimes.com/2015/12/14/can-you-justify-these-lies/?_r=0.

tell a lie? By definition, yes. He and his wife's friends will likely have to tell many lies along the way in order for the surprise to be successful. Provided that these lies do not escalate to the level of harming someone, no one has done anything seriously wrong. Rather than vilify a widely accepted cultural practice that is almost always performed with good intentions, I will simply note that there is always a possibility that intentions behind the required deception will not be realized in the way one hopes. The man's wife may have been feeling ill; she may wish she had worn a different outfit; she may have been craving some one-on-one time rather than socializing. We do not completely control the outcome of our lies, even those told with good intentions. The person who does not in fact want to be surprised will feel betrayed once she realizes that she has been deceived. The point is not that the husband's actions might have a negative outcome – this is possible for any action, including morally good actions. Rather, in the event that the surprise turns out to be unwelcome, a different light is cast, retroactively, on the husband's prior deception. It becomes more difficult to perceive the deception as good or even "harmless."

Case 12: A woman's husband drowns in a car accident when the car plunged off a bridge into a body of water. It is clear from the physical evidence that he desperately tried to get out of the car and died a dreadful death. At the hospital where his body was brought his wife asks the physician in attendance what kind of death her husband suffered. He replies, "He died immediately from the impact of the crash. He did not suffer."[26]

Clearly the physician lied. As in Case 5, above, medical practitioners must frequently make difficult decisions when communicating with their patients – or, in some cases, the patients' loved ones. We might wonder what harm could possibly be done in telling the woman something that will make her pain easier to bear. But this is an unhelpful question. "Harm" is not the criterion for determining whether a lie has been told or whether it was justified. Assuming that the lie is harmless, the fact still remains that it is not aimed at the good of truth. If we believe that the doctor–patient relationship should be built on trust, then at times painful truths will need to be spoken. Moreover, it is not obvious that the lie is entirely harmless. What if the woman were to find out the truth from another source at a later date? Would she feel betrayed by the physician's answer? Perhaps we cannot say. But that is the point. The physician

[26] Adapted from ibid.

cannot know whether the woman would prefer to hear the truth or a lie. He is not the gatekeeper of truth. Even if he is certain that the woman cannot handle the truth at the present time, it would be better to evade the question than to assume a paternalistic stance of benevolent deception.

Case 13: Agatha is interviewing for a job in a small philosophy department is asked if she intends to have children. Believing that if she says (politely) it's none of their business she will not get the job, she says she does not intend to have a family.[27]

Is the question unfair and unwarranted? Yes. Is the Agatha's response a lie? Yes. Is her lie justified? If by "justified" we mean *understandable* or *forgivable*, then yes. But insofar as it uses language in a manner that is contrary to the virtue of truthfulness, it is venially sinful. Hardly anyone would fault her for answering the way she did, but there is also a case to be made for the fact that her lie tacitly affirms the unjust hiring practices of the department. While she is not singlehandedly responsible for repairing the institutional structure that practically requires prospective employees to lie in order to get the job, her actions only reinforce the present structure.[28] Other women who apply for positions in the department will continue to be asked such questions. Should Agatha reveal her desire to have a family in the future? No. But if she possessed a well-developed habit of truthfulness, she would challenge the interviewer whether her answer to this question should have any bearing on the department's decision to hire her.

Case 14: Nathan is negotiating for a car with a salesperson. He asks Nathan about the maximum amount he is prepared to pay. Nathan says $15,000. It is actually $20,000.[29]

This is a minor, venial lie. Aquinas has a clear category for this kind of speech act: It belongs to those lies that are *officiosum*, or useful; more specifically, it is useful insofar as it profits one by saving money.[30] Typically, when we imagine cases involving money and lying, the actions we envision would be considered fraud, embezzlement, or racketeering. But this case offers a helpful reminder that not all lies involving money are grievous or mortal sins. While Nathan has not committed an injustice against the car salesman, his words are opposed to the virtue of truthfulness.

---

[27] Adapted from ibid.
[28] See Chapter 7 on the intersection of lying, truthfulness, and unjust social structures.
[29] Adapted from Dworkin, "10 Lies."
[30] See *ST* II-II.110.2. Aquinas borrows this eightfold division of lies from Augustine (see Table 6.1).

Case 15: In order to test whether arthroscopic surgery improved the conditions of patients' knees, a study is performed in which half the patients are told the procedure is being done but it is not. Little cuts are made in the knees, the doctors talk as if it is being done, sounds are produced as if the operation is being done. The patients are under light anesthesia. It turns out that the same percentage of patients report pain relief and increased mobility in the real and sham operations. The patients are informed in advance that they either will receive a real or a sham operation.[31]

No lie has been told. The last sentence of this case description is the deciding factor. Since the patients were told in advance that they *might not* be receiving the real procedure, then it would be inaccurate to call the doctors' words or actions *assertions*. If there is no assertion, there is no lie. If the doctors had performed the faux procedure without informing the patients that they may or may not be receiving the real procedure, then their actions would have involved lying and dissimulation.

This diverse, though not exhaustive, set of cases illuminates some of the finer points of application of the Thomistic framework. Some speech acts that might appear to meet my definition of lying do not, in fact, meet this definition upon closer inspection. While most of the cases that I determined to be lies are merely venial lies, the specific features of these cases reveal their flaws as moral acts. They cannot be called "good" in an unqualified sense. In order to be truthful, one must avoid even these lies. Thus far, I have shown that the Thomistic framework can cover a broad range of cases and aid our moral reasoning as we encounter endless scenarios in which we might be tempted to hide, evade, or boldly declare the truth. But some might reasonably object that this framework is rather limited in scope. After all, truthfulness is not only a concern in one-to-one personal interactions. Lying is not merely a matter of "personal morality." There are much broader, perhaps even more serious, concerns when the truth is at stake. As Kevin DeLapp and Jeremy Henkel observe, many are beginning to wonder whether "the semantic notion of truth that has been the focus for so long may be too insipid to accomplish what we ultimately want truth to do."[32] What about the societal dimensions of truthfulness? In Chapter 7, I aim to show that the framework I have developed has much to say in response this question.

---

[31] Adapted from Dworkin, "10 Lies."
[32] Kevin DeLapp and Jeremy Henkel, eds., *Lying and Truthfulness* (Indianapolis 2016), 270.

7

A Thomistic Theory of Bullshit

While the morality of lying is a perennial problem, the present generation has expressed unprecedented concern about the status of truth in public discourse.[1] Oxford Dictionaries declared the term "post-truth" as the Word of the Year in 2016. According to the *Oxford English Dictionary*, "post-truth" is an adjective defined as "relating to or denoting circumstances in which objective facts are less influential in shaping public opinion than appeals to emotion and personal belief."[2] Of course, indifference to the truth is not a new phenomenon. In 1986, philosopher Harry Frankfurt published an article titled "On Bullshit" in the *Raritan Quarterly Review*, which was subsequently published as a small book and reached the *New York Times* best seller list. Frankfurt's analysis is considered by many to be the definitive analysis of bullshit, which he defines as a "lack of connection to a concern with truth" and an "indifference to how things really are."[3] Bullshit stands in contrast to outright lying, in which case the liar is concerned with the way things really are, even as he seeks to undermine it. Yet, there is nothing particularly novel about bullshit. Frankfurt remains agnostic as to whether there is relatively more bullshit nowadays than at any other time.[4] Nonetheless, recent concerns about the status of truth in public discourse and the decline of truth as a standard of communication are not without merit. These concerns are

---

[1] This chapter has been adapted from my article, "Post-truth and Vices Opposed to Truth," in the *Journal of the Society of Christian Ethics* 37:2 (2017): 97–116.
[2] "Word of the Year 2016," English Oxford Living Dictionaries, Oxford University Press, https://en.oxforddictionaries.com/word-of-the-year.
[3] Harry G. Frankfurt, *On Bullshit* (Princeton, NJ 2005), 33–34.
[4] Ibid., 62.

grounded in the observation that not only is the exercise of bullshit widespread but also the organizing structures of our society often encourage (or even demand) individuals to become practitioners of bullshit if they wish to be successful.[5]

The purpose of the present chapter is to bring some theological analysis and conceptual order to this cacophony of concerns. The specific failures of our post-truth society result from a deeper failure – namely, to consider truthfulness as a *virtue* – and these failures come into better focus when we examine some of the predominant approaches to the ethics of lying in both academic and popular discourse. Until we embrace a fully robust notion of truth as a virtue – and a fully robust notion of bullshit as an opposing vice – we will lack the philosophical and theological resources necessary to condemn the harm done by systemic bullshit. My analysis in this chapter unfolds in three sections. The first section reclassifies bullshit as a more precise kind of moral failure that I call "truth indifference." The second section constructs an account of truth indifference as structural sin that cannot be reduced to individual actors. The third section turns to the fundamental question of why truth should be considered a virtue – and the consequences that follow when the virtue of truth is ignored or forgotten. In the course of these analyses, I offer some reflections on contemporary Christian ethics and the problem of lying, concluding that these reflections illustrate why bullshit is not an isolated cultural phenomenon.

BULLSHIT AS A VICE OPPOSED TO TRUTHFULNESS

The first methodological move I wish to make is to reclassify (and rename) what Frankfurt refers to as "bullshit." While the primary purpose of this move is to provide a more accurate diagnosis of the problem I am addressing in this chapter, I have a narrower purpose as well – namely, to place this modified notion of bullshit within Aquinas's taxonomy of the vices opposed to truthfulness (*ST* II-II.110–113). Aquinas does not, of course, list bullshit – or any of its close cousins such as humbug, poppycock, balderdash, or malarkey – among the list of vices opposed to truth in the *secunda secundae*, although he does come close. For Aquinas, as we have seen, the virtue of truthful is annexed to the cardinal virtue of justice.

---

[5] For a staggering account the prevalence of bullshit in contemporary society, see Carl T. Bergstrom and Jevin D. West, *Calling Bullshit: The Art of Skepticism in a Data-Driven World* (New York 2020).

According to the well-known definition, justice is "a habit according to which a person, with a constant and perpetual will, renders to each that which is his or her right."[6] The virtue of truthfulness is annexed to justice in light of two distinct features: It is directed to another, and it establishes a certain equality among things by equating what is in one's mind with external signs – that is, the words one uses to expresses the contents of one's mind (*ST* II-II.109.3). While we are not obligated to reveal the contents of our minds in every instance, we owe it to each other to speak truthfully whenever we do choose to speak. This is why truthfulness is a moral virtue and not an intellectual virtue: manifesting the truth is an act of the will (*ST* II-II.109.3 ad 2).

All of the vices opposed to truthfulness share a common feature in that they evince a discrepancy between what one says (or writes) and what one really believes to be true. Thus, material falsehood, while morally relevant in some cases, is not a necessary feature of sins against truth. I can utter a statement that I *believe* to be false (perhaps in hopes of harming someone), but even if I am mistaken it does not change the fact that my principle of action is a vice opposed to truth (*ST* II-II.110.1). Aquinas explains that deception belongs to the "perfection" of the lie, but this is not its specific difference. We recall that all that is required for a lie is the principle of *locutio contra mentem*, to speak against one's own mind. This may strike some as counterintuitive since it is hard to imagine what could be wrong with a lie that is not only harmless but is not even meant to deceive. Very few people today are inclined to hold such a strict view of lying. But when we examine Aquinas's hierarchy of lies, we find that they actually do track contemporary concerns to a significant extent. He notes for example, that when "the good intended is greater, the culpability of lying is diminished accordingly" (*ST* II-II.110.2). This principle dictates his eightfold division of lies, following Augustine, in order of moral gravity.[7] The most serious of these are deemed "destructive" lies (*perniciosum*) and considered mortal sins. These are lies told with the explicit intention of harming others. Next, we find, in descending order of gravity: lies told out of the mere lust for lying, jocose lies, and lies that are meant to save oneself or others (yet

---

[6] *ST* II-II.58.1: "Et si quis vellet in debitam formam definitionis reducere, posset sic dicere, quod iustitia est habitus secundum quem aliquis constanti et perpetua voluntate ius suum unicuique tribuit. Et quasi est eadem definitio cum ea quam philosophus ponit, in V Ethic., dicens quod *iustitia est habitus secundum quem aliquis dicitur operativus secundum electionem iusti*."

[7] Augustine, *De mendacio*, 25. See Table 2.1.

harm no one). An example of the last would be the Hebrew midwives in the Book of Exodus, who lied to the Egyptians in order to save the firstborn Hebrew sons. On Aquinas's interpretation, the midwives are praised for their good intention in saving the children, but the specific act of lying was not morally praiseworthy. This eightfold taxonomy reflects Aquinas's conviction that, while the moral gravity of lies can vary significantly, there can never be a *good* lie insofar as the act of lying is inherently opposed to the virtue of truth.[8]

As we saw in Chapter 4, lying is not the only vice that is opposed to truthfulness. Aquinas counts dissimulation and hypocrisy among these vices, which are demonstrated in any misrepresentation of one's own mind through external signs. The criteria here are virtually the same as lying, with the only difference being that dissimulation misleads through externals signs other than spoken or written words (*ST* II-II.111.1). Someone who impersonates a police officer, for example, commits a sin against truth even if he never utters the statement "I am a police officer." Wearing an officer's badge and assuming an officer's authority are simply lying through actions rather than words. Also counted among the vices opposed to truth are what Aquinas calls "boasting" and "irony." Boasting (*iactantia*) refers to the act of describing oneself or one's abilities in excess of what one knows to be the case. Mock-modesty (*ironia*), or what we might today call self-deprecation or false humility, occurs when one belittles oneself beyond what one knows to be true. Again, the common theme of all vices opposed to truthfulness is that they misrepresent through external signification the contents of one's mind.

What is conspicuously missing from this list of vices is Frankfurt-style bullshit (or whatever its medieval analog might be). Yet, we can imagine how this might fit into Aquinas's taxonomy without much intellectual straining. Indeed, even Thomists in the manualist tradition came close to describing something like bullshit in their works of moral theology. Writing in the first half of the twentieth century, the manualists John McHugh and Charles Callan warn, "[T]hose who do not think before speaking, or who use language carelessly or inaccurately, may be guilty of injustice and deception, or even of indirect lying."[9] While their analysis

---

[8] More precisely, a lie – no matter where it falls within this taxonomy – will be something "not good" in the sense of being a nonfitting object of the power of speech. It reflects a kind of natural badness that should not be willed.
[9] John A. McHugh and Charles J. Callan, Moral Theology: A Complete Course Based on St. Thomas Aquinas and the Best Modern Authorities, vol. 2 (London 1929), § 2389(c).

of lying mostly tracks that of Aquinas in the *secunda secundae*, McHugh and Callan are not afraid to go out on a limb and make claims that go beyond what Aquinas says in his own writings. They write, for example, "But a lie need not be entirely false, and indeed one of the most dangerous lies is what is known as a half-truth, in which some real facts are told in order to give support to pretended facts, or in which valid arguments are adduced to throw dust in the eyes as regards other arguments that are sophistical."[10]

This claim that a "half-truth" is "one of the most dangerous lies" in some ways foreshadows Frankfurt's injunction against bullshit. It also raises the question of whether half-truths and bullshit are really worse, from a moral standpoint, than outright lies. Frankfurt does not mince words:

> Both in lying and in telling the truth people are guided by their beliefs concerning the way things are. These guide them as they endeavor either to describe the world correctly or to describe it deceitfully. For this reason, telling lies does not tend to unfit a person for telling the truth in the same way that bullshitting tends to. [...] The bullshitter ignores these demands altogether. He does not reject the authority of the truth, as the liar does, and oppose himself to it. He pays no attention to it at all. By virtue of this, bullshit is a greater enemy of the truth than lies are.[11]

Is Frankfurt right that bullshit is a greater enemy of the truth than lies are? I confess that I find this phrasing to be somewhat vague. Perhaps, we can reframe the question more straightforwardly and ask whether bullshit is morally worse than lying. If we want to follow Aquinas's approach, then I think the correct answer is: it depends. Just as conventional lying can vary by degree in moral gravity, so can bullshit. In isolated instances where the individual moral agent is the primary concern, it seems appropriate to ask whether bullshitting is morally worse than lying. To be fair, Frankfurt's formulation – that "bullshit is the greater enemy of the truth than lies are" – is more apropos when bullshit is considered as a structural problem, which is an important consideration in the forthcoming analysis. But first some important qualifications and corrections to Frankfurt's notion of bullshit need to be made in order to tailor it to the specific purposes of this essay.

For reasons that will soon become clear, I will be referring to *truth indifference* instead of bullshit in what follows. While my development and use of this term is clearly indebted to Frankfurt, there are some

---

[10] Ibid., § 2389(d).
[11] Frankfurt, *On Bullshit*, 59–61.

important differences from his analysis. The first distinction between bullshit and what I am calling truth indifference is found in their precise definitions. Frankfurt claims, "What bullshit essentially misrepresents is neither the state of affairs to which it refers nor the beliefs of the speaker concerning that state of affairs. Those are what lies misrepresent, by virtue of being false."[12] But I want to claim that truth indifference emphatically *does* misrepresent the beliefs of the speaker concerning a state of affairs. Namely, truth indifference is exhibited when someone claims to believe that x is the case, when really she does not know (and, perhaps as an additional feature, does not *care* to know) if x is in fact the case. This can occur in a variety of contexts, and it does not require that the speaker harbor any deep-seated antirealist position about the possibility of truth claims, as Frankfurt seems to suggest in places.[13] Truth indifference thus meets the Thomistic criterion of *contra mentem* and therefore belongs among the list of vices opposed to truth. Yet, it is sufficiently distinguished from lying in that the speaker is unconcerned (at least for the moment) with the way things really are. Deception is not the goal of truth indifference. Or we might say that truth indifference is only concerned with deceiving the listener about the content of the speaker's *mind* – the speaker wants the listener to *think* the speaker is concerned with the truth, and she is unconcerned about whether or not the statement misleads the listener about the facts at hand.[14] In some cases, the only "fact" at hand might be a subjective expression of the speaker's mental state.[15] Take, for instance, the ubiquitous mantra of retail and service industries, "Your call is important to

[12] Ibid., 53–54.
[13] Ibid., 61–62.
[14] Frankfurt comes close to offering a definition similar to the one I am proposing when he writes, "What [the bullshitter] does necessarily attempt to deceive us about is his enterprise. His only indispensably distinctive characteristic is that in a certain way he misrepresents what he is up to" (54). But given Frankfurt's broader analysis of bullshit, it is not always clear that bullshitters directly intend to mislead about their actual beliefs. Sometimes, Frankfurt writes as if the paradigmatic bullshitter does not even think that his statement *can* have a truth value but that he is simply "playing along" according to society's mores. By articulating the notion of truth indifference as I have in this essay, I am attempting to avoid such unnecessary intellectual baggage.
[15] In *ST* II-II.70.4 ad 1, Aquinas offers some relevant remarks about the "degrees of certitude" in our assertions. While he is specifically addressing legal testimony here, the principle can be applied in a more general way to all assertions: "When giving evidence, a person should not affirm with certainty something that is not certain, as if it were known. A person should admit one's doubts using doubtful language, and express certainty using certain language."

us." The only fact in question is whether the speaker (most likely heard through an audio recording) really meant this statement when it was uttered. The point is that truth indifference is a kind misrepresentation, and thus, it is perhaps more closely related to lying than is Frankfurt's notion of bullshit.[16]

The most important distinction I wish to capture by my use of "truth indifference," however, is its systemic nature. Throughout history, there have always been bullshitters, jokesters, swindlers, and those who play fast and loose with the truth. But systemic truth indifference, as I understand it, is a unique product of modern societal structures. I think this partly explains why Frankfurt's book on bullshit is written the way it is. Just as Frankfurt acknowledges that bullshit has existed since the dawn of the human race, he also observes that we have no theory of bullshit.[17] But does it not seem odd that no one has articulated a theory until now? In the concluding section of the book, Frankfurt offers some brief speculation as to why the presence of bullshit is so great in present-day society. He writes, "Bullshit is unavoidable whenever circumstances require someone to talk without knowing what he is talking about."[18] Frankfurt offers this tantalizing suggestion without saying much more. But I believe that this insight provides a clue into what I am calling truth indifference and its systemic nature.

THE STRUCTURAL SIN OF TRUTH INDIFFERENCE

The notion of structural sin is a relatively recent development in Christian moral theology. As Jim Keenan observes, contemporary theologians "are on the verge of seeing a newer, more robust, and definitely more

---

[16] Thomas Carson has recently argued that Frankfurt is mistaken about three specific claims, namely that (1) bullshit requires the intention to deceive (at least about the speaker himself), (2) bullshit does not constitute lying, and (3) bullshitters are unlike liars in that they are unconcerned with the truth of what they say. Regarding (1), I think that Carson has a point insofar as many of Frankfurt's examples could be described as equivocation and distinguished from bullshit proper. I believe that Carson fails to make the case against (2), seeing that his counterexamples are simply lies and not bullshit. Similarly, I believe he fails to make the case against (3) because his counterexamples are all instances of equivocation. In my judgment, all of these concerns can be remedied by simply distinguishing evasion through *equivocation* from evasion through *bullshit* proper. Thus, in my discussion of Frankfurt, I have limited myself to an analysis of bullshit that is clearly distinguished from equivocation. See Thomas L. Carson, *Lying and Deception: Theory and Practice* (New York 2010), 58–63.
[17] Frankfurt, *On Bullshit*, 1.
[18] Ibid., 63.

social understanding of sin emerging that, while attentive to questions related to the voluntary and therefore to culpability, seems more interested in the fact and pervasiveness of sin as well as its roots in both the human condition and our social structures."[19] While Keenan's description emphasizes the "newness" of such approaches, there are ways to think about social and structural forms of sin that stand in continuity with older traditions. Keenan approvingly cites Oscar Romero's definition of structural sin, taken from his Second Pastoral Letter, written in 1977: "The Church has denounced sin for centuries. It has certainly denounced the sin of the individual, and it has denounced the sin which perverts relationships between human beings, particularly at the family level. But now it has reminded us of what has been fundamental from the beginning of social sin, that is to say, the crystallization of individual egoisms in permanent structures which maintain this sin and exerts its power over the great majorities."[20] The point here is that our social structures have histories, and those histories are shaped in part by the sins of the human beings composing those structures. The effects of these sins can become embedded in the very organizational structures of these institutions, creating environments in which certain sins are nourished or even inevitable.[21]

To be clear, Aquinas does not have a theory of structural sin. In his *Disputed Questions on Evil* (*De Malo*), he does not appear to consider the question of whether social structures can be sinful. While his analysis does extend beyond discrete sinful acts, into the broader domain of sin as a condition, the reader who seeks anything approaching modern conceptions of structural sin is bound to be disappointed. If anything, the reader of *De Malo* will be disposed to harbor suspicion of some theories of structural sin, given their tendency to describe "evil" in ways that ascribe agency to institutions abstracted from the human beings of which they are composed. For Aquinas, evil can have no agency of its own. Following the Augustinian notion of evil as a privation of the good, he

---

[19] James F. Keenan, "Raising Expectations on Sin," *Theological Studies* 77, no. 1 (2016): 165–180; cited at 165.
[20] Quoted in Ibid., 178.
[21] For some helpful recent work on structural sin, see *Moral Agency within Social Structures and Culture: A Primer on Critical Realism for Christian Ethics*, ed. Daniel K. Finn (Washington, DC: 2020), Daniel J. Daly, *The Structures of Virtue and Vice* (Washington, DC 2021), and David Cloutier, "Cavanaugh and Grimes on Structural Evils of Violence and Race: Overcoming Conflicts in Contemporary Social Ethics," *Journal of the Society of Christian Ethics* 37:2 (2017) 59–78.

declares that "evil is not any 'thing,' but the object attributed as 'evil' is something."[22] The closest Aquinas ever comes to describing social sin, in my estimation, is in his brief comment in the *Summa*'s treatise on law. In an article addressing the question of whether the natural law is the same in all people, he explains that sometimes knowledge of the natural law can "fail" due to the passions, or to an evil habit, or to an evil disposition of nature. As an example, he cites the Germans who "in previous times did not consider pillaging and plundering to be wrong, although it is expressly contrary to the natural law."[23] What is interesting about Aquinas's example is that it describes an entire people group. Granted, a people group is not the same thing as a social structure, but I find it intriguing that the only example he provides is meant to illustrate that an evil habit can develop across an entire society. He could have just as easily provided an example of an individual person who, over time, had developed an evil disposition and thereby eroded his or her knowledge of the natural law. Instead, he cites the Germans of ages past – and their widespread moral blindness due to a deeply ingrained habit, established through the repeated practice of plundering – as a prime example of such a failure. Perhaps this suggests that the paradigmatic instance of the natural law's failure due to moral corruption occurs when an entire society has collectively developed vicious habits.

Regardless of whether Aquinas's brief comments are meant to suggest an analysis of the social dynamics of sin, I think that there is a plausible Thomistic framework for thinking about structural sin. I want to suggest that institutions and social structures, while not moral agents per se, can possess something analogous to moral habits (virtues and vices), and that these "habits" are not reducible to the collective habits of the individuals composing the institution. If we are to take Aquinas's remarks about the Germans at face value, then we can easily imagine that a person born into such a society faces, at the very least, an uphill moral battle. When the moral environment in which one is raised bends toward certain vices, it is almost inevitable that he will also develop the same vicious habits as his own principles of action. This is not to say that these habits can never be avoided or overcome. But it would be accurate to say that the widespread influence of the relevant vices creates the conditions for the development

---

[22] *De malo* I.1: "Unde dico quod id quod est malum non est aliquid, set id cui accidit esse malum est aliquid, in quantum malum priuat nonnisi aliquod particulare bonum."
[23] *ST* I-II.94.4: "sicut apud germanos olim latrocinium non reputabatur iniquum, cum tamen sit expresse contra legem naturae, ut refert Iulius Caesar, in libro de bello Gallico."

of vicious habits in individuals. To put this in Thomistic terms: A social structure is sinful when it encourages particular vices by connecting them to genuine and necessary goods; in doing so, the natural (i.e., unchosen) objects of the will (such as health, shelter, and food) cannot be achieved without vice.

Again, I want to suggest that structural sin amounts to something more than simply a large number of people who happen to share the same vicious habits. In order for sin to be structural, the vicious "habit" must transcend the individuals (or sum of individuals) and become embedded in the institutional fabric of the structure. In Romero's terms, "the crystallization of individual egoisms" becomes ensconced "in permanent structures which maintain this sin."[24] The outcome of this effect is that it creates the conditions for the vice to flourish and that it "inclines" the structure toward vice. To be clear, I do not want to create a dichotomy between structural sin and individual sin. While it is possible that the existence of structural sin may mitigate the sin attributed to an individual's actions, these are not mutually exclusive categories. While I do not want to ascribe moral agency to social structures, I do want to affirm that they can have a causal effect in moral agency. Here I am following Daniel Finn, who writes, "Social structures are not conscious agents and so they cannot sin in any literal sense. But since they have causal effect through the choices made by persons within them, they can be described as sinful when the restrictions, enablements, and incentives those persons encounter encourage morally evil actions."[25]

Thus far, I have tried to lay the necessary groundwork for the claim that truth indifference can be understood as structural sin. By "structural truth indifference" I mean any institution or organization of people in which the vice of truth indifference is encouraged or rewarded through some combination of explicit or implicit policies, and the enforcement of this behavior is not the responsibility of any one person. Given this definition, there are certain social structures that come readily to mind. The world of advertising, for example, is one of the most obvious examples of structural truth indifference. No one doubts that the singular goal of advertising, despite its manifold truth claims, is to sell product. And advertising is so deeply imbedded in Western society that it is impossible to avoid; neither can anyone working in the industry avoid the practice

---

[24] Quoted in Keenan, "Raising Expectations on Sin," 178. See fn. 20.
[25] Daniel K. Finn, "What Is a Sinful Social Structure?" *Theological Studies* 77, no. 1 (2016): 136–164, at 154–155.

of truth indifference. It is, in fact, required. Frankfurt writes, "The realms of advertising and of public relations, and the nowadays closely related realm of politics, are replete with instances of bullshit so unmitigated that they can serve among the most indisputable and classic paradigms of the concept."[26] But what Frankfurt's analysis neglects, however, is the fact that these realms not only provide paradigm *instances* of bullshit but that those instances are very often the *inevitable products* of the environment in which they arose. This is not to say that the individuals who utter bullshit statements can claim no moral responsibility for their actions. But it is worth going beyond Frankfurt's analysis and considering whether institutions themselves can become infected, so to speak, with the vice of truth indifference. If so, how does this happen, and how should we confront it?

Before turning directly to specific cases of truth indifference, it will be helpful to consider a case that can be described as outright *lying* at the structural level. Recently, the Volkswagen corporation was caught in an emissions-cheating scandal that permeated its entire organization. Volkswagen had been installing "defeat devices" in hundreds of thousands of vehicles that were programmed to "trick" emissions testing software. As a result, they were able to sell cars that boasted impressive miles-per-gallon ratios while still (ostensibly) qualifying as low-emission vehicles. Volkswagen's competitors were mystified. Writing in *Atlantic*, Jerry Useem describes the kind of culture that was fostered at Volkswagen, observing, "You cannot unconsciously install a 'defeat device' into hundreds of thousands of cars. You need to be sneaky, and thus deliberate."[27] He cites sociologist Diane Vaughan, who coined the phrase "normalization of deviance" to describe the kind of psychological process by which entire swathes of employees perform tasks that were once classified as "not okay" but are slowly reclassified as "okay."[28] But in cases like Volkswagen, this kind of deliberation at least *begins* as conscious deliberation, even if the shift toward deception is less than a conscious choice. In cases of truth indifference, however, the deliberation that results is all the more elusive.

Finally, a brief word of clarification: What I am trying to describe in this chapter are the *conceptual* dimensions of truth indifference, especially as they manifest themselves in particular social structures. I am

---

[26] Frankfurt, *On Bullshit*, 22.
[27] Jerry Useem, "What Was Volkswagen Thinking? On the Origins of Corporate Evil – and Idiocy," *Atlantic Monthly*, January–February 2016, www.theatlantic.com/magazine/archive/2016/01/what-was-volkswagen-thinking/419127/.
[28] Ibid.

not attempting an analysis of "indifference to truth" as a broad cultural value. In other words, there might be a way to talk about what contemporary society values (or does not value) in the vein of sociological description. We might want to make the claim, for example, that Americans are simply less concerned with the truth values of the claims being made in the media they encounter on a day-to-day basis. We might then be inclined to give some sort of account of how this state of affairs came about. But this is not the kind of analysis I am interested in doing here. I am interested in truth indifference as a social and structural habit, a principle of action, which is habituated in persons or organizations. My aim in this chapter is to consider how indifference to truth, as a cultural value, can lead to structural truth indifference. I am not attempting to describe how or why our society has adopted the value of indifference to truth in the first place. In other words, I am not giving a genealogy. It is important to maintain these methodological boundaries in order to ensure that I am doing moral analysis and not sociological analysis.

THE REHABILITATION OF *VERACITAS*

Thus far, I have argued that (1) truth indifference can be understood as a vice opposed to the virtue of truth; (2) truth indifference can describe a habit in a person and, by analogy, in social structures, and in fact these two aspects of truth indifference are often concomitant; and (3) we can find prominent manifestations of structural truth indifference in current social structures relating to finance, politics, and media. At the core of this analysis, however, is the fundamental claim that truthfulness is a virtue. In what follows, I comment on what I take to be some deficiencies in the discipline of Christian ethics when engaging the ethics of lying and truthfulness.

First, a general observation regarding the status of truth indifference and the degree to which people find it morally offensive. Regarding bullshit, Frankfurt observes, "[P]eople tend to be more tolerant of bullshit than of lies, perhaps because we are less inclined to take the former as a personal affront."[29] I would add to this that people recognize the fact that bullshit and truth indifference are simply part of "the system," and we are sympathetic to those who must make truth indifferent statements as a necessary feature of their occupations – perhaps because

---
[29] Frankfurt, *On Bullshit*, 27.

most of us have been in similar situations ourselves. Thus, we do not flinch when a media relations representative offers a boilerplate apology for her corporation's malfeasances.[30] We expect insincerity and truth indifference as unfortunate but necessary outcomes of our current social structures. Frankfurt writes, "We may seek to distance ourselves from bullshit, but we are more likely to turn away from it with an impatient or irritated shrug than with the sense of violation or outrage that lies often inspire. The problem of understanding why our attitude toward bullshit is generally more benign than our attitude toward lying is an important one, which I shall leave as an exercise for the reader."[31] But what Frankfurt has chosen to bracket in his essay is central to my own concerns in this chapter.

While I have no pretense of having provided a complete genealogy of present-day structural truth indifference – let alone providing a "cure" for it – I do want to argue that contemporary ethicists lack the conceptual resources to analyze and confront it.[32] Many ethicists have proposed precepts against lying (or at least certain kinds of lies), but very few have tried to give an account of truth indifference, which falls short of lying. This is a result of failing to consider truthfulness as a virtue. It seems that even most Thomists and virtue ethicists who have written on lying fail to consider the significance of the fact that Aquinas's own analysis of lying falls within his discussion of the virtue of truthfulness.[33] Nearly every Christian ethicist writing on lying approaches the topic, either explicitly or implicitly, from a deontological or consequentialist perspective. But there is no reason why, in a Thomistic framework, that norms against lying should be incompatible with a virtue perspective.[34]

---

[30] For a relevant and insightful analysis of the ethics of apologies, see Darlene Fozard Weaver, "Apologies and Their Import for the Moral Identity of Offenders," *Journal of the Society of Christian Ethics* 36:1 (2016): 87–105.

[31] Frankfurt, *On Bullshit*, 27.

[32] Here, I should acknowledge that my own project provides an inadequate basis for combatting structural truth indifference. Many additional resources would be needed. At the very least, we would also need to develop a robust account of the role of *trust* in society. On this front, see Kevin Vallier, *Trust in a Polarized Age* (New York 2020) and Thomas O. Buford, *Trust, Our Second Nature: Crisis, Reconciliation, and the Personal* (Lanham, MD 2009).

[33] One of the most notable examples of this oversight is found in Tollefsen's *Lying and Christian Ethics*, in which the analysis of the virtue of truthfulness is confined to two pages (124–125).

[34] For a helpful analysis of the intersection of virtue (specifically the virtue of justice) and moral precepts, see Jean Porter, *Justice as a Virtue*, 38–42 and 151–152.

As I have already noted, there are some features of Aquinas's position on lying that render it unappealing to contemporary ethicists. Moreover, from one perspective, it might seem as if Aquinas has two very different concepts of lying: venial lies (sins against truth) and mortal lies (sins against neighbor). But as the foregoing analysis of truth indifference shows, we cannot be indifferent to the truth without also disposing ourselves to harm our neighbor. Aquinas's understanding of human beings as social animals, as well as his understanding of language, does not allow concerns of truth to be easily bracketed from concerns relating to one's neighbor. We may not find much in common between "benevolent" lies and malicious lies, but Aquinas shows us why both of these are sins against truth. On Aquinas's account of lying, there can never be exceptions to the prohibition against telling willful falsehoods because lying can never be *good*. There is no such thing as a "good lie" or a "virtuous lie," because the act of lying is an act against our own nature as linguistic animals, a violation of that which constitutes human flourishing. Truth is necessarily a virtue, "because to say what is true is a good act; and virtue is that which makes its possessor good, and it renders one's actions good."[35] Not all lies are equal, of course, and there are a number of factors that can mitigate the sin of lying – sometimes even reducing it to the most miniscule of venial sins.[36] But Aquinas's approach to lying provides us with a radical alternative to the predominant norm-based approaches to lying, the latter of which display a paucity of resources for understanding why lying is morally *bad*. By the same token, the virtue of truth becomes a casualty of norm-based approaches since they can offer no account of why many kinds of lies – such as benevolent or harmless lies – ought not to be told. And when truth is no longer a virtue, we are ill equipped to condemn structural truth indifference.

Many ethicists who write on lying hold to some version of the following principle: As long as you are not harming anyone, you do not owe anyone the truth. Most often, the concept of *harm* is ill defined. But for Aquinas, the virtue of truth is situated within the broader context of the virtue of justice. Moreover, the virtue of truth is grounded in our natural inclinations as social animals. It is these considerations that allow

---

[35] ST II-II.109.1: "Et talis veritas, sive veracitas, necesse est quod sit virtus, quia hoc ipsum quod est dicere verum est bonus actus; virtus autem est quae bonum facit habentem, et opus eius bonum reddit."
[36] ST II-II.110.3. See also Lawrence Dewan, "Saint Thomas, Lying, and Venial Sin."

Aquinas to write, "Since human beings are social animals, one person naturally owes another that without which the preservation of human society would not be possible."[37] This means that we owe each other not simply a duty not to harm, but the *truth*. Again, this requirement is qualified by the condition that, in order for truthfulness to be an act of virtue, it must be "clothed with due circumstances."[38] Truthfulness is the mark of a virtuous human being; the virtuous truthteller is one who only speaks the truth but also knows when, how, and where to speak it. Simply put, the virtuous truthteller values the truth and in doing so renders others their due as an act of justice. In a society in which the opposing vice – truth indifference – is cultivated, truth is devalued and bullshit is inevitable. And if structural sin, as I understand it, is something other than the direct expression of deliberate, conscious human action, then it is not difficult to imagine how a society's general stance toward truth might result in structural truth indifference.

Some philosophers and theologians writing on the ethics of lying have tried to recapture the notion of truthfulness as a virtue. Yet, nearly all of them have failed to avoid collapsing into consequentialism. This becomes clear when they are forced to confront the hard cases of lying and determine that there must be exceptions to the precept "do not lie." Rather than follow Aquinas by articulating a richly textured taxonomy of lies and deploying analytical tools like the mortal/venial distinction, these thinkers insist that lying is morally permissible in some cases, or that "lying" must be redefined so that many instances of lying are no longer considered as such.[39] These thinkers are of course free to pursue these kinds of arguments, but such approaches cannot be reconciled with an understanding of truth as a virtue. To try to reconcile them can only lead to absurd conclusions. We find this, for example, in Ronald Preston's entry on "lying" in *A New Dictionary of Christian Ethics*, in which he writes: "In order to have the discernment to know when a lie is called for, one needs to be habitually truthful."[40] Aquinas would find such a

---

[37] *ST* II-II.109.3 ad 1: "Ad primum ergo dicendum quod quia homo est animal sociale, naturaliter unus homo debet alteri id sine quo societas humana conservari non posset."

[38] *ST* II-II.109.1 ad 2: "Sed hoc non sufficit ad hoc quod sit actus virtutis, sed ad hoc requiritur quod ulterius debitis circumstantiis vestiatur, quae si non observentur, erit actus vitiosus" ("But it is not enough for this to be an act of virtue. It must also be clothed in due circumstances, which, if not observed, will render it a vicious act").

[39] For an example of the former, see Carson, *Lying and Deception*, 257–266. For an example of the latter, see Janet E. Smith, "Fig Leaves and Falsehoods."

[40] James F. Childress and John Macquarrie, eds., *A New Dictionary of Christian Ethics* (London 1986), 363.

statement unfathomable. How can the goal of a virtue contradict the very object of its habituation? If Preston's remark is reflective of the current state of Christian ethics on this topic, then this only reveals the incoherence of our current intuitions about lying.

For Aquinas, truthfulness is a virtue. This means not only that truth is something to be valued but also that truthfulness requires speaking in the right way, at the right time, and with proper regard for one's interlocutors. In order to exercise the virtue of truthfulness, one must also possess a concomitant set of virtues comprising affability, practical wisdom, and humility. When these aspects are displaced by an approach that focuses only on moral norms, or an analysis of bullshit that only considers the most obvious injustices that result when truth indifference is already firmly habituated at the structural level, then our resources as ethicists will be severely limited. What is needed is a rehabilitation of *veracitas*. Our analyses of these problems must begin with an understanding of lying and truth indifferences as distinct vices opposed to the virtue of truth. While the virtue of truth, or truthfulness (*veracitas*), is to be distinguished from truth itself (*veritas*), these terms are not bound together by mere semantic coincidence.[41] As Peter Geach writes,

> For Aquinas the *malitia* of lying consists in speaking contrary to one's own mind, *locutio contra mentem*. A man's mind is of course not a rule or measure of truth, but unless he is exceptionally corrupt he at least desires to orient his mind to Truth. And Truth is God, even though in aiming at truth one may not explicitly realise this. So *locutio contra mentem* of its nature makes it harder to orient oneself to God.[42]

This is not an instance of theological sleight of hand. Rather, it is a powerful reminder that we must be mindful of the ultimate end to which our (truthful) language is oriented. If structural truth indifference is a vice, then we must be more attentive to the ways in which it inhibits the virtue of truthfulness in all areas of our lives.

---

[41] Aquinas clarifies the different meanings of "truth" in *ST* II-II.109.1. For a fascinating and, at times, troubling exploration of the tension between these two senses of "truth," see Bernard Williams, *Truth & Truthfulness* (Princeton, NJ 2002).
[42] Peter Geach, "Truth, Truthfulness, and Trust," 57.

Conclusion

TRUTHFULNESS AS A HABIT

"What is the harm in lying?" This question often serves as a rough-and-ready litmus test for the would-be liar. In situations in which it appears advantageous to lie, many people feel justified in doing so if it does not harm anyone as a result. And it seems that academic philosophers are just as eager as ordinary folk to embrace this principle. Writers like Sissela Bok have made it the touchstone of their ethical ruminations on the permissibility of lying. "Truthful statements are preferable to lies in the absence of special considerations," Bok avers.[1] What are these special considerations? One must consider "the effects of undiscovered lies on the choices of liars and dupes" and "the impact of discovered and suspected lies on trust and social cooperation."[2] Lest these criteria seem too subjective, she counsels any would-be liar to conduct a Rawlsian thought experiment: Would a jury of one's peers find the lie under consideration to be justified, given the circumstances? If so, then one may proceed. If not, the lie is most likely impermissible.[3]

The problem with Bok's position is that it is too reasonable. That is to say, her position is so wildly sensible that it allows us to neglect the philosophical, linguistic, and ethical difficulties that present themselves when we reflect on the value of truth. It only reinforces our moral blind spots. It uncritically accepts the assumption that the morality of lying is strictly

---

[1] Sissela Bok, *Lying: Moral Choice in Public and Private Life*, 30.
[2] Ibid.
[3] See Chapter 7, "Justification," in Bok, *Lying*, 90–106.

a matter of justice. When this assumption serves as one's starting point, it should come as no surprise that harmless or beneficial lies are deemed morally permissible. While, according to Bok, truthful statements should generally be prioritized over lies, this principle (which she refers to as "the principle of veracity"[4]) is only one of a competing set of principles that may come into conflict in difficult situations.

While the principle of veracity in some ways echo Aquinas's virtue of *veracitas*, or truthfulness, it is only a pale imitation. For Bok, the value of truthfulness is found in its avoidance of harm and its contribution to the maintenance of social institutions.[5] Its value is therefore wholly negative: It prevents harm and it prevents institutions from collapsing. But it cannot give us a positive account of why it is simply good to be truthful. Aquinas, like Bok, believes that truthfulness helps us to avoid injustice, and he believes that truthfulness plays an important role in maintaining valuable social structures (*ST* II-II.109.3 ad 1).[6] But more importantly, he believes that truthfulness is a virtue because it makes its possessor a *good person*: "Truth, or truthfulness, must necessarily be a virtue, because to say what is true is a good act; and virtue is that which makes its possessor good, and renders one's actions good."[7] The object of *veracitas* is truth (*veritas*) itself. Truthfulness in our speech promotes knowledge of the truth, and, as Aristotle reminds us, "All human beings by nature desire to know."[8] This does not mean that truth is strictly an individual good. Indeed, we do not have to "extend" the value of truth to the social realm – it is inherently social, for the simple reason that human beings are social animals. The natural function of language is to *communicate*, and communication relies on a shared assumption of truthfulness among members of a linguistic community. It is in this sense that *veracitas* is a social virtue.

---

[4] Bok, *Lying*, 30.
[5] Bok writes, "[T]rust in some degree of veracity functions as a *foundation* of relations among human beings; when this trust shatters or wears away, institutions collapse," *Lying*, 31.
[6] The maintenance of social institutions is not an intrinsic good, since it is possible for social institutions to be evil. A gang, for example, may rely on truthfulness among its members in order to flourish. As I argued in Chapter 7, many institutions actually require a *disregard* for truth in order to thrive.
[7] *ST* II-II.109.1: "Et talis veritas, sive veracitas, necesse est quod sit virtus, quia hoc ipsum quod est dicere verum est bonus actus; virtus autem est quae bonum facit habentem, et opus eius bonum reddit."
[8] Aristotle, *Metaphysics*, Books 1–9, Loeb Classical Library, 271, trans. Hugh Tredennick (Cambridge, MA 1933), I.1.

Veracitas is more than a description or property of certain speech acts. It is a habit – a habit that resides in a person even when she is not speaking. For Bok, "being truthful" is synonymous with expressing the truth with words. On this view, there are some instances in which one should not be truthful. For Aquinas, however, "being truthful" is synonymous with possessing the habit, or virtue, of *veracitas*. The virtuous person who possesses the habit of *veracitas* does not reveal the truth indiscriminately to anyone she encounters. Rather, she knows *when* and *how* to express the truth (*ST* II-II.109.1 ad 2). She knows when to exercise prudence and she holds the truth back (*dissimulatio*) when appropriate (*ST* II-II.110.3 ad 4). But neither does she willingly tell any falsehoods; she does not utter statements that assert what is contrary to her own mind. This is not always easy. Very frequently, it will be easier and much more convenient to tell a lie than to tell the truth – and the temptation will be even more powerful when we know that no one will be directly harmed by our lies. Some people will like us less for being truthful. As Iago laments in Shakespeare's *Othello*,

> O wretched fool
> That lov'st to make thine honesty a vice!
> O monstrous world! Take note, take note, O world,
> To be direct and honest is not safe.[9]

Yet, like all virtues, the virtue of *veracitas* is a constant and stable feature of a person's character. Since the virtue of *veracitas* incorporates the exercise of prudence by its very definition, and since sometimes being truthful means remaining silent, there is no instance (*pace* Bok) in which truthfulness, rightfully understood, is inappropriate.

Any lie, no matter its end or purpose, is opposed to the virtue of *veracitas*. No lie can arise from this virtue nor can it contribute to its cultivation. In this sense, there are no "harmless" lies. It is true that many lies do no injustice to one's interlocutor. But every time we make a conscious, willing decision either to tell the truth or to tell a lie, we either exercise the virtue of *veracitas* or we work against it. In the case of the person who disregards this virtue and tells harmless, white lies whenever convenient, "[A] soul that should be a mirror of Truth is covered with hundreds of tiny scratches."[10] Many people intuitively share

---

[9] William Shakespeare, *The Oxford Shakespeare: Othello: The Moor of Venice*, ed. Michael Neill (New York 2008), Act 3, Scene 3. The irony here is that these words are spoken by the most deceitful character in the play.
[10] Peter Geach, "Truth, Truthfulness, and Trust," 57.

this understanding of the intrinsic value of truthfulness, even if they cannot articulate it. Parents will correct young children who tell bald faced lies, for example, even if the lie is harmless and deceives no one. What are they trying to teach their children if not the inherent importance of truthfulness? When we care about raising children who will develop into truthful persons, we are not only concerned about avoiding harm – our aim is for them to become good human beings. These observations suggest that we must first develop a coherent notion of truthfulness before we can assess the morality of lying. As I have argued, the virtue of truthfulness tells us something about the purposes of human language. A Thomistic framework that places *veracitas* in its rightful place can generate a more precise taxonomy of speech acts, demonstrating the ways in which these acts and their corresponding habits are opposed to the virtues of truth and justice.

MORTAL AND VENIAL LIES

The Christian tradition has consistently recognized that lying is a sin. Even in the earliest periods of the Christian church, however, there were prominent figures who maintained that some lies may be justified and that the prohibition against lying may come into conflict with other obligations.[11] These were exceptional cases, and lies were only permitted as a last resort. Later, in the Western tradition, some theologians and moral manualists attempted to redefine lying in such a way as to allow for certain falsehoods. Against these, Aquinas maintained the Augustinian definition of lying as "speaking against one's mind," as well as the Augustinian position that no lie is without sin. What most of Aquinas's interpreters have missed, however, is the important difference between him and Augustine on the nature of lying. Whereas Augustine believes that all lies violate the eighth commandment of the Decalogue, Aquinas posits the radical idea that lying *per se* is only venially sinful. Lies that violate the Decalogue are always something more than just "lies": they bear false witness *against one's neighbor*, and we call such actions slander, gossip, perjury, and so on. Augustine begrudgingly acknowledges that some lies are venial sins, but he considers these to be exceptions rather than the norm – they participate less fully in the nature of lying than other, more serious lies. But for Aquinas, the nature of lying is simply to speak *contra mentem*, against one's mind, and oftentimes that is

---

[11] See Boniface Ramsey, "Two Traditions on Lying."

all there is to it. We do not intend to harm anyone; we simply say what we believe to be false because it is convenient or brings us pleasure. Such lies are sins against truthfulness, but it is not the sort of sin that will separate one from God's charity.

If lying is venially sinful, then it is not a sin against justice. To be consistent, Aquinas must address the sin of lying without reference to the Decalogue, and he is the first major figure in Christian history to do so. He marshals antique sources to aid in this endeavor: Cicero, who provides the conceptual link between truth and justice, and Aristotle, who provides the vocabulary for truthfulness as a virtue. Aquinas does not simply restate their positions, however; the notion of *veracitas* he develops is uniquely his own. What this allows him to do is to explain why lying – even mild, harmless lying – is a sin against truth. At the same time, it allows him to narrow, with unprecedented precision and clarity, the scope of lies that violate the eighth commandment. It is only these lies, which are mortal sins, that are truly "impermissible," insofar as they transgress the eternal law. The result is that Aquinas's position addresses and, to some degree, accommodates the concerns of the minority strand in the Christian tradition that considers some lies permissible. While proponents of this tradition may still find his position unsatisfying, Aquinas's interpreters would do well to recognize that he is closer to this strand of thought than has been previously recognized.

Aquinas's distinction between mortal and venial lies also has an advantage in that it maps onto moral intuitions held by many people today. While most people sense that there is something wrong with lies that cause harm to others, it is not easy to give an account of why so-called "harmless" lies are problematic. Aquinas would be sympathetic to this epistemological gap. He would point out that mortal lies are a clear violation of justice, and as such they run against the first principle of practical reason: "Pursue good and avoid evil" (*ST* I-II.94.2). It is less clear, however, that lies that are merely opposed to truthfulness (but not opposed to justice *per se*) are morally problematic. Aquinas can give an account of why this this is so, but it does not change the fact, on his view, that lying can never be a morally good act. *Veracitas* is a virtue annexed to justice, and our obligation to speak truthfully has the nature, not of legal debt, but of moral debt. To understand this requires a deep probe into human nature, the functions of human language, and the conditions of postlapsarian humanity – in other words, the tasks of the present volume.

THE THOMISTIC INSIGHT

Aquinas's great insight on the morality of lying is that lies are not first and foremost sins against justice. They are sins against *veracitas*, which is closely related to justice but should not be conflated with it. This insight – novel in Aquinas's day and neglected in our own – is the impetus for this book. One of the inherent difficulties with such a project is that present ethical discourse has wedded *moral wrongdoing* to the notion of *harm*. The monogamous relationship between these two concepts allows for no other partners. As a result, we find it difficult to conceive of truthfulness as a virtue, since violations of truthfulness do not necessarily cause harm to anyone.[12]

Moral philosophers and theologians have struggled to translate Aquinas's position on lying into the idiom of contemporary philosophical discourse. The difficulty in translating Aquinas's insight for our own day is only compounded by the fact that his insights regarding the virtue of *veracitas* are closely related to another concept that is completely alien to contemporary ethical discourse: the distinction between mortal and venial sin. This distinction is precluded (perhaps by definition) from the realm of moral philosophy, and it is quickly becoming extinct in the realm of moral theology. Readers will likely have noticed that this book deploys this distinction without reservation or modification. This practice reflects two closely related convictions, namely, a conviction that it is best to avoid "translating" Aquinas's thought, whenever possible, and a conviction that the mortal–venial distinction is worth rehabilitating. I cannot adequately defend these convictions here, but I do hope that Chapters 1–7 will have the effect of persuading at least a few readers that this is a fruitful approach to a complex set of moral questions.

Much has been written on Aquinas's position on lying, but no one has adequately accounted for the nuances or the implications of this position. Many of his readers have missed the great Thomistic insight, which is found in the combination of two principles: (1) all lies are sins against truth and yet (2) many lies are so minimally sinful that they can only be considered "bad" in a highly qualified sense. This dual commitment serves as the cornerstone of my project. Most contemporary Christian ethicists, however, err in defending one of these principles at

---

[12] For a representative example of this way of thinking about lying and harmfulness, see Bernard Gert, *Common Morality: Deciding What to Do* (New York 2004), 40-42.

the expense of the other. John Skalko, for example, attempts to defend Aquinas's prohibition of lying as an exceptionless moral norm, but in so doing he equates all lying with murder: "If you can lie for the sake of the common good, then why can you not murder?"[13] Julius Dorszynski, on the other hand, elevates the notion of one's "right to the truth" to the extent that a lie told to an unjust aggressor is entirely without sin.[14] These claims reflect divergent intuitions about the nature of lying; both are at odds with Aquinas, albeit for different reasons. Some of Aquinas's defenders, in striving to maintain the strictness of his prohibition, have also sought to answer difficult cases by allowing speech acts like equivocation to fall outside the definition of lying. In short, they want to decrease the scope of moral action we call "lying" while emphasizing its wrongness. My framework essentially inverts this relationship: I aim to expand its scope while minimizing its wrongness – or, at least, I wish to minimize the moral significance of certain lies, without calling them permissible or good.

Aquinas believes that not even beneficent lies can be called morally good. This claim is undoubtedly the most contentious feature of his view. But the fact that this claim is far from obvious – indeed, it will be difficult for many people to grasp – lends credence to Aquinas's position. This claim is difficult to understand not only because Aquinas's intellectual context is so removed from our own. It is difficult because the finer points of practical reasoning are often a challenge to discern. Venial lies are very minor sins. The more minor the sin in question, the more difficult it will be to pinpoint the nature of its sinfulness. This is due, in part, to the reality that we live in a fallen world. On a daily basis, the postlapsarian world presents us with scenarios in which sin appears to be the most reasonable course of action. Many of these scenarios simply would not exist in the state of paradise. Aquinas's anthropology of postlapsarian humanity also accounts for the *fomes peccati*, or the "spark of sin," which St. Paul describes in Chapter 7 of his Epistle to the Romans (*ST* I-II.91.6). Our fallen appetites often lead us not only to make bad moral decisions but also to arrive at incorrect moral judgments.[15] Since lying is opposed to the virtue of truthfulness, a lie can never be a good action. To perform a morally bad action is to be out of step with reason. But lying quite frequently seems to us to be the reasonable thing to do.

[13] Skalko, "Why Did Aquinas Hold That Killing Is Sometimes Just, But Never Lying?" 234.
[14] Dorszynski, *Catholic Teaching about the Morality of Falsehood*, 94.
[15] See *De malo* III.9 and *ST* I-II.94.4.

The theological and anthropological contours of Aquinas's thought are often lost on contemporary philosophers who engage his writings on lying. This is true not only of his critics but of his defenders. It is not difficult to see why. If one feels bound by the strictures of analytic philosophy to bracket theological notions such as *sin*, then one will either attempt to carry on without these features of Aquinas's arguments or attempt to "translate" them into the idiom of contemporary philosophical discourse. I believe these attempts not only do a disservice to Aquinas's thought; they are a disservice to contemporary ethical discourse. The purpose of this book has been to demonstrate the perennial relevance of Aquinas's thought on the morality of lying. The framework I have developed does not seek to translate Aquinas's concepts – it seeks to rehabilitate them. This rehabilitation demands that we begin our moral analysis of lying, not with a set of moral conundrums or abstract principles, but with the virtue of truthfulness.

Bibliography

ANCIENT AND MEDIEVAL SOURCES

Albert the Great. *Super Ethica*, in Alberti Magni Opera omnia (Editio Coloniensis), eds. Beate Geyer, et al. (Münster 1951).
Al-Ghazali, Abu. An Exposition of the Reality of Truthfulness, Its Meaning and Levels, in *Al-Ghazali on Intention, Sincerity and Truthfulness: Kitab al-niyya wa'l-ikhlas wa'l-sidq*, trans. Anthony Shaker (Cambridge 2013), 85–98.
Alighieri, Dante. *The Divine Comedy: Inferno*, trans. Anthony Esolen (New York 2003).
Aquinas, Thomas. *Summa theologiae*, in Sancti Thomae de Aquino Opera omnia, vols 4–12 (Rome 1888–1906).
Aquinas, Thomas. *Scriptum super Sententia magistri Petri Lombardi*, vol. 3, ed. M. F. Moos (Paris 1933).
Aquinas, Thomas. *Quaestiones disputatae de malo*, in Quaestiones disputatae, vol. 2, ed. P. Bazzi (Turin 1953).
Aquinas, Thomas. *Super primam Epistolam ad Corinthios lectura*, in *Super epistolas S. Pauli lectura*, 8th rev. edn, vol. 1, ed. Raphael Cai (Turin 1953).
Aquinas, Thomas. *Super epistolam ad Galatas lectura*, in *Super epistolas S. Pauli lectura*, 8th rev. edn, vol. 1, ed. Raphael Cai (Turin 1953).
Aquinas, Thomas. *Super epistolam ad Romanos lectura*, in *Super epistolas S. Pauli lectura*, 8th rev. edn, vol. 1, ed. Raphael Cai (Turin 1953).
Aquinas, Thomas. *Sententia super Peri hermeneias* (Turin 1955).
Aquinas, Thomas. *Liber de veritate catholicae Fidei contra errores infidelium seu Summa contra Gentiles* (Turin 1961).
Aquinas, Thomas. *Expositio super Iob ad litteram*, in Sancti Thomae de Aquino Opera omnia, vol. 26 (Rome 1965).
Aquinas, Thomas. *Quaestiones disputatae de veritate*, in S. Thomae Aquinatis opera omnia ut sunt in indice thomistico, vol. 3, ed. Roberto Busa (Stuttgart-Bad Cannstatt 1980).
Aquinas, Thomas. *Quaestiones de quolibet*, in *S. Thomae Aquinatis opera omnia ut sunt in indice thomistico*, vol. 3, ed. Roberto Busa (Stuttgart-Bad Cannstatt 1980).

Aquinas, Thomas. *Sententia libri Ethicorum*, in *S. Thomae Aquinatis opera omnia ut sunt in indice thomistico*, vol. 4, ed. Roberto Busa (Stuttgart-Bad Cannstatt 1980).
Aquinas, Thomas. *Sancti Thomae de Aquino in psalmos Davidis expositio*, in *S. Thomae Aquinatis opera omnia ut sunt in indice thomistico*, vol. 6, ed. Roberto Busa (Stuttgart-Bad Cannstatt 1980).
Aquinas, Thomas. *Collationes in decem preceptis, in Jean-Pierre Torrell, "Les Collationes in decem preceptis de saint Thomas d'Aquin. Edition critique avec introduction et notes," Revue des Sciences philosophiques et théologiques* 69 (1985): 5–40 and 227–263.
Aristotle. *Metaphysics*, Books 1–9 (Loeb Classical Library), 271, trans. Hugh Tredennick (Cambridge, MA 1933).
Aristotle. *Nicomachean Ethics* (Loeb Classical Library), trans. H. Rackham (Cambridge, MA 1934).
Aristotle. *Categories, On Interpretation, and Prior Analytics* (Loeb Classical Library), trans. H. P. Cook and Hugh Tredennick (Cambridge, MA 1938).
Aristotle. *Nicomachean Ethics*, trans. W. D. Ross, in *The Complete Works of Aristotle*, ed. Jonathan Barnes (New York 1991).
Augustine of Hippo. *De magistro*, in *S. Aurelii Augustini Opera Omnia*, in Patrologiae Cursus Completus Series Latina, 32, ed. Jacques-Paul Migne (Paris 1841).
Augustine of Hippo. *Letter 28*, in *S. Aurelii Augustini Opera Omnia*, in Patrologiae Cursus Completus Series Latina, 33, ed. Jacques-Paul Migne (Paris 1865).
Augustine of Hippo. *Letter 40*, in *S. Aurelii Augustini Opera Omnia*, in Patrologiae Cursus Completus Series Latina, 33, ed. Jacques-Paul Migne (Paris 1865).
Augustine of Hippo. *De doctrina christiana*, in *S. Aurelii Augustini Opera Omnia*, in Patrologiae Cursus Completus Series Latina, 34, ed. Jacques-Paul Migne (Paris 1865).
Augustine of Hippo. *Contra mendacium*, in *S. Aurelii Augustini Opera Omnia*, in Patrologiae Cursus Completus Series Latina, 40, ed. Jacques-Paul Migne (Paris 1865).
Augustine of Hippo. *De mendacio*, in *S. Aurelii Augustini Opera Omnia*, in Patrologiae Cursus Completus Series Latina, 40, ed. Jacques-Paul Migne (Paris 1865).
Augustine of Hippo. *Enchiridion de fide, spe et charitate*, in *S. Aurelii Augustini Opera Omnia*, in Patrologiae Cursus Completus Series Latina, 40, ed. Jacques-Paul Migne (Paris 1865).
Augustine of Hippo. *On Christian Teaching*, trans. R.P.H. Green (New York 2008).
Augustine of Hippo. *The City of God*, 2 vols, trans. William Babcock (Hyde Park, NY 2012–2013).
Benedict. *The Rule of St. Benedict* (New York 2008).
Bonaventure. Commentarius in IV Libros Sententiarum III, in *Opera Omnia* 1–4 (Quaracchi, Italy 1882–1889).
Bonaventure. *Collationes de decem praeceptis*, in *Opera omnia*, 5 (Quaracchi, Italy 1891).
Chrysostom, St. John. *On the Priesthood*, trans. Graham Neville (Crestwood, NY 1977).

Cicero. *On Invention; Best Kind of Orator; Topics* (Loeb Classical Library), 386, trans. H. M. Hubbell (Cambridge, MA 1940).
de Peñafort, Raymond. *Summa S. Raymundi de Peniafort, cum glossis Joannis de Friburgo, secunda editio auctior et correctior* (Avignon 1715).
Gratian. *Decretum magistri Gratiani*, in *Corpus iuris canonici*, eds. E. Richer and Emil A. Friedberg, 2nd ed. (Leipzig 1879; repr. Graz 1959).
Hugh of St. Victor. *De sacramentis christianae fidei*, in Patrologiae Cursus Completus Series Latina, 176, ed. Jacques-Paul Migne (Paris 1854).
Jerome. *St. Jerome's Commentaries on Galatians, Titus, and Philemon*, trans. Thomas P. Scheck (Notre Dame, IN 2010).
Lombard, Peter. *Sententiarum libri quatuor*, in Patrologiae Cursus Completus Series Latina, 192, ed. Jacques-Paul Migne (Paris 1855).
William of Auxerre. *Summa aurea* III, in *Magistri Guillelmi Altissiodorensis*, Summa Aurea, Vol. 3, ed. Jean Ribaillier, Spicilegium Bonaventurianum (Paris 1980).

MODERN AND CONTEMPORARY SOURCES

Agamben, Giorgio. *The Sacrament of Language: An Archeology of the Oath*, trans. Adam Kotsko (Stanford, CA 2011).
Alter, Robert. *The Art of Biblical Narrative* (New York 2011).
Altholz, Josef L. "Truth and Equivocation: Liguori's Moral Theology and Newman's Apologia," *Church History* 44:1 (1975): 73–84.
Anderson, Matthew Lee. "(When) Is there a Christian Responsibility to Gossip?," *Journal of the Society of Christian Ethics* (forthcoming).
Anonymous. "Review of the Works of St. Alphonsus Maria de Liguori," *The Dublin Review* 37:74 (1854) Art. III: 326–403.
Anscombe, Gertrude Elizabeth Margaret. "Two Moral Theologians," in *Faith in a Hard Ground: Essays on Religion, Philosophy and Ethics by G.E.M. Anscombe*, eds. Mary Geach and Luke Gormally, 157–169 (Charlottesville, VA 2008).
Arbib, Michael. "Toward the Language-Ready Brain: Biological Evolution and Primate Comparisons," *Psychonomic Bulletin and Review* 24 (2017): 142–150.
Ashworth, Jennifer E. "Signification and Modes of Signifying in the Thirteenth-Century Logic: A Preface to Aquinas on Analogy," *Medieval Philosophy and Theology* 1 (1991): 39–67.
Ashworth, Jennifer E. "Aquinas on Significant Utterance: Interjection, Blasphemy, Prayer," in *Aquinas's Moral Theory: Essays in Honor of Norman Kretzman*, eds. Scott MacDonald and Eleonore Stump, 207–234 (Ithaca, NY 2008).
Aumann, Jordan, OP. "The Theology of Venial Sin," *Proceedings of the Catholic Theological Society of America* 10 (1955): 74–94.
Austin, John Langshaw. *How to Do Things with Words* (Cambridge, MA 1962).
Austin, Nicholas, SJ. *Aquinas on Virtue: A Causal Reading* (Washington, DC 2017).
Austriaco, Nicanor Pier Giorgio. "On the Limits of Abstraction: A Response to Professor Marie Georg," *American Catholic Philosophical Quarterly* 95:1 (2021): 145–148.

Austriaco, Nicanor Pier Giorgio. "Thomistic Thoughts about Thought and Talk," *American Catholic Philosophical Quarterly* 95:1 (2021): 117–129.

Babington, Charles. "Clinton Reply in License Case: Testimony 'Not Legally False,'" The Washington Post, May 9, 2000.

Baker, Peter. *Breach: Inside the Impeachment and Trial of William Jefferson Clinton* (New York 2012).

Banks, Erik. *See no Evil: Uncovering the Truth Behind the Financial Crisis* (New York 2011).

Bergstrom, Carl T. and Jevin D. West, *Calling Bullshit: The Art of Skepticism in a Data-Driven World* (New York 2020).

Berlinger, Nancy. "What Is Meant by Telling the Truth: Bonhoeffer on the Ethics of Disclosure," *Studies in Christian Ethics* 16:2 (2003): 80–92.

Bhattacharjee, Yudhijit. "Why We Lie," *National Geographic* 231:6 (June 2017): 36–52.

Blum, Susan D. "Truth," *Journal of Linguistic Anthropology* 9 (1999): 255–258.

Blum, Susan D. *Lies That Bind: Chinese Truths, Other Truths* (Lanham, MD 2007).

Bok, Sissela. *Lying: Moral Choice in Public and Private Life*, 2nd ed. (New York 1999).

Boller, Paul F. *Presidential Campaigns: From George Washington to George W. Bush*, rev. ed. (New York 2004).

Bonhoeffer, Dietrich. "What Is Meant by 'Telling the Truth'?" in *Ethics*, trans. Neville Horton Smith, 358–368 (New York 1995).

Bowlin, John. *Tolerance among the Virtues* (Princeton, NJ 2016).

Boyle, Joseph. "The Absolute Prohibition of Lying and the Origins of the Casuistry of Mental Reservation: Augustinian Arguments and Thomistic Developments," *American Journal of Jurisprudence* 44:1 (1999): 43–65.

Boyle, Nicholas. "Truth Telling, the Media, and Society," *New Blackfriars* 98:1073 (2017): 19–33.

Braaten, Carl E. "Sins of the Tongue," in *I am the Lord Your God: Christian Reflections on the Ten Commandments*, eds. Carl E. Braaten and Christopher R. Seitz, 206–217 (Grand Rapids, MI 2005).

Brock, Stephen L. *Action and Conduct: Thomas Aquinas and the Theory of Action* (Edinburgh 1998).

Brock, Stephen L. *The Light That Binds: A Study in Thomas Aquinas's Metaphysics of Natural Law* (Eugene, OR 2020).

Brodie-Brosnan, J. "Father Vermeersch on Mental Restrictions," *The Irish Ecclesiastical Record* 18 (1921): 602–609.

Brodie-Brosnan, J. "Father Vermeersch on the Malice of Lying," *The Irish Ecclesiastical Record* 18 (1921): 266–274.

Buford, Thomas O. *Trust, Our Second Nature: Crisis, Reconciliation, and the Personal* (Lanham, MD 2009).

Butler, John. "Truthfulness and Thomism in Medical Practice," *National Catholic Bioethics Quarterly* 12:4 (2012): 633–651.

Carson, Thomas L. *Lying and Deception: Theory and Practice* (New York 2010).

Casagrande, Carla and Silvana Vecchio. *Les péchés de la langue : Discipline et éthique de la parole dans la culture medieval* (Paris 1991).

Catholic Church. *Catechism of the Catholic Church*, 1st ed. (Washington, DC 1994).
Catholic Church. *Catechism of the Catholic Church: Revised in Accordance with the Official Latin Text Promulgated by Pope John Paul II*, 2nd ed. (Washington, DC 1997).
Childress, James F. and John Macquarrie, eds. *A New Dictionary of Christian Ethics* (London 1986).
Chisholm, Roderick M. and Thomas D. Feehan. "The Intent to Deceive," *The Journal of Philosophy* 74:3 (1977): 143–159.
Chomsky, Noam. *Aspects of the Theory of Syntax* (Cambridge, MA 1965).
Clem, Stewart. "Lying to the Nazi at the Door: A Thomistic Reframing of the Classic Moral Dilemma," *Journal of Religious Ethics* 49:1 (2021): 6–32.
Clem, Stewart. "Post-truth and Vices Opposed to Truth," *Journal of the Society of Christian Ethics* 37:2 (2017): 97–116.
Clem, Stewart. "Speaking Truthfully: A Thomistic Perspective on the Peculiar Origins of Human Language," in *The Evolution of Human Wisdom*, eds. Celia Deane-Drummond and Agustín Fuentes, 109–126 (Lanham, MD 2017).
Cloutier, David. "Cavanaugh and Grimes on Structural Evils of Violence and Race: Overcoming Conflicts in Contemporary Social Ethics," *Journal of the Society of Christian Ethics* 37:2 (2017): 59–78.
Cohen, Ted. *Jokes: Philosophical Thoughts on Joking Matters* (Chicago, IL 1999).
Colish, Marcia. "Rethinking Lying in the Twelfth Century," in *Virtue and Ethics in the Twelfth Century*, eds. István Bejczy and Richard Newhauser, 155–173 (Boston, MA 2005).
Corran, Emily. "Hiding the Truth: Exegetical Discussions of Abraham's Lie from Hugh of St. Victor to Stephen Langton," *Historical Research*, 87:235 (Feb 2014): 1–17.
Corran, Emily. *Lying and Perjury in Medieval Practical Thought: A Study in the History of Casuistry* (New York 2018).
Couenhoven, Jesse. *Stricken by Sin, Cured by Christ: Agency, Necessity, and Culpability in Augustinian Theology* (New York 2013).
Courtois, Gérard. "Mensonge et parjure selon saint Thomas d'Aquin," *Rue Descartes* 8/9 (1993): 85–97.
Cuneo, Terrence. *Speech & Morality: On the Metaethical Implications of Speaking* (New York 2014).
Cunningham, Stanley B. *Reclaiming Moral Agency: The Moral Philosophy of Albert the Great* (Washington, DC 2008).
Daly, Daniel J. *The Structures of Virtue and Vice* (Washington, DC 2021).
Deacon, Terrence W. *The Symbolic Species: The Co-Evolution of Language and the Brain* (New York 1997).
Debey, Evelyne et al. "Lying Relies on the Truth," *Cognition* 132 (2014): 324–334.
Decosimo, David. "Just Lies: Finding Augustine's Ethics of Public Lying in His Treatments of Lying and Killing," *Journal of Religious Ethics* 38:4 (2010): 661–697.
Decosimo, David. *Ethics as a Work of Charity: Thomas Aquinas on Pagan Virtue* (Stanford, CA 2014).

Deely, John. *Intentionality and Semiotics: A Story of Mutual Fecundation* (Scranton, PA 2007).
Deely, John. *Realism for the 21st Century: A John Deely Reader*, ed. Paul Cobley (Scranton, PA 2009).
De Haan, Daniel D. "Linguistic Apprehension as Incidental Sensation in Thomas Aquinas," *Proceedings of the American Catholic Philosophical Association* 84 (2011): 179–196.
DeLapp, Kevin and Jeremy Henkel, eds. *Lying and Truthfulness* (Indianapolis 2016),
DeLetter, P., SJ. "Venial Sin and Its Final Goal," *Thomist* 16:1 (1953): 32–70.
Denery II, Dallas G. *The Devil Wins: A History of Lying from the Garden of Eden to the Enlightenment* (Princeton, NJ 2015).
Dessalles, Jean-Louis. "Why Talk?" in *The Social Origins of Language*, eds. Danny Dor, Chris Knight, and Jerome Lewis (New York 2014).
Dewan, Lawrence, OP. "St. Thomas, Lying, and Venial Sin," in *Wisdom, Law, and Virtue: Essays in Thomistic Ethics*, 374–386 (New York 2008).
Donagan, Alan. "Consistency in Rationalist Moral Systems," *The Journal of Philosophy* 81 (1984): 291–309.
Donze, Caroline. "Breaking the Seal of Confession: Examining the Constitutionality of the Clergy-Penitent Privilege in Mandatory Reporting Law," *Louisiana Law Review* 78:1 (2017): 268–310.
Dorszynski, Julius. *Catholic Teaching about the Morality of Falsehood* (Washington, DC 1948).
Dougherty, Michael V. *Moral Dilemmas in Medieval Thought: From Gratian to Aquinas* (New York 2011).
Dunbar, Robin. *Grooming, Gossip, and the Evolution of Language* (Cambridge, MA 1996).
Dworkin, Gerald. "Are These 10 Lies Justified?" The New York Times (December 14, 2015), https://opinionator.blogs.nytimes.com/2015/12/14/can-you-justify-these-lies/?_r=0.
Ellul, Jacques. *Propaganda: The Formation of Men's Attitudes*, trans. Konrad Kellen and Jean Lerner (New York 1965).
Evans, Angela D., and Kang Lee. "Emergence of Lying in Very Young Children," *Developmental Psychology* 49:10 (2013): 1958–1963.
Feehan, Thomas D. "Augustine on Lying and Deception," *Augustinian Studies* 19 (1988): 131–139.
Feehan, Thomas D. "The Morality of Lying in St. Augustine," *Augustinian Studies* 21 (1990): 67–81.
Feehan, Thomas D. "Augustine's Own Examples of Lying," *Augustinian Studies* 22 (1991): 165–190.
Finn, Daniel K. "What Is a Sinful Social Structure?," *Theological Studies* 77:1 (2016): 136–164.
Finn, Daniel K., ed. *Moral Agency within Social Structures and Culture: A Primer on Critical Realism for Christian Ethics* (Washington, DC 2020).
Flannery, Kevin, SJ. *Acts amid Precepts: The Aristotelian Logical Structure of Thomas Aquinas's Moral Theory* (Washington, DC 2001).

Flannery, Kevin, SJ. "Being Truthful with (or Lying to) Others about Oneself," in *Aquinas and the Nicomachean Ethics*, eds. Tobias Hoffman, Jörn Müller, and Matthias Perkams, 129–145 (New York 2013).
Flannery, Kevin, SJ. "Anscombe on Two Jesuits and Lying," in *The Moral Philosophy of Elizabeth Anscombe*, eds. Luke Gormally, David Albert Jones, and Roger Teichmann, 192–211 (La Vergne, TN 2016).
Foot, Philippa. "Moral Dilemmas Revisited," in *Moral Dilemmas and Other Topics in Moral Philosophy*, 175–188 (New York 2003).
Frankfurt, Harry G. *On Bullshit* (Princeton, NJ 2005).
Gauthier, R. Antoine, and Jean-Yves Jolif. *L'Éthique à Nicomaque*, 4 vols, 2nd ed. (Leuven 2002).
Geach, Peter. "Truth, Truthfulness, and Trust," in *Truth and Hope*, 47–66 (Notre Dame, IN 2001).
George, Marie. "A Rambutan by Any Other Name Would Taste as Sweet: Response to Professor Nicanor Pier Giorgio Austriaco, OP," *American Catholic Philosophical Quarterly* 95:1 (2021): 149–152.
George, Marie. "Does Knowing What Things Are Require Language (as a System of Physical or Imaginable Signs)?" *American Catholic Philosophical Quarterly* 95:1 (2021): 131–144.
Gert, Bernard. *Common Morality: Deciding What to Do* (New York 2004).
Greasley, Kate. "The Morality of Lying and the Murderer at the Door," *Law and Philosophy* 38:5–6 (2019): 439–452.
Greenwald, Glenn. "A Clinton Fan Manufactured Fake News That MSNBC Personalities Spread to Discredit WikiLeaks Docs," Intercept (December 9, 2016), https://theintercept.com/2016/12/09/a-clinton-fan-manufactured-fake-news-that-msnbc-personalities-spread-to-discredit-wikileaks-docs/.
Grice, Paul. "Presupposition and Conversational Implicature," in *Radical Pragmatics*, ed. Peter Cole, 183–198 (New York 1981).
Grice, Paul. "Logic and Conversation," in *Studies in the Way of Words*, 22–40 (Cambridge, MA 1989).
Griffiths, Paul J. *Lying: An Augustinian Account of Duplicity* (Grand Rapids, MI 2004).
Guevin, Benedict M. "When a Lie Is Not a Lie: The Importance of Ethical Context," *Thomist* 66 (2002): 267–274.
Hamblin, Charles L. *Fallacies* (London 1970).
Hauerwas, Stanley. *Sanctify Them in Truth: Holiness Exemplified* (Nashville, TN 1999).
Hauerwas, Stanley. *The Hauerwas Reader*, ed. John Berkman (Durham, NC 2001).
Hearne, Vicki. *Adam's Task: Calling Animals by Name* (New York 1987).
Houtman, Cornelius. *Exodus* (Leuven 2000).
Heer, Jeet. "Donald Trump Is Not a Liar: He's Something Worse: A Bullshit Artist," New Republic (December 1, 2015), https://newrepublic.com/article/124803/donald-trump-not-liar.
Heyman, Gail D., Anna S. Hsu, Genyue Fu, and Kang Lee. "Instrumental Lying by Parents in the US and China," *International Journal of Psychology* 48:6 (2013): 1176–1184.

Hume, David. *A Treatise Concerning Human Nature*, eds. David Fate Norton and Mary J. Norton (New York 2000).

Hursthouse, Rosalind. *On Virtue Ethics* (New York 1999).

Ibbotson, Paul and Michael Tomasello. "Language in a New Key," *Scientific American* 315:5 (2016): 70–75.

Pope Innocent XI. "Sixty-Five Propositions Condemned in the Decree of the Holy Office, March 2, 1679," in *Enchiridion symbolorum, definitionum et declarationum de rebus fidei et morum*, ed. Heinrich Denzinger, 2101–2167 (San Francisco, CA 2012), Latin-English, 43rd ed.

Jefferson, Thomas. *The Writings of Thomas Jefferson*, vol. 13, eds. Andrew A. Lipscomb and Albert Ellery Bergh (Washington, DC 1903).

Jensen, Steven J. *Sin: A Thomistic Psychology* (Washington, DC 2018).

Jonsen, Albert R. and Stephen Toulmin. *The Abuse of Casuistry: A History of Moral Reasoning* (Berkeley, CA 1988).

Kant, Immanuel. "On a Supposed Right to Lie from Philanthropy," trans. M. J. Gregor, in *Immanuel Kant, Practical Philosophy*, eds. A. W. Wood and M. J. Gregor, 611–615 (Cambridge 1996).

Karg, Katja, Martin Schmelz, Josep Call, and Michael Tomasello. "Chimpanzees Strategically Manipulate What Others Can See," *Animal Cognition* 18 (2015): 1069–1076.

Keenan, James F., SJ. "Raising Expectations on Sin," *Theological Studies* 77:1 (2016): 165–180.

Kemp, Kenneth W. and Thomas Sullivan. "Speaking Falsely and Telling Lies," *Proceedings of the American Philosophical Association* 67 (1993): 151–170.

King, Martin Luther, Jr. "Letter from a Birmingham Jail," in *Why We Can't Wait* (Boston 2011).

Kirk, Kenneth. *Conscience and Its Problems: An Introduction to Casuistry* (Louisville, KY 1999).

Knight, Chris. "Ritual/Speech Coevolution: A Solution to the Problem of Deception," in *Approaches to the Evolution of Language: Social and Cognitive Bases*, eds. James R. Hurford, Michael Studdert-Kennedy, and Chris Knight, 68–91 (New York 1998).

Konner, Melvin. *The Tangled Wing: Biological Constraints on the Human Spirit* (New York 1982).

Korsgaard, Christine M. "The Right to Lie: Kant on Dealing with Evil," *Philosophy & Public Affairs* 15:4 (1986): 325–349.

Kreeft, Peter. "Why Live Action Did Right and Why We All Should Know That," CatholicVote.org (February 18, 2011), www.catholiceducation.org/en/religion-and-philosophy/apologetics/why-live-action-did-right-and-why-we-all-should-know-that.html.

Kurtscheid, Bertrand. *A History of the Seal of Confession*, trans. F. A. Marks (London 1927).

Kurtzleben, Danielle. "With 'Fake News,' Trump Moves from Alternative Facts to Alternative Language," NPR (February 17, 2017), www.npr.org/2017/02/17/515630467/with-fake-news-trump-moves-from-alternative-facts-to-alternative-language.

Labourdette, Michel, OP. *Grand cours de théologie morale, 4: Vices et péchés (IaIIae, qu. 71–89)* (Paris 2017).
Labourdette, Michel, OP. *Grand cours de théologie morale, 13: La religion (IaIIae, qu. 80–122)* (Paris 2018).
Lewis, Michael. "The Origins of Lying and Deception in Everyday Life," *American Scientist* 103:2 (2015): 128–135.
Lottin, Odon. "Le concept de justice chez les théologiens du moyen âge avant l'introduction d'Aristote," *Revue Thomiste* 44 (1938): 511–521.
Lyn, Heidi, Jamie L. Russell, David A. Leavens, Kim A. Bard, Sarah T. Boysen, Jennifer A. Schaeffer, and William D. Hopkins. "Apes Communicate about Absent and Displaced Objects: Methodology Matters," *Animal Cognition* 17 (2014): 85–94.
Macagno, Fabrizio. "The Presumptions of Meaning: Hamblin and Equivocation," *Informal Logic*, 31:4 (2011): 367–393.
MacIntyre, Alasdair. "Moral Dilemmas," *Philosophy and Phenomenological Research* 50, Supplement (1990): 367–382.
MacIntyre, Alasdair. "Truthfulness, Lies, and Moral Philosophers," in *The Tanner Lectures on Human Values*, vol. 17, ed. Grethe B. Peterson, 309–369 (Salt Lake City 1994).
MacIntyre, Alasdair. *Dependent Rational Animals: Why Human Beings Need the Virtues*. (Chicago, IL 1999).
MacIntyre, Alasdair. *After Virtue: A Study in Moral Theory*, 3rd ed. (Notre Dame, IN 2007).
MacIntyre, Alasdair and John Finnis. "Pastoral Concerns: Faith, Natural Law and Virtue," in *The Twenty-Fifth Anniversary of Vatican II: A Look Back and a Look Ahead*, ed. Russell E. Smith, 250–262 (Dallas, TX 1990).
McCabe, Herbert, OP. *God Matters* (New York 2005).
McCluskey, Colleen. *Thomas Aquinas on Moral Wrongdoing* (New York 2017).
McEntyre, Marilyn Chandler. *Caring for Words in a Culture of Lies* (Grand Rapids, MI 2009).
McHugh, John A. and Charles J. Callan. *Moral Theology: A Complete Course Based on St. Thomas Aquinas and the Best Modern Authorities*, vol. 2 (London 1929).
McNicholl, A. J., OP. "The Ultimate End of Venial Sin," *Thomist* 2 (1940): 373–409.
Maheshwari, Sapna. "How Fake News Goes Viral: A Case Study," The New York Times. www.nytimes.com/2016/11/20/business/media/how-fake-news-spreads.html.
Mahon, James. "Kant on Lies, Candour and Reticence," *Kantian Review* 7 (2003): 102–133.
Mamet, David. *Glengarry Glen Ross: A Play* (New York 1994).
Mann, William E. "To Catch a Heretic – Augustine on Lying," *Faith & Philosophy* 20:4 (October 2003): 479–495.
Marshall, Bruce D. "'We Shall Bear the Image of the Man of Heaven': Theology and the Concept of Truth," in *Rethinking Metaphysics*, eds. L. Gregory Jones and Stephen E. Fowl, 93–117 (Oxford 1995).
Marshall, Bruce D. *Trinity and Truth* (New York 2000).
Matthews, Gareth B. *Augustine* (Malden, MA 2005).

Mattison, William C., III. "A New Look at the Last End: Noun and Verb, Determinate Yet Capable of Growth," *Journal of Moral Theology* 8:2, Special Issue (2019): 95–113.
Milbank, John and Catherine Pickstock. *Truth in Aquinas* (New York 2001).
Milgrom, Jacob. *Leviticus 17–22* (New York 2000).
Miller, Christian B. *Honesty: The Philosophy and Psychology of a Neglected Virtue* (New York 2021).
Miller, Patrick D. *The Ten Commandments* (Louisville, KY 2009).
Müller, Gregor. *Die Wahrhaftigkeitspflicht und die Problematik der Lüge: Ein Längsschnitt durch die Moraltheologie und Ethik unter besonderer Berücksichtigung der Tugendlehre des Thomas von Aquin und der modernen Lösungsversuche* (Freiburg 1962).
Myers, Jason A. "Law, Lies and Letter Writing: An Analysis of Jerome and Augustine on the Antioch Incident (Galatians 2:11–14)," *Scottish Journal of Theology* 66:2 (2013), 131.
Nemeth, Charles. *Aquinas in the Courtroom: Lawyers, Judges, and Judicial Conduct* (Westport, CT 2001).
New York Times Editorial Staff. "Truth and Lies in the Age of Trump," editorial, *New York Times* (December 10, 2016), www.nytimes.com/2016/12/10/opinion/truth-and-lies-in-the-age-of-trump.html.
Newhauser, Richard G. *The Treatises on Vices and Virtues in Latin and the Vernacular* (Turnhout, Belgium 1993).
Newman, John Henry. *Parochial and Plain Sermons* (San Francisco, CA 1997).
Norman, Matthew. "Whoever Wins the US Presidential Election, We've Entered a Post-Truth World – There's No Going Back Now," Independent, November 8, 2016. www.independent.co.uk/voices/us-election-2016-donald-trump-hillary-clinton-who-wins-post-truth-world-no-going-back-a7404826.html.
O'Brien, Thomas C. "Appendix 3: Venial Sin (1ae2ae 89)," in *Summa theologiae*, Vol. 27, 118–124 (New York 1974).
O'Callaghan, John. *Thomistic Realism and the Linguistic Turn: Toward a More Perfect Form of Existence* (Notre Dame, IN 2003).
Oesterle, John A. "Another Approach to the Problem of Meaning," *The Thomist* 7:2 (1944): 233–263.
O'Gorman, Ned. "'Telling the Truth:' Dietrich Bonhoeffer's Rhetorical Discourse Ethic," *Journal of Communication and Religion* 28 (2005): 224–248.
Petri, Thomas, OP and Michael A. Wahl. "Live Action and Planned Parenthood: A New Test Case for Lying," *Nova et Vetera* 10:2 (2012): 437–462.
Porter, Jean. *Ministers of the Law: A Natural Law Theory of Legal Authority* (Grand Rapids, MI 2010).
Porter, Jean. *Justice as a Virtue: A Thomistic Perspective.* (Grand Rapids, MI 2016).
Porter, Steven L. and Jason Baehr. "Becoming Honest: Why We Lie and What Can Be Done About It," in *Integrity, Honesty, and Truth Seeking*, eds. Christian B. Miller and Ryan West, 182–204 (New York 2020).
Preston, Ronald. "Lying," in *A New Dictionary of Christian Ethics*, eds. James F. Childress and John Macquarrie (London 1986).
Pruss, Alexander. "Lying and Speaking Your Interlocutor's Language," *Thomist* 63 (1999): 439–453.

Pruss, Alexander. "The Case against False Assertions," First Things (September 22, 2011), www.firstthings.com/web-exclusives/2011/09/the-case-against-false-assertions.
Puffer, Matthew. "Retracing Augustine's Ethics: Lying, Necessity, and the Image of God," *Journal of Religious Ethics* 44:4 (2016): 685–720.
Radzik, Linda. "Gossip and Social Punishment," *Res Philosophica* 93:1 (2016): 185–204.
Ramsey, Boniface. "Two Traditions on Lying and Deception in the Ancient Church," *Thomist* 49 (1985): 504–533.
Rappeport, Alan. "'What Is Aleppo?' Gary Johnson Asks, in an Interview Stumble," New York Times (September 8, 2016).
Ray, Roger D. "Christian Conscience and Pagan Rhetoric: Augustine's Treatises on Lying," *Studia Patristica* 22 (1987): 2321–2325.
Rehbock, Theda. "Don't Lie! ... Why Not?: How to Argue for Truthfulness in Medical Practice," *Cambridge Quarterly of Healthcare Ethics* 21:2 (2012): 177–187.
Rhonheimer, Martin. *Natural Law and Practical Reason: A Thomist View of Moral Autonomy*, trans. Gerald Malsbary (New York 2000).
Richard, Claude, Yvette Lajeunesse and Marie-Thérèse Lussier. "Therapeutic Privilege: Between the Ethics of Lying and the Practice of Truth," *Journal of Medical Ethics* 36:6 (2010): 353–357.
Robinson, Marilynne. *Gilead* (New York 2006).
Russell, Jeremiah and Michael Promisel. "Truth, Lies, and Concealment: St. Augustine on Mendacious Political Thought," *The Review of Politics* 79 (2017): 451–473.
Saul, Jennifer. *Lying, Misleading, and What Is Said* (New York 2012).
Scott-Phillips, Thomas. "Nonhuman Primate Communication, Pragmatics, and the Origins of Language." *Current Anthropology* 56:1 (2015): 56–80.
Searle, John. *Speech Acts: An Essay in the Philosophy of Language* (New York 1969).
Shakespeare, William. *The Merchant of Venice* (New York 2008).
Shakespeare, William. *Othello: The Moor of Venice* (New York 2008).
Sherwin, Michael, OP. *By Knowledge & by Love: Charity and Knowledge in the Moral Theology of St. Thomas Aquinas* (Washington, DC 2005).
Shiffrin, Seana Valentine. *Speech Matters: On Lying, Morality, and the Law* (Princeton, NJ 2014).
Skalko, John. *Disordered Actions: A Moral Analysis of Lying and Homosexual Activity* (Neunkirchen-Seelscheid 2019).
Skalko, John. "Why Did Aquinas Hold That Killing Is Sometimes Just, But Never Lying?" *Proceedings of the American Catholic Philosophical Association* 90 (2017): 227–241.
Smith, Janet E. "Fig Leaves and Falsehoods," *First Things* 214 (June/July 2011): 45–49.
Smith, Lesley. *The Ten Commandments: Interpreting the Bible in the Medieval World* (Boston, MA 2014).
Smith, Randall B. *Aquinas, Bonaventure, and the Scholastic Culture of Medieval Paris* (New York 2021).

Southern, Richard William. *The Making of the Middle Ages* (New Haven, CT 1953).
Sullivan, Evelin. *The Concise Book of Lying* (New York 2001).
Stump, Eleonore. "The Non-Aristotelian Character of Aquinas's Ethics: Aquinas on the Passions," *Faith & Philosophy* 28:1 (2011): 29–43.
Synan, Edward A. "Thomas Aquinas: Propositions and Parables," in *The Gilson Lectures on Thomas Aquinas*, ed. James P. Reilly, 107–124 (Toronto 2008).
Taylor, Charles. *A Secular Age* (Cambridge, MA 2007).
Tessman, Lisa. *Moral Failure: On the Impossible Demands of Morality* (New York 2014).
Tessman, Lisa. *When Doing the Right Thing Is Impossible* (New York 2017).
Tierney, Brian. *The Idea of Natural Rights: Studies on Natural Rights, Natural Law, and Church Law 1150–1625* (Grand Rapids, MI 1997).
Timmermann, Felix and Emanuel Viebahn. "To Lie or Mislead?" *Philosophical Studies* 178:5 (2021): 1481–1501.
Tollefsen, Christopher O. *Lying and Christian Ethics.* (Cambridge, UK 2014).
Tomasello, Michael. *Origins of Human Communication.* (Cambridge, MA 2008).
Torrell, Jean-Pierre, OP. *Saint Thomas Aquinas, Vol. 2: Spiritual Master*, trans. Robert Royal (Washington, DC 2003).
Torrell, Jean-Pierre, OP. *Aquinas's Summa: Background, Structure, & Reception*, trans. Benedict M. Guevin (Washington, DC 2005).
Torrell, Jean-Pierre, OP. *Saint Thomas Aquinas, Vol. 1: The Person and His Work*, 3rd ed., trans. Matthew K. Minerd and Robert Royal. (Washington, DC 2022).
Useem, Jerry. "What Was Volkswagen Thinking? On the Origins of Corporate Evil – and Idiocy," The Atlantic Monthly, January/February 2016, www.theatlantic.com/magazine/archive/2016/01/what-was-volkswagen-thinking/419127/.
Vallier, Kevin. *Trust in a Polarized Age.* (New York 2020).
Vermeersch, Arthurus. De mendacio et necessitatibus commercii humani, Parts 1 and 2, *Gregorianum* 1:1 (1920): 11–40.
Vermeersch, Arthurus. De mendacio et necessitatibus commercii humani, Part 3: Necessitatibus commercii humani quo pacto providendum sit, *Gregorianum* 1:3 (1920): 425–474.
Verschuere, Bruno, et al. "The Ease of Lying," *Consciousness and Cognition* 20 (2011): 908–911.
Wawrykow, Joseph P. *God's Grace and Human Action: "Merit" in the Theology of Thomas Aquinas* (Notre Dame, IN 1995).
Weaver, Darlene Fozard. "Apologies and Their Import for the Moral Identity of Offenders," *Journal of the Society of Christian Ethics* 36:1 (2016): 87–105.
Weaver, Paul H. *News and the Culture of Lying* (New York 1994).
Webster, John. "Sins of Speech," *Studies in Christian Ethics* 28:1 (2015), 35–48.
Westberg, Daniel. *Right Practical Reason: Aristotle, Action, and Prudence in Aquinas* (New York 1994).
White, Kevin. "The Virtues of Man the *Animal Sociale*: *Affabilitas* and *Veritas* in Aquinas," *Thomist* 57:4 (1993), 641–653.
Williams, Bernard. *Truth & Truthfulness: An Essay in Genealogy* (Princeton, NJ 2002).

Williams, Rowan. *The Edge of Words: God and the Habits of Language* (London 2014).
Wippel, John F. "Truth in Thomas Aquinas," *The Review of Metaphysics* 43:2 (1989): 295–326.
Wippel, John F. "Truth in Thomas Aquinas, Part II," *The Review of Metaphysics* 43:3 (1990): 543–567.
Wittgenstein, Ludwig. *Culture and Value: A Selection from the Posthumous Remains*, trans. Peter Winch (New York 1998).
Wittgenstein, Ludwig. *Philosophical Investigations*, 3rd ed., trans. G. E. M. Anscombe (Malden, MA 2001).
Zagorin, Perez. *Ways of Lying: Dissimulation, Persecution, and Conformity in Early Modern Europe* (Cambridge, MA 1990).
Zembaty, Jane S. "Aristotle on Lying," *Journal of the History of Philosophy* 31:1 (1993): 7–29.

Index

Abelard, Peter, 74
Abraham, 38, 45, 128, 129, 136, 139
Acts of the Apostles, 38, 41
Agamben, Giorgio, 86
Albert the Great, 63
Al-Ghazali, Abu, 132
Alter, Robert, 38
Altholz, Josef, 133
Ambrose of Milan, 39, 120, 139
Ananias and Sapphira, 38
Andronicus, 74
Anscombe, Elizabeth, 119, 135, 141, 152
Aquinas, Thomas. *See also* justice; lying; sin; virtue
   lying in Aquinas's early works, 61–71
   on charity, 77–79, 106, 111
   on equivocation, 128
   on humans as social animals, 100
   on law, 77
   on moral dilemmas, 153
   on sins of speech, 77–90
   on the Decalogue and lying, 61–71
   use of Aristotle, 63–66, 74
Aristotle
   on boasting, 118
   on *epieikeia*, 74
   on humans as social animals, 101
   on language, 28, 91, 124
   on truthfulness, 63–66, 69, 70
Ashworth, E. Jennifer, 88, 93
assertion. *See* language: assertion, *See also* lying: and assertion
Athanasius of Alexandria, 39, 129

Augustine of Hippo
   correspondence with Jerome, 41–42
   definition of lying, 43
   hierarchy of lies, 48
   on hiding the truth, 100
   on humans as social animals, 101, 125, 138
   on lying, 32–35, 40–51, 115–116, 126, 157
   on the eighth commandment, 189
Aumann, Jordan, 69
Austin, J. L., 82
Austin, Nicholas, 64
Austriaco, Nicanor Pier Giorgio, 124

Babington, Charles, 131
Baehr, Jason, 2
Baker, Peter, 130
Basil of Caesarea, 39
Benedict of Nursia, 67
Bergstrom, Carl, 171
Berlinger, Nancy, 13
boasting, 65, 69, 75, 117, 173
Bok, Sissela, 3, 186–187
Bonaventure, 57–58
Bonhoeffer, Dietrich, 13
Bowlin, John, 73
Boyle, Joseph, 111
Brock, Stephen, 78, 81
Brodie-Brosnan, J., 134
Buford, Thomas, 30, 182
bullshit, 170–176
Butler, John, 163

Callan, Charles, 115, 173
Carson, Thomas, 176
Casagrande, Carla, 63
Cassian, John, 39, 40
Catechism of the Catholic Church, 13, 22, 114
Catholicism, 13, 15–21, 132, See also *Catechism of the Catholic Church*
Chisholm, Roderick, 105
Chrysostom, John, 39–40
Cicero, 74–75, 190
Clement of Alexandria, 39
Clinton, Bill, 130
Cloutier, David, 177
Cohen, Ted, 105
Colish, Marcia, 39, 52, 115
confession, sacrament of, 84
consequentialism, 21, 114, 144, 145, 150, 184
Corran, Emily, 2, 46
Couenhoven, Jesse, 159
Courtois, Gérard, 112
Cuneo, Terence, 124
Cunningham, Stanley, 63
cursing, 61, 89

Daly, Daniel, 177
Dante, 138
De Haan, Daniel, 92
de Peñafort, Raymond, 43, 57
Decalogue. See Ten Commandments
deception. See lying: and deception
Decosimo, David, 50–51, 63, 64
Deely, John, 94
DeLapp, Kevin, 169
DeLetter, P., 69
Denery, Dallas, 4–5, 54, 105
Deuteronomy, 45, 83
Dewan, Lawrence, 109, 146–150
dissimulation, 38, 100, 119–122, 128, 141, 156, See also hypocrisy
Donagan, Alan, 153
Donze, Caroline, 85
Dorszynski, Julius, 14, 39, 163, 164
Dougherty, M. V., 153
Dublin Review, The, 133
duplicity. See lying *and* dissimulation

Ecclesiasticus, 68
Ephesians, Epistle to the, 45
equivocation. See language: equivocation, See also language: mental reservation

eschatology, 108
Exodus, 12, 17, 18, 47, 78, 82, 85, 107

fairy tales, 126, 161
fall of humanity, 15–21, 110, 151–153, 159, 192
false witness, 13, 67, 85, 175, 189, See also Ten Commandments
falsehood
    formal falsehood as insufficient condition for lying, 103–104
    formal vs. material, 96, 155, 157
Feehan, Thomas, 44, 60, 105
Finn, Daniel, 179
Flannery, Kevin, 64, 65, 71, 128, 143, 146–149, 151
flattery, 67
Foot, Philippa, 153
Frankfurt, Harry, 170–176
Frontinus, 120

Galatians, Epistle to the, 41
Gauthier, R. A., 65
Geach, Peter, 96, 139, 142, 157, 162, 185
Genesis, 38, 45, 129, 138, 156
George, Marie, 124
Giuliani, Rudy, 7
gossip, 61, 67, 89
Gratian, 52–55
Greasley, Kate, 139
Gregory the Great, 17, 107–108
Grice, Paul, 127
Griffiths, Paul, 32–35, 50–51, 109, 136, 141, 144, 152
Grotius, Hugo, 14
grumbling, 67
Guevin, Benedict, 24

Hamblin, C. L., 125, 131, 137
Hauerwas, Stanley, 99
Hebrew midwives, 17–18, 34, 47, 106–108, 159
Hebrews, Epistle to the, 38
Henkel, Jeremy, 169
Hilary of Poitiers, 39
Hosea, 78
Houtman, Cornelius, 45
Hugh of St. Victor, 46, 52, 55
Hume, David, 29
Hursthouse, Rosalind, 151
hypocrisy, 121–122, 156

image of God. *See imago Dei*
imago Dei, 33, 35
impersonation, 119, 173
Innocent XI, 133
insult, 61
intention
  and remaining silent, 150
  to deceive. *See* lying: and deception
  to harm, 9, 32, 47, 58, 67, 77, 88, 106, 113, 116, 156, 159, 183, 184, 191
irony (*ironia*). *See* mock-modesty
Isaac, 156
is-ought fallacy, 29

Jacob, 156
James, Epistle of, 38
Jefferson, Thomas, 101
Jehu, 119
Jensen, Steven, 69
Jerome, 41–42
John Damascene, 93
John, Gospel of, 50, 68, 139
jokes, 105, 116, 118, 127, *See also* lying: jocose lies
Jolif, J. Y., 65
Jonsen, Albert, 85
justice. *See also* lying: and justice
  and charity, 77, 159
  general and particular, 80

Kant, Immanuel, 36
Keenan, James, 176
Kemp, Kenneth, 14
King, Martin Luther, Jr., 80
Kings, Second Book of, 119
Kirk, Kenneth, 136
Kreeft, Peter, 3, 166
Kurtscheid, Bertrand, 85

Labourdette, Michel, 69, 135
Langton, Stephen, 46
language. *See also* lying: as *contra mentem*; lying: and linguistic context
  and human nature, 101
  and the Trinity, 32–35, 109
  and thought, 25–26, 28, 32, 42, 87, 124
  assertion, 104–105, 111, 114, 123–138, 142, 155
  conversational implicature, 127
  equivocation, 123–138, 158
  in animals, 93, 101, 125

jokes. *See* jokes
meaning, 123–138
mental reservation, 132–135, 158
private language, 123, 125, 130, 132, 137–138
senses of "word" (*verbum*), 92, 96
signification, 87, 93, 98, 104, 123–138, 141
silence, 135, 140–144, 150
theological significance of, 32–35, 49
utterances, 94, 104, 157
vagueness, 135, 140, 158, 162
Leviticus, 78
Liguori, Alphonsus, 133
Live Action, 165
Lombard, Peter, 52–55, 61
Lottin, Odon, 74
lying. *See also* language: equivocation
  and assertion, 19, 114, 123–138
  and Catholic moral theology, 13, 15–22
  and deception, 19, 43–44, 102–104, 155
  and dissimulation. *See* dissimulation
  and justice, 24, 31, 32, 61, 70–76, 159, 172, 183, 191
  and linguistic context, 22–24, 104, 123–138, 158, 162
  and the right to know the truth, 13–14, 146, 158, 163
  as *contra mentem*, 43, 50, 54, 65, 96, 103, 119, 155, 158, 175
  as violation of a moral norm, 25–27, 31, 113, 145–146, 152
  Christian perspectives on, 12–15, 33, 189
  compared to murder or theft, 19–21, 113–114, 192
  definition of, 2–3, 42, 91, 102–105, 128
  doctors lying to patients, 163, 167, 169
  habitual, 113
  in the Bible, 38, 140
  in wartime, 17, 51, 120, 119–121, 156
  jocose lies, 48, 52, 63, 119, 158
  necessary conditions for, 105
  perverted faculty argument against, 26–32
  to the Nazi, 13, 18, 22–25, 138–153, 159

MacIntyre, Alasdair, 39, 144–146
Macrobius, 74
Mann, William, 43
Marshall, Bruce, 96
Matthew, Gospel of, 45, 66, 120

Mattison, William, 109
Mayeux v. Charlet, 85
McCabe, Herbert, 109
McCluskey, Colleen, 2, 4
McHugh, John, 115, 173
McNicholl, A. J., 69
mental reservation. *See* language: mental reservation
Milbank, John, 95
Milgrom, Jacob, 45
Miller, Christian, 2, 75
Miller, Patrick, 45
mockery, 61, 89, 117
mock-modesty, 64, 65, 69, 75, 173
moral dilemmas, 138–153
and virtue ethics, 151
moral object, 18–20, 102, 109, 137, 148
mortal sin. *See* sin: mortal and venial
Müller, Gregor, 44, 51
Myers, Jason, 41

natural law, 72, 77, 80, 81, 178
New Natural Law, 26, 28, 30
Nemeth, Charles, 82
New Natural Law. *See* natural law: New Natural Law
Newhauser, Richard, 53
Newman, John Henry, 99
Nicholas of Lyra, 45
Nimrod, 138
nonverbal deception. *See* dissimulation

O'Brien, T. C., 69
O'Callaghan, John, 93, 124
O'Gorman, Ned, 13
Oesterle, John, 123
Origen, 39, 40

Paul the Apostle, 41–42, *See also* individual entries for Pauline epistles
perjury, 67, 85
perverted faculty argument. *See* lying: perverted faculty argument against
Peter of Spain, 93
Peter the Chanter, 46
Petri, Thomas, 165
Pickstock, Catherine, 95
Pierce, C. S., 105
Planned Parenthood, 165
Platonism, 94, 132
Porter, Jean, 72, 76, 79, 80, 182

Porter, Steven, 2
postlapsarian condition. *See* fall of humanity
post-truth. *See* truth: post-truth
Preston, Ronald, 36, 184
pretending, 104, 114, 126
private language. *See* language: private language
prophecy, 46, 139
Pruss, Alexander, 21–25, 117
Psalms, 13, 45, 47, 53, 79, 87
Puffer, Matthew, 33

Radzik, Linda, 89
Rahab, 38
Ramsey, Boniface, 5, 39, 44, 108
Ray, Roger, 41, 42
Rehbock, Theda, 163
Rhonheimer, Martin, 3, 25
Robinson, Marilynne, 137
Romans, Epistle to the, 49, 87, 192
Romero, Oscar, 177

Sánchez, Thomas, 132
Santa Claus, 162–163
sarcasm, 126
Saul, Jennifer, 140
Searle, John, 82
Shakespeare, William, 127, 188
Sherwin, Michael, 78
Shiffin, Seana Valentine, 139
signification, 156
silence. *See* language: silence
sin. *See also* fall of humanity
as contrary to law, 109–111, 148, 150, 152, 157, 190
fomes peccati, 17, 192
hamartiology, 32
mortal and venial, 6, 21, 26, 32, 48, 69, 77, 88, 106, 109–112, 146–153, 157, 159, 189–190
sins of speech. *See* Aquinas, Thomas: on sins of speech, *See also* boasting; bullshit; cursing; false witness; flattery; gossip; grumbling; hypocrisy; insult; lying; mockery; mock-modesty; perjury
Skalko, John, 3, 14, 20, 29–32, 113, 128, 192
slander, 61, 67, 82, 89
Smith, Janet, 3, 14–21, 110, 152
Smith, Lesley, 59
Smith, Randall B., 2

Southern, R. W., 2, 53
structural sin. *See* truth-indifference
Stump, Eleonore, 64
Sullivan, Evelin, 38
Sullivan, Thomas, 14
surprise parties, 166
Synan, Edward, 117

Taylor, Charles, 4
Ten Commandments, 12, 44, 36–59, 78, 189
  Jewish interpretations, 45
Tessman, Lisa, 153
Tierney, Brian, 72
Tollefsen, Christopher, 3, 6, 14, 25–29, 143–144, 182
Torrell, Jean-Pierre, 2, 66, 76
Toulmin, Stephen, 85
Tower of Babel, 138
Trinity. *See* language: and the Trinity
Trump, Donald, 7
truth
  and falsity, 96, 126
  as conformity between intellect and thing, 94, 97
  as it relates to truthfulness, 97–99
  as the aim of truthfulness, 98
  correspondence theory of, 96
  God as, 95
  half-truths, 174
  living the, 99
  of being, 94
  post-truth, 170
  right to know the. *See* lying: and the right to know the truth
  true utterances, 94, 97, 139
truthfulness
  and concealing the truth, 100, 128, 135, 141, 156, 165
  and due circumstances, 98, 184
  as a mean between excess and deficiency, 98
  as a moral debt, 100, 110, 141
  as other-regarding, 100
  virtue of, 25, 31, 33, 74, 98–111, 156, 185–189
truth-indifference, 174–181

Useem, Jerry, 180

Vallier, Kevin, 182
Vaughan, Diane, 180
Vecchio, Silvana, 63
venial sin. *See* sin: mortal and venial
veracitas. *See* truthfulness
veritas. *See* truth
Vermeersch, Arthur, 3
Vermeersch, Arthurus, 134
virtue
  and the will, 98, 100, 107, 141
  of justice. *See* lying: and justice
  of religion (*religio*), 73, 86, 106
  of truthfulness. *See* truthfulness: virtue of
  perfection of, 108
Volkswagen emissions scandal, 180
vows, 62, 164

Wahl, Michael, 165
warfare. *See* lying: in wartime
Wawrykow, Joseph, 107
Webster, John, 21, 87
Werner, Karl, 117
West, Jevin, 171
Westberg, Daniel, 78
White, Kevin, 76, 102
William of Auxerre, 52, 56
Williams, Bernard, 185
Williams, Rowan, 104, 142
Wippel, John, 94
Wisdom, Book of, 45
Wittgenstein, Ludwig, 112, 123, 125

Zagorin, Perez, 104, 132
Zembaty, Jane, 28, 65

For EU product safety concerns, contact us at Calle de José Abascal, 56–1°, 28003 Madrid, Spain or eugpsr@cambridge.org.

www.ingramcontent.com/pod-product-compliance
Ingram Content Group UK Ltd.
Pitfield, Milton Keynes, MK11 3LW, UK
UKHW040655220625
459949UK00011B/267